Frommer's®

YELLOWSTONE &
GRAND TETON
NATIONAL PARKS

12th Edition

By Elisabeth Kwak-Hefferan

FrommerMedia LLC

FROMMER'S STAR RATINGS SYSTEM

Every hotel, restaurant, and attraction listed in this guide has been ranked for quality and value. Here's what the stars mean:

★ Recommended
★★ Highly Recommended
★★★ A must! Don't miss!

AN IMPORTANT NOTE

The world is a dynamic place. Hotels change ownership, restaurants hike their prices, museums alter their opening hours, and buses and trains change their routings. And all of this can occur in the several months after our authors have visited, inspected, and written about these hotels, restaurants, museums, and transportation services. Though we have made valiant efforts to keep all our information fresh and up-to-date, some few changes can inevitably occur in the periods before a revised edition of this guidebook is published. So please bear with us if a tiny number of the details in this book have changed. Please also note that we have no responsibility or liability for any inaccuracy or errors or omissions, or for inconvenience, loss, damage, or expenses suffered by anyone as a result of assertions in this guide.

Previous page: View from the waterfall at Yellowstone Canyon.
This page: Grand Teton.

CONTENTS

Grizzly family at Grand Teton.

A LOOK AT YELLOWSTONE & GRAND TETON

As flagships of the National Park System, Yellowstone and Grand Teton National Parks are symbols of the great outdoors: magnificent, awe-inspiring monuments to unbridled nature and the American frontier as it once was. Join in the collective *"Ahh!"* at Old Faithful's timely gushes, or gaze in rapt wonder at the churning rainbow hues of the Grand Prismatic Spring. Fish, kayak, or canoe on Jenny Lake or the Snake River, or hike to jaw-dropping views of the Teton Range. Stay in a historic lodge, rough it in a log cabin, or sleep under the stars in a back-country campground. Join a ranger-led trek, go horse-back riding to a fireside cookout, or, in winter, discover the parks' pristine, snow-blanketed depths via snowcoach. However you choose to explore Yellowstone and Grand Teton, our guidebook will help you organize your trip and make the memories of a lifetime. Enjoy the adventure!

Crowds thrill to an eruption of Old Faithful, a geothermal geyser that spouts water up to 184 feet in the air approximately every 90 minutes.

YELLOWSTONE

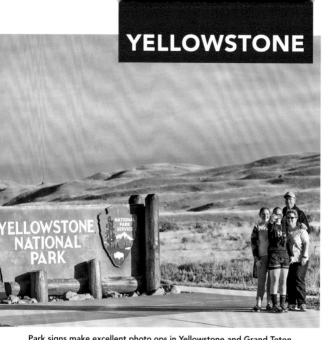

Park signs make excellent photo ops in Yellowstone and Grand Teton.

The Grand Canyon of the Yellowstone is a visual feast of plunging poly-chrome rock walls and powerful waterfalls.

Humans have been an inseparable aspect of these lands for more than 11,000 years. Today, some 27 tribes have historic ties to Yellowstone.

Lamar Valley is a popular wildlife viewing spot, with multiple pullouts along the park road for sighting Yellowstone megafauna like bison, grizzlies, and elk.

Park rangers lead entertaining and informative talks and hikes throughout the parks.

Steaming, 125-foot-deep Grand Prismatic Spring (p. 38) gets its brilliant colors from heat-loving organisms called thermophiles.

Bighorn sheep deserve their name, but they're also famous for their agility on rocky, mountainous terrain like Mount Washburn (p. 74) and the Gallatin Range.

Palette Spring at Mammoth Hot Springs (p. 70). Mammoth is a constantly shifting geological area, where old springs may dry up suddenly and new ones appear just as rapidly.

Soaring timber-and-stone walls and a massive fireplace make the Old Faithful Inn (p. 138) one of Yellowstone's most beloved lodgings.

Winter in the park means fewer crowds, as well as opportunities for cross-county skiing and snowshoeing. Park rangers lead free snowshoe walks (p. 95) from the Mammoth and West Yellowstone areas several times a week.

Campgrounds (p. 139) in Yellowstone range from remote pack-in/out back-country sites to enormous tent and RV villages with modern facilities.

Kayakers can take a closer look at geothermal vents like Fishing Cone (p. 59) in the West Thumb Geyser Basin on the shores of Yellowstone Lake.

GRAND TETON

Near Jenny Lake, the popular hike to Hidden Falls (p. 120) crosses Cascade Creek and leads to a 200-foot cascade.

Bison crossing in front of the historic T.A. Moulton Barn, an early-20th-century homestead framed against the Teton Range.

Paintbrush wildflowers bloom along a park trail.

A hiker in Granite Canyon, Grand Teton. Even during the park's busiest periods, backcountry hikes (p. 114) allow visitors to quickly escape the crowds and reach isolated lakes, meadows, and streams.

Each summer, Native American artists display their work at the Colter Bay Visitor Center (p. 97), the busiest hub on the park's north end.

Both Yellowstone and Grand Teton offer incredible opportunities for fly-fishing.

Moose sightings are most frequent at the edges of ponds and valley bottoms, where they feed on willows and water plants, especially along the Moose-Wilson Road and near the Jackson Lake Lodge (p. 150) in Grand Teton.

It's worth the strenuous climb from the Lupine Meadows trailhead to experience the wildflowers, wildlife, and wide-open views of Amphitheater Lake (p. 119) and the surrounding mountains.

Autumn along the Snake River, with the Teton Range in the background.

Staying at the Jenny Lake Lodge (p. 151) includes a five-course gourmet dinner in the celebrated restaurant (non-guests can reserve a table, too).

GATEWAYS TO YELLOWSTONE & GRAND TETON

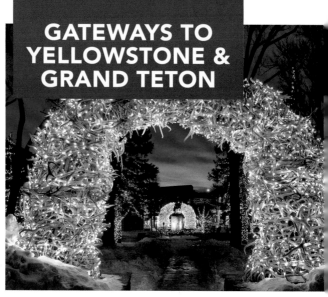

The town square in Jackson Hole bedazzles with an iconic arch made of elk antlers, strung with holiday lights during the winter season. It's one of four elk antler arches manning the entrances to the square, aka George Washington Memorial Park.

A parade is one of the main events of the ropin' and ridin' Cody Stampede, the annual rodeo festival held in Cody, Wyoming, around July 4th since 1919.

Summer rafting trips on the Snake River range from peaceful float trips to challenging Class II and III rapids. Several top-notch outfitters (p. 175) are based in Jackson.

Horse-drawn sleds bring visitors close to the thousands of elk that graze every winter at the National Elk Refuge (p. 178) near Jackson.

The Sage Lodge (p. 169) in Pray, Montana, sits on the banks of the Yellowstone River and has its own fly-fishing school.

The Whitney Western Art Museum, at the Buffalo Bill Center of the West in Cody, Wyoming (p. 199), holds works by renowned Western artists like Charles M. Russell and Frederic Remington.

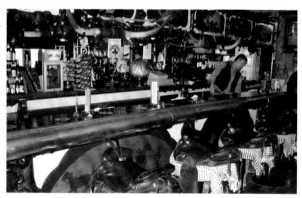

Western dancing, live entertainment, and a raucous good time are on tap at the Million Dollar Cowboy Bar (p. 195), Jackson's most famous watering hole.

Skiers admiring the mountain views at the Grand Targhee Ski Resort, in Jackson, Wyoming, which offers some 2,600 acres of skiable terrain.

INTRODUCING YELLOWSTONE & GRAND TETON

Yellowstone and Grand Teton National Parks are life-list destinations for millions of people—not just Americans—the world over. That's because you won't find scenery like this anywhere else on the planet: No other region combines rare geothermal fireworks, skyscraping mountains, glaciers, and a huge variety of wildlife such as grizzly bears, wolves, elk, and moose in one spot the way the Greater Yellowstone Ecosystem does. Here, you can spend days getting lost among the geysers and hot springs, gazing up at or down from towering peaks, marveling at incredible waterfalls and carpets of wildflowers, and scoping for that next thrilling wildlife sighting. These two exceptional parks have something for everyone—and as soon as you check this place off your life list, you're bound to start dreaming about your next visit.

Creatures great and small thrive in Yellowstone and Grand Teton national parks. In the wilderness of Yellowstone's southern corners, grizzlies feed on cutthroat trout during the annual spawning run to the Yellowstone headwaters; in the soft blue depths of Octopus Pond, microbes of enormous scientific value incubate and develop; in the mountain ridges, gray wolves make their dens and mountain lions hunt bighorn sheep. In Grand

Teton, bald eagles and ospreys soar above the banks of the Snake River, moose munch their way through meadows, and elk and bison traverse the park on the same roads as visitors.

When John Colter, a scout for Lewis and Clark, first wandered this way in 1807, his descriptions of geysers, sulfurous hot pools, and towering waterfalls drew jeers and suspicion. No one doubts him now, but these are still places you should see for yourself. Today's explorers come in camper vans and on bicycles, aboard snowmobiles and telemark skis, and in such numbers that the parks sometimes seem to groan under the strain.

In the early days of Yellowstone, first established as a national park in 1872, visitors were so sparse that their unregulated activities—catching 100 trout at a time, washing their underwear in the hot pools—left few noticeable scars. Now, with millions of people visiting the parks annually, the strain on everything from sewer systems to fish populations is immense. Yet while there are problems, these parks still radiate extraordinary beauty: the jagged Tetons, the glassy surface of Jenny Lake, the awe-inspiring Grand Canyon of the Yellowstone, the towering Obsidian Cliff, the steamy meandering of the Firehole River. Wildlife that most Americans see only in zoos wanders freely here, from the grizzly to the river otter, the trumpeter swan to the rufous hummingbird. Aspen groves, fields of lupines, the howls of coyotes and wolves—all testify to the resilience and vitality of the Greater Yellowstone Ecosystem, which extends outside the borders of the park to Grand Teton and beyond.

This is not just a paradise for sightseers—it's a scientific preserve as well. The hot pools support a population of unique microbes known as thermophiles and extremophiles, and studies of the elk herds and grizzlies have yielded crucial information on habitat needs and animal behavior. The rocks of Yellowstone present the Earth turned inside out, making it a treasure trove for geologists.

Most visitors will see or know little of this. They park in a pullout on U.S. 191/89/26 to pose in front of Grand Teton, or they sit on crowded benches to watch Old Faithful erupt. If you have more time, however, we suggest that you take little sections of these parks—just the Jenny Lake area in Grand Teton, say, or Yellowstone's northeast corner, the Lamar

Valley—and savor them in all their fine detail, rather than embark on a madcap race to see every highlight.

Above all, get out of your car and away from the road, into the wild heart of the backcountry. These parks embody our country's beginnings: as a landscape of wilderness, of challenging and rugged extremes, and of extraordinary bounty and beauty. Use this guide as a set of footprints to help you find your way there.

A LOOK AT YELLOWSTONE

Yellowstone was a novel idea when it was named the country's first national park, but the notion had staying power. In 2022, the park celebrated its 150th year—a testament to the enduring popularity of this place. And no wonder: What other national park in the world boasts an assortment of some 10,000 thermal features, including more than 300 geysers? Even when the rest of North America was still largely wilderness, Yellowstone was unique. Its collection of geo-thermal features is richer and more concentrated than any other in the world, with mud pots, geysers, and hot springs of all colors and sizes. Plus, Yellowstone has a waterfall that's twice as tall as Niagara Falls and a canyon deep and colorful enough to be called "grand." Sure, other parks have great hiking trails and beautiful geologic formations—Grand Teton is pretty spectacular in its own right, as is Yosemite—but unlike many other parks, a sizable percentage of the geology in Yellowstone is reachable by visitors in average physical shape.

Ever focus your camera lens on an untamed grizzly bear or a bald eagle? What about a wolf? Thousands of visitors have these experiences here every year. Protected from development by the national park and surrounding forests, Yellowstone is home to herds of bison and elk, packs of wolves, flocks of trumpeter swans, schools of Yellowstone cutthroat trout, and plenty of subtler beauties, such as wildflowers and hummingbirds.

The park's appeal is not limited to the visual senses; you'll smell it, too. Yellowstone has more than 1,100 species of native plants. When wildflowers cover the meadows in spring, their fragrances are overpowering. The mud pots and fumaroles have their own set of odors, though many are less pleasing than that of a wild lily.

Your ears will be filled with the sounds of geysers noisily spewing forth thousands of gallons of boiling water into the blue Wyoming sky. After sunset, coyotes break the silence of the night with their high-pitched yips.

You can spend weeks hiking Yellowstone's backcountry or fishing its streams, but you can also see the highlights from behind the wheel in a day or two. The park's road system passes most of the key attractions and is filled with wildlife commuting from one grazing area to another; many visitors to Yellowstone tour the park without hitting a trail. But even though driving through the park will certainly create vivid memories, visitors who choose to stay in their cars are short-changing themselves.

Yellowstone slows down in fall and then reawakens as a winter destination come December, when cross-country skiing, snowshoeing, and snowmobiling are the prime pursuits. There's no cozier place than the lobby of the Old Faithful

Snow Lodge, one of two hotels in the park's interior that stays open during Yellowstone's long, cold, and snowy winter season. We highly recommend a visit when snow covers the ground—you'll often have the park to yourself. But dress appropriately (read: no fewer than three layers) and be ready to incur an extra expense in the form of snowcoach fare.

A LOOK AT GRAND TETON

Because the magnificent mountains of the Teton Range stand so tall, with the park curling snugly at their feet, visitors sometimes fail to appreciate the surrounding environment of rivers and high valley floor. The Tetons are a geologically young range of old Precambrian granite, abrupt and sharp-edged as they knife up from the Snake River Valley along a 40-mile-long fault sculpted over the course of the last 13 million years, with help from geological upheaval, retreating glaciers, and erosion (the Great Smoky Mountains, by comparison, uplifted some 270 million years ago). The result is a masterpiece. Many visitors regard Grand Teton National Park—with its shimmering lakes, thickly carpeted forests, and towering peaks blanketed with snow most of the year— as more dramatically scenic than its northern neighbor.

It's also a very accessible park. You can appreciate its breathtaking beauty on a quick drive-by or take to the trails and waterways in search of backcountry lakes and waterfalls. The Tetons themselves are especially popular with mountain climbers, who scale them year-round.

The Tetons and the valley below have a dynamic relationship. Elk and other wildlife migrate from the high country down to the open grasslands to forage during the winter; in spring, snowmelt curls across the valley floor and west through a gap in the mountains, and the moraines and alluvial soils that slough off the mountains provide rich soil for the pastures below.

Visitors can float and fish the lively Snake River; visit the National Elk Refuge; hike in nearby ranges, such as the Wind River or the Gros Ventre; or play cowboy at one of the dude and guest ranches that dot the valley of Jackson Hole. Skiers and snowboarders have a blast on the slopes here, as well as at Grand Targhee on the other side of Teton Pass. And the chic town of Jackson, with its antler-arched square and its busy shops, offers everything from fly-fishing outfitters to classy art galleries to rowdy two-stepping crowds at cowboy bars.

MAKING THE MOST OF YOUR TRIP

Yellowstone and Grand Teton are not just photo ops and zoos where the animals roam free. Both parks are works in progress; they are living, breathing wilderness areas. Plant your feet in a comfortable pair of walking or hiking shoes, find a trailhead, and set off into the woods with a sack lunch and a big bottle of water. Better yet, if you can afford the time, plan an excursion by boat around Shoshone Lake or to the south end of Yellowstone Lake, to areas few visitors ever see. Grand Teton has its fair share of isolated spots, too—even on the far shore of popular Jenny Lake, where you'll be rewarded with a pristine, forested glade with nothing to distract you but wild moose and an awe-inspiring mountaintop.

If you're more adventurous, take a whitewater trip down Snake River Canyon or let a guide take you up to Grand Teton's summit. In Yellowstone, sleep under the stars and listen to the wolves howling at Slough Creek Campground; or backpack for a week on the Thorofare Trail.

You'll never plumb the absolute depths of these parks—no one ever will. You could spend your whole life trying, though, and have a wonderful and illuminating time doing it.

THE best OF YELLOWSTONE & GRAND TETON

A "best of" list could never do justice to Yellowstone and Grand Teton. These are just starting points, the best of the excellent accommodations and dining the parks offer, as well as unique sightseeing and recreational opportunities. Some involve backcountry expeditions; others can be enjoyed from behind a windshield. In the wildly diverse environments of these two parts, you can be as adventurous as you want—climbing peaks or spending the night deep in the wilderness—or soak in the more civilized side of the parks at grand lodges and enchanting roadside overlooks.

The Best Views

You'll never get it all in a camera lens, but you can try. Just don't get too caught up in Instagramming your trip: Compose some memorable shots, then put down the camera and take in the scenery with nothing between you and the view.

o **Grand Canyon of the Yellowstone** (Yellowstone): Here, plunging polychrome rock walls frame two of the most powerful waterfalls for hundreds of miles: the 308-foot **Lower Falls** and 109-foot **Upper Falls.** Excellent views await along both the North and South Rims of the canyon, but **Artist Point,** at the end of South Rim Drive, offers a picture-perfect distant look at Lower Falls. On the North Rim, **Inspiration Point** delivers an equally impressive view. See "Yellowstone: The Extended Tour" in chapter 3.

o **Lamar Valley** (Yellowstone): If it's wildlife you seek, then make tracks to this expansive valley on the park's northeast side. Your chances of spotting at least some of Yellowstone's charismatic megafauna—including grizzly bears, wolves, elk, and bison—are very high, especially if you visit at dawn or dusk. Multiple pullouts along the park road provide vantage points to set up your spotting scope or binoculars. See "Yellowstone: The Extended Tour" in chapter 3.

o **Mount Washburn** (Yellowstone): For one of the finest top-down views over Yellowstone, hike to the top of this 10,243-foot summit. From the windswept peak, you'll see the Grand Canyon of the Yellowstone slicing into the earth, the rolling Lamar and Hayden valleys, and all the way to the Tetons. See "Day Hikes" in chapter 4.

o **Yellowstone Lake** (Yellowstone): Sunrise over Yellowstone Lake is stunningly beautiful (especially if there's fog on the lake), whether you watch it from the sunroom at the **Lake Yellowstone Hotel,** the front porch at **Lake Lodge,** or, even better, from a campsite along the southern wilderness shore. For an equally spectacular sunset view, drive 10 miles east of the hotels to **Lake Butte Overlook.** See "Yellowstone: The Extended Tour" in chapter 3.

o **Cathedral Group** (Grand Teton): The three central mountains of the Teton Range rarely disappoint, except on the unusual occasion when weather gets in the way (although clouds tend to accent rather than obscure their majesty). A number of pullouts on both the inner and outer park roads grant a lovely view of them, but the **Cathedral Group Turnout** on the Jenny Lake Scenic Drive is particularly special. See "The Highlights" in chapter 5.

o **Oxbow Bend** (Grand Teton): Don't miss the view of 12,605-foot Mount Moran reflected in a wide bend of the Snake River—especially in fall, when the aspens and willows go golden. See "Touring Grand Teton" in chapter 5.

The Best Thermal Displays

Yellowstone has more thermal features—geysers, mud pots, hot springs, and steam vents—than the rest of the world combined. When you're angling for a good shot of a colorful pool or a belching mud pot, obey the signs; otherwise, you might find yourself (quite literally) on shaky ground. For details on Yellowstone's steamy sights, see "Yellowstone: The Extended Tour" in chapter 3.

o **Upper Geyser Basin** (Yellowstone): Home to the mega-famous Old Faithful Geyser as well as enough other thermal features to form the largest concentration of geysers in the world, Upper Geyser Basin is a can't-miss destination. This is why you're here, right?

o **Norris Geyser Basin** (Yellowstone): The park's oldest and hottest thermal area encompasses a dynamic collection of geysers, steaming hot springs, and hissing steam vents. Change is constant here, remaking this remarkable area year by year and day by day.

o **Mammoth Hot Springs Terraces** (Yellowstone): Here you can observe Mother Nature going about the business of mixing and matching heat, water, limestone, and rock fractures to sculpt the landscape. This is one of the most colorful areas in the park; its tapestries of orange, pink, yellow, green, and brown, formed by masses of bacteria and algae, seem to change colors before your eyes. The mineral-rich hot waters that flow to the surface here do so at an unusually constant rate, roughly 750,000 gallons per day.

The Best Day Hikes

Just a few hundred yards off the road, things get a lot less crowded, and you'll have the views and the wildlife (almost) to yourself. Getting out of the car and into the wilds is always worthwhile, but these shorter trips are the best of the best for those not doing extended, multiday hikes.

o **Mount Washburn Trail** (Yellowstone): Starting at Dunraven Pass, south of Tower Junction, this walk to the fire lookout atop Mount Washburn offers unsurpassed views of both parks, plus the opportunity to see mountain wildlife, such as bighorn sheep. See p. 74.

o **Lone Star Geyser Trail** (Yellowstone): This gentle, 5-mile hike along the Firehole River presents several places to stop and take in the scenery, go fishing, and—at the endpoint—view an active, medium-size geyser. It is also one of a few bicycle-friendly trails in Yellowstone, and in the winter, it's a popular cross-country-skiing trail. See p. 78.

o **Upper Pebble Creek Trail** (Yellowstone): Explore the less-traveled, peak-heavy northeastern part of the park on this wildflower-filled ramble to cliff views and creekside hiking. See p. 73.

o **Amphitheater Lake Trail** (Grand Teton): We promise: Climbing the switchbacks up to this cirque-cradled, high-country lake is well worth the effort. See p. 119.

The Best Backcountry Trails

To see the true heart of the parks, load up a backpack and spend a night or more in the wilderness. These remote areas make for unforgettable backpacking destinations, whether you're up for an overnight or a real multiday epic.

o **Thorofare Trail** (Yellowstone): This hike will take you deeper into road-free wilderness than you can get anywhere else in the lower 48 states. You'll spend a few nights on the trail, climbing up to the park's southern border and beyond to the Yellowstone River's headwaters, a high valley bursting with wildlife. Early in the summer, if the snow has melted, the cutthroat spawning run attracts grizzlies and coyotes. It's not for the faint of heart. See "Exploring the Backcountry" in chapter 4.

- **Bechler Region** (Yellowstone): The park's remote "Cascade Corner" features plentiful waterfalls, soakable hot springs, and riverside hiking. Several different out-and-back or loop options are possible, and you can even plan a long-haul hike from Bechler all the way to Old Faithful. See "Exploring the Backcountry" in chapter 4.
- **Cascade/Paintbrush Canyon Loop** (Grand Teton): Perhaps the most popular trail in Grand Teton, the Cascade/Paintbrush Canyon Loop, which starts on the west side of Jenny Lake, winds northwest 9.5 miles on the Cascade Canyon Trail to Lake Solitude and the Paintbrush Divide, then returns past Holly Lake on the 10-mile Paintbrush Canyon Trail. The payoff comes at the highest point, Paintbrush Divide, which offers marvelous views of Jackson Hole and Leigh Lake. See "Exploring the Backcountry" in chapter 6.

The Best Campgrounds

If you stay in developed campgrounds in the parks, the outdoor life is pretty civilized. You'll have running water and, in most cases, flush toilets, plus the opportunity to meet fellow campers.

- **Slough Creek & Pebble Creek Campgrounds** (Yellowstone): These two small, primitive campgrounds in the Lamar Valley are prized for their proximity to excellent trout fishing and wildlife-watching. Plus, they're much quieter than some of the other giant campgrounds in the park for a real away-from-it-all vibe. See p. 140.
- **Lewis Lake Campground** (Yellowstone): The park's southernmost campground has private-feeling sites tucked into the trees near the shores of Lewis Lake, making it great for paddlers or boaters. See p. 142.
- **Indian Creek Campground** (Yellowstone): Smallish, quiet, and close to top-shelf fishing and elk and bison viewing, Indian Creek is another option that really makes you feel like you're getting off the beaten track. See p. 140.
- **Jenny Lake Campground** (Grand Teton): Situated near the edge of the lake from which it takes its name, Jenny Lake Campground is nestled among spruce and fir trees just a short walk away from the South Jenny Lake area. It's

the perfect place to spend the night if you plan to hike around the lake to Hidden Falls or up Cascade Canyon the next day. See p. 153.

The Best Places to Eat in the Parks

The parks' restaurants aren't as much about five-star dining (with one notable exception) as they are about kicking back in a friendly, one-of-a-kind atmosphere to enjoy hearty fare. Chapter 7 has the details on all these options.

o **Old Faithful Inn Dining Room** (Yellowstone; ☏ **307/344-7311**): Don't miss a chance to linger over a meal under the soaring stone-and-timber architecture of the park's coolest hotel. The menu leans toward steak, seafood, and local favorites, such as bison. See p. 147.

o **Lake Yellowstone Hotel Dining Room** (Yellowstone; ☏ **307/344-7311**): A tinkling piano, Victorian details, and large picture windows over the lake give this restaurant Yellowstone's most elegant air. See p. 146.

o **Jenny Lake Lodge Dining Room** (Grand Teton; ☏ **307/543-3100**): This luxurious dining room stands head and shoulders above the rest with its expertly prepared, five-course prix fixe dinner. Expect lots of local ingredients, creative flavors, and impeccable service—and prices to match the top-quality dining. Lodge guests get breakfast and dinner with the cost of their room, but non-guests can also make reservations. See p. 157.

o **The Mural Room** (Grand Teton; ☏ **307/543-3463**): Jackson Lake Lodge's signature restaurant is known even more for its fantastic window views looking out over the Tetons than it is for its (quite good) food. See p. 156.

The Best Places to Sleep in the Parks

In-park lodging ranges from rustic old classics to sleek modern hotels, and some are true gems. Chapter 7 has the details on all.

o **Old Faithful Inn** (Yellowstone; ☏ **307/344-7311**): One peek into this early-1900s masterpiece, and you'll know why it's the most-requested hotel in the park. From the grand stone fireplace to soaring timber-and-stone walls and charmingly old-fashioned rooms, Old Faithful Inn is unlike any other hotel out there, in a national park or otherwise. See p. 138.

○ **Lake Yellowstone Hotel** (Yellowstone; ⓒ **307/344-7311**): If you're looking to do up your park vacation in style, this is your choice: Lovingly restored Colonial Revival details, a graceful sunroom with lake views, and carefully curated guest rooms make this the most upscale hotel at Yellowstone. See p. 136.

○ **Roosevelt Lodge Cabins** (Yellowstone; ⓒ **307/344-7311**): Deluxe it isn't: This complex of very rustic cabins is as simple as it gets. But its authentic frontier atmosphere, proximity to corrals for horseback rides, and prime location smack at the start of the Lamar Valley make this less-crowded lodge one of the most memorable places to bunk. See p. 135.

○ **Jenny Lake Lodge** (Grand Teton; ⓒ **307/543-3100**): We challenge you to find a better, more luxurious hotel in any national park. Guests stay in fancy cabins, come together for A-list meals, and enjoy free perks like horseback rides and front-lawn yoga sessions. See p. 150.

The Best Places to Eat Outside the Parks

You might be practically in the wilderness out here, but the park's gateway towns boast some mighty fine dining choices. See chapter 8 for details on all the establishments listed below.

○ **In Jackson, Wyoming:** It's tough to pick just one favorite in the culinary capital of Wyoming, but **Snake River Grill** (ⓒ **307/733-0557**) has long been the preferred stop of locals and guests alike for its inventive, genre-blending dishes, ranging from Asian-style noodles to quail. It's a splurge, but a worthy one. See p. 191.

○ **In Cody, Wyoming: Trailhead** (ⓒ **307/578-8510**) may play up its wood-fired pizzas, but that's just the tip of the iceberg at this homey spot serving housemade pastas, seafood, and steaks, too. See p. 206.

○ **Near Gardiner, Montana: Chico Dining Room** (ⓒ **406/333-4933**), the restaurant at a beloved hot springs resort, offers a refined dining experience in the middle of nowhere. What better way to finish a day (or kick off an evening) of thermal relaxation than with a superb meal and a glass of wine from the extensive list here? See p. 169.

The Best Places to Sleep Outside the Parks

In high season, park rooms are at a premium and sell out quickly. Chapter 8 has all the details on these fine alternatives in the park gateway towns.

o **In Jackson, Wyoming:** The **Wort Hotel** (✆ 307/733-2190; p. 186) is a Jackson landmark with comfortable "New West"–style rooms and a town institution of a watering hole, the **Silver Dollar Bar.** The modern **Hotel Jackson** (✆ 307/733-2200; p. 184) marries high design with comfortable Western touches.

o **In Gardiner, Montana:** Carefully designed rustic-meets-modern suites and plentiful amenities make the boutiquey **Wonderland Lodge** (✆ 406/224-2001; p. 167) the best night's sleep in town.

o **In Cody, Wyoming:** Centered on a serene green courtyard, the vintage-but-improved **Chamberlin Inn** (✆ 307/587-0202; p. 203) features charming, historic rooms and apartments with serious literary cred: Ernest Hemingway once stayed here (and you can sleep in his room).

The Best Things to See & Do Outside the Parks

Don't assume that a Yellowstone and Grand Teton vacation must be confined to within park boundaries. Here are a few area attractions worth checking out. See chapter 8 for details.

o **In Cody, Wyoming:** The **Buffalo Bill Center of the West** (✆ 307/587-4771) is the best museum in the region—make that five museums, as you can check out exhibits in wings dedicated to Native Americans, natural history, art, firearms, and Buffalo Bill Cody himself. See p. 199.

o **In Jackson, Wyoming:** Glimpse some of the finest artistic interpretations of the natural world at the fantastic **National Museum of Wildlife Art** (✆ 307/733-5771; p. 180), which houses 1,300 pieces within its red-sandstone walls. At the top of the **Jackson Hole Aerial Tram** (✆ 307/739-2753;

p. 180), at Jackson Hole Mountain Resort, you can see the Tetons from an elevation of more than 10,000 feet. And riding it is essentially a cheat code for hikers who want to explore the gorgeous, high-elevation trails without the stiff climb.

o **In West Yellowstone, Montana:** No mere roadside wildlife park, the **Grizzly & Wolf Discovery Center** (© **406/646-7001**) is a nonprofit sanctuary for bears and wolves where you can see the magnificent animals up close while learning about their lives, habitats, and the threats they face. See p. 159.

The Best Scenic Drives

Though we encourage you to get out and explore on foot whenever possible, the parks offer fantastic scenic drives for those disinclined or unable to hoof it. But do take advantage of the many opportunities to pull over and gaze at the wonders before you.

o From the most beautiful part of Yellowstone (the northeast corner), through **Silver Gate** and **Cooke City** and up to the dizzying heights of **Beartooth Pass,** the **Beartooth Highway** (U.S. 212) drive is nothing short of spectacular. If that's not enough, you can extend the trip to **Red Lodge, Montana,** or head down to **Cody, Wyoming,** and connect to the East Entrance Road (see below). See chapter 3.

o The **East Entrance Road** is the second-most scenic way to approach Yellowstone (behind the Beartooth Highway, above). Wind through gorgeous Shoshone Canyon, top out on 8,530-foot **Sylvan Pass,** and then cruise down from the high country to sweeping views over **Yellowstone Lake.** See chapter 3.

o A twisting, narrow road climbs Grand Teton's **Signal Mountain** to a fine 360-degree view of the valley and surrounding peaks. On the way up, you'll see wildflowers and birds; from the top, you can study the moraines and potholes left by retreating glaciers. See chapter 5.

THE PARKS IN DEPTH

I n Yellowstone and Grand Teton National Parks, spectacular scenery combines with millennia of human history to create what we consider the real American West. The land is uncluttered and the setting is one of rugged beauty: from the remote wilderness of Yellowstone's Thorofare country to the soaring peaks of the Teton Range and the geothermal activity sprouting from below the surface of the Earth.

YELLOWSTONE & GRAND TETON NATIONAL PARKS TODAY

The struggle to balance recreation and preservation is as old as the parks themselves, and it's an issue that rears its head in questions about the visitor experience, wildlife management, and what activities should be allowed within the parks. How can the park preserve the wilderness feel of the place while keeping its doors open to more than 4 million people every year? What's to be done about controversial populations of bison and wolves? How is climate change threatening the ecosystems here? These and other issues pose management challenges but also prove the parks are as dynamic as they've ever been.

Bison, Bears & Wolves

In the frontier West—where bison seemed to be everywhere, grizzly bears were fearsome, and wolves regularly raided livestock—wildlife was treated as more of a nuisance than a national treasure. Eventually, the bison and grizzly populations around Yellowstone and Grand Teton were whittled down to near-extinction, and ranchers and federal agents completely eradicated wolves by the 1930s.

It took some intensive management to bring grizzlies and bison back to reasonably healthy numbers in the area. Now the wolves, which were reintroduced from Canada in 1995, are reaping the benefits of the ungulate herds that have enjoyed a nearly predator-free environment for quite some time. But these high-profile species—called "charismatic megafauna" by biologists—are not out of the woods yet, given the pressures of development around the parks.

Yellowstone biologists manage bison numbers in the park to average about 5,000 animals, and, naturally, the bison pay no mind to the parks' invisible boundaries. In the winter, when the snow is deep, they leave the park to forage at lower elevations, sometimes in ranch pastures inhabited by domestic cattle. Some ranchers fear that the bison will spread brucellosis, a virus that can be transmitted to cattle, causing infected cows to abort their unborn calves. There have been no documented cases of bison-to-cattle transmission, but the perceived threat to livestock still worries state officials and other stakeholders. Currently, the park transfers some animals to various tribal lands to help restore Indigenous cultures' historic ties to bison. And federal, state, and tribal agencies slaughter some bison each winter as a population control measure. The practice is controversial—in the winter of 2022-23, a tribal hunt harvested more than 1,100 bison, drawing particular pushback. Park and state officials continue to search for some middle ground with animal-rights activists.

Wolves are another sore point with area ranchers, who worry that a booming wolf population threatens their livestock (and wolves do sometimes prey on cows and sheep). Wolf advocates, on the other hand, argue that restoring the natural wolf population returns the ecosystem to its original, balanced state. The reintroduction has been astonishingly successful. Rapidly reproducing, feeding on elk in Yellowstone's Lamar Valley, wolves now number about 124 in Yellowstone (and about 352 total statewide), and the packs have spread as far south as Grand Teton, where several have produced pups. Gray wolves were delisted from the endangered-species lists in Montana and Idaho in 2011, and after some legal wrangling, also delisted in Wyoming in 2017.

Grizzly bears once teetered on the brink of extinction in the parks, but they've slowly made a comeback, reaching an estimated population of 150 to 200 in the park and nearly 1,000 in the Yellowstone area. (Wolves have helped because their hunting results in more carcasses to scavenge.) Because of this success, in 2007 the U.S. Fish and Wildlife Service removed the grizzly from the threatened species list for the Yellowstone area, a decision reversed in 2010. The yo-yo continued in 2017, when the agency again delisted grizzlies; a 2018 court order then restored their protection under the Endangered Species Act.

A Burning Issue

After years of suppressing every fire in the park, Yellowstone, in 1988, was operating under a new "let it burn" policy, based on scientific evidence that fires were regular occurrences before the settlement of the West and part of the natural cycle of a forest. That philosophy faced the ultimate test the same year, when nearly one-third of Yellowstone burned in a series of uncontrollable wildfires. These violent conflagrations scorched more than 700,000 acres, leaving behind dead wildlife, damaged buildings, injured firefighters, and ghostly forests of stripped, blackened tree trunks.

Today the park may be healthier than it was before the 1988 fires. Saplings have sprouted from the long-dormant seeds of lodgepole pines (fire stimulates the pine cones to release their seeds), and green shrubs, sometimes as thick as one million saplings per acre, are steadily replacing the old, tinder-dry forest undergrowth. Visitors who want to better understand the effects of the fires of 1988 should check out the exhibits at the Grant Village Visitor Center; the coverage there is the best in the park.

The Changing Climate

Wildfire in the park didn't stop being an issue when the 1988 fires went out, of course. Though wildfire has been a natural part of the ecosystem for thousands of years, climate change has been supercharging these blazes, causing more frequent, hotter, and more destructive fires and extending the wildfire season. Fire (and its associated smoke) are just one aspect of a changing climate that park managers—and visitors—must grapple with now and as far into the future as we can imagine.

Scientists have already documented changing conditions, including melting glaciers, shifting streamflow patterns, and more extreme weather events. In turn, these changes have begun to affect park vegetation, forest health, animal populations, and park infrastructure. Recent research has predicted that the Yellowstone ecosystem will see more drought and extreme heat, less snow and earlier snowmelt, and accelerated wildfires over the next few decades—but how bad things get depends on how quickly the globe can rein in fossil fuel emissions.

LOOKING BACK: YELLOWSTONE & GRAND TETON HISTORY

Yellowstone National Park

Humans have been a part of the landscape that is now the park for at least 11,000 years. The Tukudika people, a band of the Mountain Shoshone, lived in this area for millennia. Their name, which means "eaters of the mountain sheep," points to the band's primary meat source: bighorn sheep. The

DATELINE

18,000 B.C.	Earliest evidence of humans in Wyoming.
11,000 B.C.	Earliest evidence of humans in Montana.
1620s	Arrival of the Plains Indians.
1807	John Colter explores the Yellowstone area, going as far south as Jackson Hole.
1867	The Union Pacific Railroad enters Wyoming.
1869	A party led by David Folsom undertakes the first modern exploration of Yellowstone.
1871	The Hayden Expedition surveys Yellowstone.
1872	Yellowstone is established as the nation's first national park.
1876	Warriors from the Sioux, Lakota, and Cheyenne tribes defeat General George A. Custer and

Tukudika traveled within the Yellowstone region, hunting and gathering plants; they spent their summers in the higher country and moved to the lower regions during the colder months. Archaeological sites within the park have yielded signs of their ancient civilization, including soapstone (steatite) bowls and obsidian arrowheads quarried from what's now Obsidian Cliff. The Tukudika lived in Yellowstone until the late 19th century, when they were forcibly removed to the Wind River Shoshone and Fort Hall Shoshone-Bannock reservations. Today, 27 current tribes have historic ties to Yellowstone, including the Crow (Apsáalooke), Nez Perce (Nimiipuu), Salish (Séliš), Kootenai (Ktunaxa), and Sioux (Lakota).

The first explorer of European descent to lay eyes on Yellowstone's geothermal wonders was probably John Colter, who broke away from the Lewis and Clark Expedition in 1806 and spent 3 years wandering a surreal landscape of mud pots, mountains, and geysers. When he described his discovery on his return to St. Louis, no one believed him. Miners and fur trappers followed in his footsteps, reducing the plentiful beaver population of the region to almost zero and occasionally making curious reports of a sulfurous world still sometimes called "Colter's Hell."

The first significant exploration of what would become the park took place in 1869, when a band of Montanans, led by David Folsom, completed a 36-day expedition. The group

his troops at the Battle of the Little Bighorn (Montana).	**1889** Montana, on November 8, becomes the 41st state in the Union.
1877 Chief Joseph of the Nez Perce surrenders to U.S. soldiers in the Bear Paw Mountains after a flight that took his tribe though Yellowstone.	**1890** Wyoming becomes the nation's 44th state.
	1929 Grand Teton National Park is established, consisting of only the main peaks of the Cathedral Range.
1883 The Northern Pacific Railroad crosses Montana.	

continues

traveled up the Missouri River and into the park's heart, where they documented the falls of Yellowstone, mud pots, Yellowstone Lake, and Fountain Geyser. Two years later, an expedition led by U.S. Geological Survey director Ferdinand V. Hayden brought back evidence of Yellowstone's wonders, in astonishing photographs by William Henry Jackson.

A debate began over the potential for commercial development and exploitation of the region, as crude health spas and thin-walled "hotels" went up near the hot springs. There are various claimants to the idea of a national park—members of the Folsom party later told an oft-disputed story about thinking it up around a campfire in the Upper Geyser Basin—but the idea gained steam as Yellowstone explorers hit the lecture circuit back East. In March 1872, President Ulysses S. Grant signed legislation declaring Yellowstone the nation's first national park.

The Department of the Interior got the job of managing the new park. With no budget and no clear idea of how to take care of a wilderness preserve, many mistakes were made in the early years. Inept superintendents granted favorable leases to friends with commercial interests in the tourism industry. Poachers ran amok and decimated the wildlife population. A laundry business near Mammoth went so far as to clean linens in a hot pool.

By 1886, things were so bad that the U.S. Army took control of Yellowstone; iron-fisted management practices

1950 National forest and private lands are added to Grand Teton National Park, forming the park's current boundaries.	**2007** The U.S. Forest Service removes the Greater Yellowstone grizzly bear population from the threatened species list.
1988 Five fires break out around Yellowstone, blackening approximately one-third of the park.	**2008** The gray wolf population in the Northern Rockies hits 1,600; the species is no longer listed as endangered.
1995 Gray wolves are reintroduced into Yellowstone National Park.	**2009** Montana has its first legal wolf hunting season since reintroduction in 1995.

protected the park from those intent on exploiting it. (However, the military did participate in the eradication of the plateau's wolf population.) By 1916, efforts to make the park more visitor-friendly had begun to show results: Construction of the first roads had been completed, and guest housing was available in the area. Stewardship of the park was then transferred to the newly created National Park Service, which remains in control to this day.

Grand Teton National Park

Unlike Yellowstone, Grand Teton can't boast of being the nation's first park and a model for parks the world over. The creation of the smaller, southern neighbor was the result of a much more convoluted process over 50 years.

The first signs of human habitation in the Grand Teton region date back at least 11,000 years. Among the tribes who hunted here in the warmer seasons were the Blackfeet (Niitsitapi), Crow (Apsáalooke), Gros Ventre (A'aninin), and Shoshone, who came over the mountains from the Great Basin to the west. They spent summers here hunting and raising crops, before heading to warmer climes for the winter.

Trappers and explorers, who first arrived in the valley in the early 1800s, were equally distressed by the harsh winters and short growing seasons, which made Jackson Hole a marginal place for farming and ranching. Among these early visitors were artist Thomas Moran and photographer William

2010 Court rulings return the grizzly bear to the threatened species list and the gray wolf to the endangered species list.

2011 The U.S. Congress returns gray wolf management to the states, effectively delisting the species again in Wyoming and Montana.

2011 A grizzly bear kills a visitor near the Grand Canyon of the Yellowstone, the first bear-related fatality in the park in more than 20 years.

2016 Several visitors are fined for walking into Grand Prismatic Hot Spring, then posting the crime online.

continues

Henry Jackson, whose images awoke the country to the Tetons' grandeur. Homesteaders quickly realized that their best hope was to market the unspoiled beauty of the area, which they began doing in earnest in the early 20th century.

The danger of haphazard development soon became apparent. There were hot dog stands along the roads, a dance hall at Jenny Lake, and buildings going up on prime habitat. In the 1920s, after some discussion about how the Grand Teton area might be protected, Yellowstone Park officials and conservationists went to Congress. Led by local dude ranchers and Yellowstone superintendent Horace Albright, the group was able to protect only the mountains and foothills, leaving out Jackson Lake and the valley. Wyoming's congressional delegation—and many locals—were vehemently opposed to enclosing the valley within park boundaries.

Then, in 1927, something called the Snake River Land Company started buying ranches and homesteads at the base of the Tetons. The company turned out to be a front for John D. Rockefeller, Jr., one of the richest men in the world, working with the conservationists. He planned to give the land to the federal government and keep a few choice parcels for himself. But Congress wouldn't have it, and Rockefeller made noises about selling the land, about 35,000 acres, to the highest bidder. In the 1940s, President Franklin D. Roosevelt created the Jackson Hole National Monument out of Forest Service lands east of the Snake River. That paved the way for

2017 The U.S. Fish and Wildlife Service takes the Yellowstone grizzly bear population off the threatened species list.

2018 A court ruling returns Yellowstone grizzlies to the threatened species list.

2022 Catastrophic flooding in the northern part of Yellowstone destroys roads and backcountry trails, closing sections of the park for weeks or months.

2024 A rare hydrothermal explosion at Black Diamond Point destroys sections of boardwalk and closes Biscuit Basin for the season.

Rockefeller's donation, and in 1950, Grand Teton National Park expanded to its present form.

WHEN TO GO

Summer, autumn, and winter are the best times to visit the Northern Rockies. The days are sunny, the nights are clear, and humidity is low. A popular song once romanticized "Springtime in the Rockies," but that season lasts for about two days in early June. The rest of the season conventionally known as "spring" is likely to be chilly and spitting snow or rain; trails will still be clogged with snow and mud.

Typically, from mid-June on, you can hike, fish, camp, and watch wildlife—except in the higher elevations, which cling to snow well into July. Wildflowers bloom at the lower elevations in early summer, beginning in May in the lower valleys and plains. In the higher elevations, they open up in July. But late summer (Aug and Sept) brings the risk of "smoke season," or smoke from regional or local wildfires settling in the area, obscuring the views and choking up anything with lungs. In bad years, when air quality plummets, being outdoors is inadvisable.

Autumn is not just the time when the aspens turn gold; it's also when rates for gateway motels and restaurants are lower and roads become less crowded. That allows you to pay more attention to the wildlife, which is busy fattening up for the winter.

Winter is glorious, although it's not for everyone. It can be very cold, but the air is crystalline, the snow is powdery, and the skiing is fantastic. If you drive in the parks' vicinity in winter, *always* carry cold-weather clothing, sleeping bags, food, flashlights, and other safety gear. Every local resident has stories about being caught unprepared in wintry weather.

The Climate

The region is characterized by long, cold winters and short, relatively mild summers. There is not a lot of moisture, winter or summer, and the air is dry, except for the brief wet season in March and April.

Don't expect the kind of **spring** you get in lower elevations. Cold and snow can linger into April and May—blizzards can hit the area even in mid-June—although temperatures are generally warming. The average daytime readings are in the 40s or 50s (4°–15°C), gradually increasing into the 60s or 70s (16°–26°C) by early June. So, during spring, a warm jacket, rain gear, and water-resistant walking shoes could be welcome traveling companions.

The area is rarely balmy, but temperatures during the middle of the **summer** are typically 75° to 85°F (24°–29°C) in the lower elevations and are especially comfortable because of the lack of humidity. Remember, too, that the atmosphere is thin at this altitude, so sunscreen is a must. Nights, even during the warmest months, will be cool, with temperatures dropping into the low 40s (4°–9°C), so you'll want to include a jacket in your wardrobe. Because summer thunderstorms are common, you'll probably be glad you've included a waterproof shell or umbrella.

As **fall** approaches, temperatures remain mild but begin to cool, so you'll want to carry an additional layer of clothing. The first heavy snows typically fall in the valley by November 1 (much earlier in the mountains) and continue through March or April. Aspen trees turn bright yellow; cottonwoods turn a deeper gold.

During **winter** months, you need long underwear, heavy shirts, vests, coats, warm gloves, and thick socks. Temperatures can be anywhere from the single digits (negative teens Celsius) to the 30s (–1° to 4°C) during the day, and subzero overnight temperatures are common. Ultracold air can cause lots of health problems, so drink fluids, keep an extra layer of clothing handy, and don't overexert yourself.

For up-to-date weather information and road conditions, call ☏ **307/344-2117** (Yellowstone) or ☏ **511** (in-state mobile) or visit www.wyoroad.info or **www.nps.gov/grte/planyourvisit/roads.htm**.

Avoiding the Crowds

Between the Fourth of July and Labor Day (early Sept), the Northern Rockies come to life. Flowers bloom, fish jump, bison calves frolic—and tourists converge. Park roads are crowded with trailers, and well-known spots are jammed with a significant portion of the millions who make the trek to Montana and Wyoming every year. Your best bet: Travel before June 15, if possible, or after mid-September. Labor Day used to represent a reliable slowdown in visitation, but

SEASONAL ROAD openings & closings

In Yellowstone Traveling Yellowstone's roads during the spring months can be a roll of the dice because openings may be delayed for days (even weeks) at a time, especially at higher altitudes. There is always some section of road in Yellowstone under construction, so call ahead and get a road report (📞 **307/344-2117**). It's irritating, but don't take it out on the road workers; they often labor through the night to cause as little inconvenience as possible.

The only road open year-round is the north entrance to **Mammoth Hot Springs.** From Mammoth, an access road to the northeast entrance and **Cooke City** is plowed throughout the winter season. This service for Cooke City residents gives visitors a great opportunity to see wildlife in winter in the Lamar Valley. Just be mindful of the weather; the road is often slick with ice.

Snowplowing begins in early March. In Yellowstone, the first roads open to motor vehicles (usually by the end of April) include **Mammoth-Old Faithful, Norris-Canyon,** and **West Yellowstone-Madison.** If the weather cooperates, the **East Entrance-Lake** and **Lake-Canyon** open in early May, followed by the **South Entrance-Lake, Lake-Old Faithful,** and **Tower-Tower Fall** in mid-May. **Tower-Canyon** over Dunraven Pass typically opens last—by the end of May, unless there's a late-season snowfall.

The **Chief Joseph Highway,** connecting the entrances in Cooke City, Montana, and Cody, Wyoming, often opens by mid-May. The **Beartooth Highway,** between Cooke City and Red Lodge, Montana, is generally open by Memorial Day weekend.

Winter road closures typically begin in mid-October, when the Beartooth Highway closes. Depending on the weather, most other park roads remain open until the park season ends in early November.

In Grand Teton Because Grand Teton has fewer roads and they're at lower elevations, openings and closings are more predictable. **Teton Park Road** opens to conventional vehicles and RVs around May 1. The **Moose-Wilson Road** opens to vehicles around May 15. Roads close to vehicles on November 1, although they never close for nonmotorized use.

in recent years, people have continued filling the park well into the fall season. If you can't come in the off-season, then visit the major attractions at off-peak hours when others are eating or sleeping. Or, as I suggest over and over, abandon the pavement for the hiking trails, a foolproof way to shake the hordes.

Whenever you come, give these parks as much time as you can; you'll experience more at an unhurried pace.

Yellowstone's Average Monthly Temperatures (High/Low)

	JAN	FEB	MAR	APR	MAY	JUNE	JULY	AUG	SEPT	OCT	NOV	DEC
°F	29/10	34/13	40/17	49/26	60/34	70/41	80/47	78/45	69/37	56/29	39/19	31/12
°C	-2/-12	1/-11	4/-8	9/-3	16/1	21/5	27/8	26/7	21/3	13/-2	4/-7	-1/-11

Grand Teton's Average Monthly Temperatures (High/Low)

	JAN	FEB	MAR	APR	MAY	JUNE	JULY	AUG	SEPT	OCT	NOV	DEC
°F	26/1	31/3	39/12	49/22	61/31	71/37	81/42	80/40	70/32	56/23	38/14	27/2
°C	-3/-17	-1/-16	4/-11	9/-6	16/-1	22/3	27/6	27/4	21/0	13/-5	3/-10	-3/-17

Holidays

Banks, government offices, post offices, and many stores, restaurants, and museums are closed on the following legal national holidays: January 1 (New Year's Day), the third Monday in January (Martin Luther King, Jr. Day), the third Monday in February (Presidents' Day), the last Monday in May (Memorial Day), June 19 (Juneteenth), July 4 (Independence Day), the first Monday in September (Labor Day), the second Monday in October (Columbus Day), November 11 (Veterans Day/Armistice Day), the fourth Thursday in November (Thanksgiving Day), and December 25 (Christmas Day). The Tuesday after the first Monday in November is Election Day, a federal government holiday in presidential-election years (held every 4 years, and next in 2028). The parks are always open on holidays, but visitor centers are often closed.

RESPONSIBLE TRAVEL

Heavy summer auto traffic and the annual impact of millions of human beings have raised questions about the sustainability of these national parks. But a visit to Yellowstone and Grand Teton can be a relatively green vacation. In Yellowstone, concessionaire **Xanterra Travel Collection** (www. yellowstonenationalparklodges.com; ✆ **307/344-7311**) has implemented numerous environmental initiatives, including a recycling/composting program, sourcing food for its restaurants locally and sustainably, and reducing water and energy use. The Old Faithful Snow Lodge was built in part from reclaimed wood from the sawmill that cut the timber for the Old Faithful Inn, and Canyon Lodge's buildings are LEED-certified. Campgrounds have recycling bins. In Grand Teton, the **Grand Teton Lodge Company** (www.gtlc.com; ☏ **307/543-3100**) has implemented sustainability programs to lessen the human impact on the park. A 2015 remodel of Jackson Lake Lodge added water- and energy-conserving fixtures and incorporated recycled materials, and the company's Epic Promise initiative sets a goal of net zero emissions and net zero waste to landfills by 2030.

Yellowstone has installed Level 2 electric vehicle charging stations at Old Faithful, Lake Village, Canyon Village, and Mammoth; EV plugs are also in West Yellowstone and Gardiner. At Grand Teton, Signal Mountain Lodge offers EV charging. Switching to an electric vehicle for your park road trip not only eliminates pollution from the tailpipe, but also slashes carbon emissions that are causing climate change.

Perhaps the best way to look at sustainability is to go off the grid on an overnight backpacking trip. The website of the outdoor-ethics organization **Leave No Trace** (www.lnt.org) provides useful tips for backpackers on how to leave a campsite in the same condition that they found it. Backpacking is

GENERAL RESOURCES FOR green TRAVEL

In addition to the resources for Yellowstone and Grand Teton listed above, the following websites provide valuable, wide-ranging information on sustainable travel.

o **Responsible Travel** (www.responsibletravel.com) is a great source of sustainable travel ideas; the site is run by a spokesperson for ethical tourism in the travel industry.

o **Sustainable Travel International** (www.sustainabletravel.org) promotes ethical tourism practices and manages a directory of sustainable properties and tour operators around the world.

o The **Green Hotels Association** (www.greenhotels.com) recommends green-rated member hotels around the world that fulfill the association's stringent environmental requirements.

o For information on sustainable outdoor recreation, visit **Tread Lightly!** (www.treadlightly.org).

a refreshing counterpoint to modern life that gives perspective on the issues of sustainability and personal energy dependence. For more on backpacking, see "Special Permits" in chapter 10, and the sections on each park's backcountry in chapters 4 and 6.

TOURS

Academic Trips

One of the best ways to turn a park vacation into an unforgettable experience is to join an educational program. There are no finals in these courses; it's just a relaxed, informative way to spend time outdoors.

Yellowstone Forever ★★★ (www.yellowstone.org; © 406/848-2400), formerly the Yellowstone Association Institute, operates at the historic Lamar Buffalo Ranch in the northeast part of the park and at other locations in the vicinity. It typically offers a slew of courses every year, covering everything from winter wildlife tracking to wilderness medicine to the history of fur trappers on the plateau. Prices are reasonable, and some classes are targeted to families and youngsters. For an in-depth experience, choose a Field Seminar with a stay at the ranch or the Gardiner Yellowstone Overlook Field Campus. Customizable hiking, geology, and wildlife-watching **private tours** with a naturalist start at $710 per day, including transportation. The organization has also teamed with the Xanterra Travel Collection to offer 4- to 5-night **Lodging & Learning** packages, which include days spent exploring trails with guides coupled with nights at comfortable lodgings throughout the park.

The **Teton Science Schools** ★★ (www.tetonscience.org; © 307/733-1313) is a venerable institution that offers summer and winter programs. Classes review the ecology, geology, and wildlife of the park, with photography and tracking workshops offered as well. Classes cater to different age groups, and the emphasis is on experiential, hands-on learning.

The Teton Science Schools' **Wildlife Expeditions** includes trips in open-roof vans, on rafts, in sleighs, and by foot. These tours bring visitors closer to wildlife than they're likely to get on their own. Wildlife Expeditions offers trips ranging from a half-day sunset safari ($179) to private, full-day park tours (about $1,875 for up to 9 people).

Adventure Trips

For a detailed list of outfitters, guides, and equipment rental providers categorized by activity, see the "Other Activities" sections in chapters 4 and 6.

In addition, **AdventureBus** (www.adventurebus.com; *℃* **909/633-7225**) offers trips on its customized buses with an emphasis on outdoor adventures in Yellowstone and Grand Teton. The rate is about $1,350 per person for a weeklong trip. **Austin Adventures** (www.austinadventures.com; *℃* **844/399-8868**) offers guided multiday tours that include biking, hiking, and rafting in and around Yellowstone and Grand Teton. Six-day trips start around $4,999 per adult. **Backroads** (www.backroads.com; *℃* **800/462-2848**) offers a variety of guided multiday trips involving horseback riding, hiking, cycling, and rafting in and around Yellowstone and Grand Teton. The rate is about $4,199 to $7,099 per person for 4- to 6-day trips staying in park lodges. And **Escape Adventures** (www.escapeadventures.com; *℃* **800/596-2953** or 702/596-2953) offers 5- and 6-day road cycling/mountain biking tours of Grand Teton and Yellowstone that also include rock climbing, rafting, and hiking. The rate starts at $1,999 per person (camping) and $4,099 per person (park lodgings).

EXPLORING YELLOWSTONE

Get used to the idea right now: Yellowstone is a colossal park, and you'd never see everything here if you tried for a lifetime. Just embrace the fact that *anything* you choose to do while you're here will be fascinating, wondrous, and 100% worth your time. Whether you go off in search of wolves and bears, tour the geyser basins, hike the trails, or cruise the park roads, Yellowstone is guaranteed to blow your mind.

Grand Loop Road, the 154-mile, figure-eight road looping through the heart of the park, connects most of the major and minor attractions, and you're bound to spend some time cruising it. But stop frequently and get out of the car: Exploring the park's highlights and, even better, getting out into the backcountry on a hiking trail will enrich your trip by leaps and bounds.

You *could* visit Yellowstone for a single day—and if that's your only chance, by all means, take it—but you need a minimum of 3 days to really get a feel for the place. A week or more is even better. Hit up the must-sees, such as **Old Faithful, Grand Canyon of the Yellowstone, Mammoth terraces, Lamar Valley,** and **Yellowstone Lake,** but also check out some of the lesser-known but still incredible destinations. Attend a ranger-led program or sign up for a class with **Yellowstone Forever** (p. 67) for an in-depth experience. Consider spending a night under the stars, either in a drive-in campground or deep in the backcountry. The farther you go from the road, the more solitude you'll enjoy, and the more the park's wild heart will be revealed to you.

ESSENTIALS

ACCESS/ENTRY POINTS   Yellowstone has five entrances. The **north entrance,** near Mammoth Hot Springs, is located just south of Gardiner, Montana, and U.S. 89. In the winter, this is the only access to Yellowstone by car.

The **west entrance,** just outside the town of West Yellowstone, Montana, on U.S. 20, is the closest entry to Old Faithful. Inside the park, you can turn south to Old Faithful or north to the Norris Geyser Basin. This entrance is open to wheeled vehicles from late April to early November, depending on snow levels, and to snowmobiles and snowcoaches from mid-December to mid-March.

About 64 miles north of Jackson, Wyoming, the **south entrance,** on U.S. 89/191/287, approaches Yellowstone from Grand Teton National Park. On the way, drivers get panoramic views of the Teton Range. Once in the park, the road skirts the Lewis River to the south end of Yellowstone Lake, at West Thumb and Grant Village. It's open to cars from early to mid-May to early November, and to snowmobiles and snowcoaches from mid-December to mid-March.

The **east entrance,** on U.S. 14/16/20, 53 miles west of Cody, Wyoming, is open to cars from early May to early November and to snowmobiles and snowcoaches from late December to mid-March. The drive over Sylvan Pass is one of the most scenically stunning approaches to the park, but it might make you nervous if you're not used to mountain driving.

The **northeast entrance,** at Cooke City, Montana, is closest to the Tower-Roosevelt area, 29 miles to the west. This entrance is open to cars year-round, but from mid-October (when the Beartooth Highway closes) until around Memorial Day, the only route to Cooke City is through Mammoth Hot Springs. When it's open, the drive from Red Lodge to the park is a grand climb among the clouds.

VISITOR CENTERS   The park has five major visitor and information centers, each with a different offering.

The **Albright Visitor Center** (© **307/344-2263**), at Mammoth Hot Springs, is open daily year-round (9am–5pm). It houses an info desk, backcountry office, and wildlife exhibits.

Yellowstone National Park

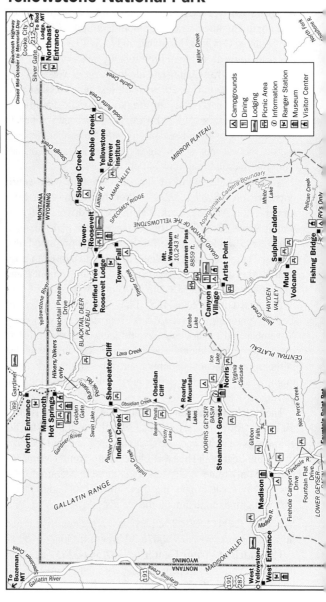

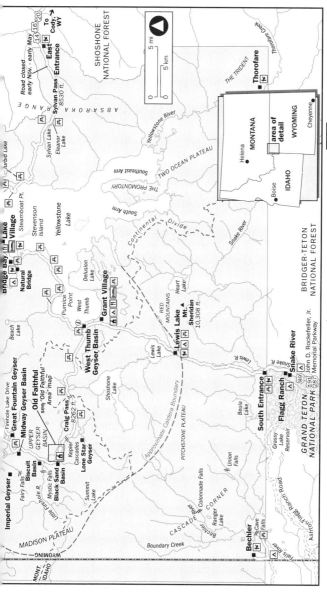

33

The **Canyon Visitor Education Center** (☎ **307/344-2550**), in Canyon Village, is one of the park's most expansive, interactive facilities, with excellent exhibits on the park's supervolcano. It's open in summer daily (8am–6pm), and the friendly rangers are used to dealing with crowds.

The park's newest visitor center, the **Old Faithful Visitor Education Center** (☎ **307/344-2750**), has picture-perfect views of Old Faithful, exhibits on how the geothermal features work, and a Young Scientist area for budding geologists. It displays projected geyser-eruption times, making it a good first stop for those looking to see Old Faithful. It's open daily, in summer 8am to 8pm and in winter from mid-December to mid-March 9am to 5pm.

The **Fishing Bridge Visitor Center** (☎ **307/344-2109**), near Fishing Bridge on the north shore of Yellowstone Lake, has an excellent display that focuses on the park's bird life. You can get information and publications here as well. It's open in summer daily 8am to 6pm.

The **Grant Visitor Center** (☎ **307/344-2109**) has publications, videos, and a fascinating exhibit on the role of fire in Yellowstone. It's open in summer daily 8am to 6pm.

Park literature and helpful staff are also found at several small information stations: the **Madison Information Station** (☎ 307/344-2109; summer daily 9am–4:30pm); the **Museum of the National Park Ranger** (☎ 307/344-2109; summer daily 10am–4pm) and the **Norris Geyser Basin Museum and Information Station** (☎ 307/344-2109; summer daily 9am–5pm), both at Norris; the **West Thumb Information Station** (☎ 307/344-2109; summer daily 9am–5pm); and the **West Yellowstone Visitor Information Center,** 30 Yellowstone Ave. (☎ 307/344-2876; summer daily 8am–8pm, limited hours the rest of the year). In Gardiner, **Yellowstone Forever,** 308 Park St. (www.yellowstone.org; ☎ 406/848-2400), contains a small gift shop with books and other visitor info.

ENTRANCE FEES A 7-day pass costs $35 per private vehicle. A 7-day snowmobile or motorcycle pass costs $30, and someone who comes in on bicycle, skis, or foot will pay $20 for 7 days. The National Park Service offers several free days or weeks every year; for this year's schedule, check www.nps.gov/planyourvisit/fee-free-parks.htm.

If you're lucky enough to visit Yellowstone more than once a year, the $70 annual pass is the way to go. Even better, pick up the $80 **America the Beautiful Annual Pass** (free for U.S. military members), which grants entry to all national parks and most other federal fee areas for a year. Other special passes include the **Lifetime Senior Pass,** for a one-time fee of $80, for those ages 62 and up; the **Access Pass,** free for those with permanent disabilities; and the free **Annual 4th Grade Pass** for American 4th graders and their families. Buy any pass at any entrance to the park.

CAMPING FEES   Fees for camping in Yellowstone range from $20 to $39 per night, depending on amenities. RV sites run up to $89 per night. For information on camping, see "Where to Camp in Yellowstone" in chapter 7. In most cases, reservations are required at all campgrounds in both parks.

SPECIAL REGULATIONS & WARNINGS   More detailed information about the following rules can be requested from the park rangers, at visitor centers throughout the park, or at **www.nps.gov/yell**.

o **Bicycles:** Bicycles are allowed on the park's roadways and a few gravel roads, but not on trails or boardwalks. Spring (early Apr) and fall (Nov) are some of the best times for cycling, as the park opens the roads to bikes before and after cars are allowed. Come prepared for nasty weather. Helmets and bright clothing are recommended because of the narrow, winding park roads and the presence of large RVs with poor visibility.

o **Camping:** A person may camp in the park for no more than 30 days in any given year, and no more than 14 days during the summer season (except at Fishing Bridge RV Park, where neither limit applies). Food, garbage, and food utensils must be stored in a hard-sided vehicle or locked in a campground's bearproof locker when not in use.

o **Defacing park features:** Collecting, removing, or destroying any natural or archaeological objects is prohibited, including picking wildflowers or collecting rocks. Only dead-and-down wood of wrist size or smaller can be collected for backcountry campfires, and only when and where such fires are allowed.

o **Firearms:** As of 2010, firearms are allowed in national parks (shooting them remains illegal, however). Those in possession of a firearm must have a legal license from their state of residence. Firearms are prohibited in marked facilities.

o **Littering:** Littering in the national parks is strictly prohibited—if you take it in, you take it out. Throwing coins or other objects into thermal features is illegal.

o **Motorcycles:** Motorcycles and motor scooters are allowed only on park roads. No off-road or trail riding is allowed. Driver's licenses and license plates are required.

o **Pets:** Pets must always be leashed and are prohibited in the backcountry, on trails, on boardwalks, and in thermal areas. If you tie up a pet and leave it, you're breaking the law. Service animals, however, can go on trails and boardwalks in developed areas and, with a permit, the backcountry.

o **Smoking:** No smoking is allowed in thermal areas, on trails, in buildings, or within 25 feet of any building entrance.

o **Snowmobiling:** The park offers limited permits to private snowmobilers via a lottery system; for details, see p. 94.

o **Swimming:** Swimming or wading is prohibited in thermal features or in streams whose waters flow from thermal features in Yellowstone. Swimming elsewhere is discouraged due to the cold water, swift currents, and unpredictable weather.

o **Wildlife:** It is unlawful to approach within 100 yards of a bear or wolf or within 25 yards of other wildlife. Feeding any wildlife is illegal. Wildlife calls, such as elk bugles or other artificial attractants, are forbidden.

THE HIGHLIGHTS

Yellowstone is an enormous park with a staggering number of attractions to see. The park's absolute highlights are accessible via the Grand Loop Road, and you can visit most of them in a few days. Tailor your itinerary to your interests—perhaps wildlife, thermal features, or major scenic hotspots—and hit the road. It takes roughly 30 minutes to drive between major junctions, but traffic and herds of bison crossing the road can significantly lengthen travel time. Be patient. *Tip:* Hit the road early—we're talking sunrise—to ensure you'll get a parking spot at some of the most popular destinations. Note that RVs and vehicles with trailers will have an especially tough time in the parking lots, so leave your rig behind if possible.

The Upper Loop

MAMMOTH HOT SPRINGS The first attraction you'll hit coming in from the north, Mammoth's beautifully sculpted travertine terraces (the **Upper and Lower terraces ★★** are described in "Yellowstone: The Extended Tour," p. 45) are well worth a stroll. History buffs will appreciate the **Albright Visitor Center** and **Fort Yellowstone,** a collection of preserved buildings from the 1890s and early 1900s.

NORRIS GEYSER BASIN ★★ Norris is Yellowstone's hottest, most acidic thermal area and a wonderful place to wander two adjoining basins, Back Basin and Porcelain Basin. You'll see examples of geysers, steam vents, and hot springs with colorful bacterial mats, plus the **Norris Geyser Basin Museum.**

CANYON VILLAGE AREA An absolute must-see, the **Grand Canyon of the Yellowstone River ★★★** plunges more than 1,000 feet from rim to river and features two stunning waterfalls. Gaze at the polychromatic rock layers from several lookouts and hike the North or South Rims. Several fantastic day hikes and overnight trails launch from this area.

TOWER-ROOSEVELT AREA As the closest road junction to the **Lamar Valley ★★★,** this is ground zero for spotting wolves, bears, bison, elk, and plenty more species. Nearby **Tower Fall ★** is one of the park's most impressive front-country cascades; an overlook is accessible via a short, paved path.

The Lower Loop

OLD FAITHFUL AREA Probably the world's most famous geyser, **Old Faithful ★★★** shouldn't be missed—but the rest of the spouters and hot springs in **Upper Geyser Basin ★★★** are equally impressive. Walk the boardwalks for a look at this unique concentration of hydrothermal action (more than 150 features within 1 sq. mile). Explore the incredible **Old Faithful Inn** or eat at **Old Faithful Snow Lodge.** One of the park's best visitor centers is also here, along with some great hiking trails.

LAKE VILLAGE AREA Huge, lovely, and very cold, 20-mile-long **Yellowstone Lake** ★★ offers plenty of adventure: scenic boat tours, paddling opportunities, and shoreline camping. Stop by the historical, elegant **Lake Yellowstone Hotel,** or grab a beer on the front porch of **Lake Lodge.** Nearby **Bridge Bay Marina** offers boat rentals and guided fishing trips. Just north, **Hayden Valley** ★★ is another great place to look for bears and bison.

MIDWAY GEYSER BASIN Yellowstone's largest hot spring, **Grand Prismatic Spring** ★★, resembles a portal to another world: a shockingly blue pool ringed by bright yellows, greens, and oranges. A boardwalk swings you past the steaming spring, or you can get the aerial view via the nearby **Grand Prismatic Overlook Trail.** The **Fairy Falls Trail** also takes off from here.

IF YOU HAVE ONLY 1 OR 2 DAYS

There are two ways to approach a time-crunched visit to Yellowstone, both of which have their merits. One, choose one area to explore in depth, take your time absorbing the sights, and get out on a backcountry trail. If that's your cup of tea, skip on to "Yellowstone: The Extended Tour" to choose your destination. But if you'd rather pack as many sights into the day as humanly possible, the following itineraries are for you. Keep in mind that patience and flexibility are key to pulling off this whirlwind.

1 DAY Get an early start: This greatest-hits tour of the lower loop of Grand Loop Road covers 94 to 124 miles and encompasses five major attractions, leaving little time for dallying. Begin from the popular west entrance and cruise along the **Madison River,** where you can see the forest recovering from the 1988 fires. You'll also spot ducks and trumpeter swans on the river, and grazing elk and bison. Turn north at Madison Junction and stop at **Norris Geyser Basin** to walk the boardwalks through both the larger, geyser-packed Back Basin and the smaller, bleached-white Porcelain Basin. Plan to spend at least an hour here, perhaps a bit more if you want to see the **Norris Geyser Basin Museum.**

Get back in the car and proceed east to the **Canyon Village** area (a good spot for a snack or to stop by the visitor center). Then continue down the road to **South Rim Drive** for a peek at the **Grand Canyon of the Yellowstone,** including the awe-inspiring **Upper Falls** and **Lower Falls.** Hike part of the South Rim Trail for rimside views or go straight to **Artist Point** for a picture-perfect view of Lower Falls.

Next stop: **Hayden Valley.** Drive south and keep an eye out for bison and bears roaming near the Yellowstone River. Just beyond is the **Lake Village** area, your best bet for lunch. Dine at Lake Yellowstone Hotel or picnic along the shore. The lake will be your companion along the next stretch of road, curving southwest to **West Thumb.** Hop out and walk the boardwalk through this small lakeside geyser basin.

Press west, crossing the Continental Divide twice, to the **Old Faithful** area. You'll easily catch Old Faithful itself at least twice, as it erupts every 68 to 94 minutes (check at the Old Faithful Inn or the visitor center for the next predicted show). In between eruptions, stroll the boardwalk through **Upper Geyser Basin** to gaze at more than a hundred other thermal features. If you're lucky enough to score a room at Old Faithful Inn, Old Faithful Snow Lodge, or Old Faithful Lodge, this is your stopping point. If you'd rather sleep alfresco, head back north to Madison or Norris campgrounds.

2 DAYS   With a second day, you can tack on the sights of the upper loop to your plan (the loop itself is 70 miles long, although visiting the Lamar Valley will add 15–20 more miles out and back). If you spent the night at Old Faithful, make your way north to Norris (stop by **Midway Geyser Basin** to see **Grand Prismatic Spring** en route). From there, continue north to **Mammoth Hot Springs.** Get out and walk the upper and lower terraces to watch travertine formations being built before your eyes. Stop by **Albright Visitor Center** for background on park history and wildlife, then take the self-guided tour of **Fort Yellowstone.**

Next, the road swings east. Take the one-way **Blacktail Plateau Drive** for even better wildlife-spotting opportunities than you already have on the road, then press on into the **Lamar Valley.** This wide, rich expanse is home to most of the park's major wildlife species; dawn and dusk are the best times to look for them, especially wolves.

Backtrack to **Tower-Roosevelt** and make a quick stop to see **Tower Fall** from the overlook. The next stretch is one of the park's most scenic: a winding road that climbs to 8,859-foot Dunraven Pass, delivering sweeping views the whole way up and down. You'll end up back at Canyon Village.

YELLOWSTONE: THE EXTENDED TOUR

If you have the option, extend your visit to 4 or 5 days (or even longer): You'll see so much more, will have the time to get out and hike a few trails, and will be able to soak in the scenery without feeling quite so rushed.

A stop at any of the park **visitor centers** is an excellent way to kick off your trip. Most have exhibits on Yellowstone's wildlife, geothermal features, volcanic activity, or history, plus brochures and maps. Rangers are on hand to answer questions, provide info on current conditions, and make insider suggestions based on your particular fancy. Note that the park has 10 centers and information stations (see "Essentials," earlier in this chapter), but some might be closed if you visit off-season. **Albright Visitor Center** at Mammoth and the **West Yellowstone Visitor Information Center** are open year-round.

You can begin a Yellowstone tour from any of the park's five entrances, but this itinerary assumes you'll be starting from the most popular one, the west entrance, and driving clockwise around **Grand Loop Road.** Simply adjust the order of attractions if you jump in at any other point.

West Yellowstone to Norris

Closest entrance: West Yellowstone (west entrance)

Distances: 14 miles from West Yellowstone to Madison; 14 miles from Madison to Norris

The west entrance road takes you through a lush valley along the **Madison River.** The distant peaks of the Gallatin Range beckon to the northwest, and bison and elk frequently browse in the grasses here. This is also a prime spot to see the lingering effects of the historic 1988 wildfires that burned 36% of the park. The **Two Ribbons Trail,** one of the first pullouts you'll reach, offers a .8-mile accessible boardwalk through a forest of blackened trunks, heat-shattered boulders, and fresh new growth. Lodgepole pines have what are called *serotinous cones,* which are sealed in a sticky resin and depend on the high temperatures of wildfire to melt the resin and expose and drop their seeds—and evidence of the success of this adaptation is all around.

Next, keep your eyes peeled for the entrance to **Riverside Drive,** a secluded paved road about 6 miles from the entrance station. The road doubles back west along the Madison and grants access to several ideal fly-fishing spots. This river is known for its top-notch trout waters and remains on the warm side year-round, thanks to upstream hot springs. Riverside Drive also makes for a quiet escape for a picnic.

As you continue toward Madison Junction, you'll see more vivid evidence of the 1988 fires and, odds are, a herd of bison that hang out during summer months. As frightening as the fires were, they had their advantages: There is evidence that the 1988 fires burned hotter here because the old lodgepole pines had been infected by beetles, decimating the trees long before the fires blazed. The good news is that the fire killed the beetles and re-mineralized the soil. When temperatures exceeded 500°F (260°C), pine seeds were released from serotinous pine cones, quickening the regrowth cycle.

Another lovely pullout on the south side of the road features an interpretive display about the major explorer parties in the region and the 1877 Nez Perce retreat. A band of Nez Perce traveled through this area trying to escape the U.S. Army, which wanted to force them onto a reservation; the Army caught up with them about 40 miles south of the Canadian border. Beyond, the **Mount Haynes Overlook** has a boardwalk down to the Madison River, where bulbous Mount Haynes looms just across the water.

Hiking options are limited on this segment, but you can stretch your legs on the 1-mile (round-trip) **Harlequin Lake Trail,** a mellow uphill hike to the lily pad–covered lake. The trailhead is about 1½ miles west of Madison Junction. The **Purple Mountain Trail** is a more challenging 6-miler (round-trip) that gains 1,500 feet on the way to a gorgeous overlook of the Madison and Gibbon rivers. Pick this one up a ¼ mile north of Madison Junction.

Madison Junction marks the place where the Firehole and Gibbon rivers meet, flowing together to form the

Madison River. (The Madison meets the Jefferson and Gallatin rivers about 183 miles away to form the mighty Missouri River.) These are excellent trout waters. The sprawling **Madison Campground** sits here in a lodgepole forest with river views; it's one of Yellowstone's most popular options. The **Madison Information Station,** just south, has a ranger on hand, kid-friendly animal exhibits, and trail guides.

You're now on Grand Loop Road. The next 14-mile section follows the Gibbon River through a canyon lined with flaky magenta rock. The river was named for General John Gibbon, who explored here in 1872 but whose dubious claims to fame were as the cavalry leader who buried Custer's army and who chased Chief Joseph and the Nez Perce from the park as they attempted to escape to Canada.

Make sure to stop at 84-foot **Gibbon Falls,** a lacy fan of water cascading off the edge of the Yellowstone Caldera rim (it's one of the few places in the park where the caldera boundary is in plain sight). Continue past **Beryl Spring** (better thermals await) and hike 2 miles (round-trip) to **Monument Geyser Basin** if you're up for a steep challenge. The trail leads to a mostly extinct thermal area littered with ancient white geyser cones.

The last attraction before Norris, **Artists' Paintpot ★** holds a series of milky-white and bluish pools alongside gurgling mud pots spitting glop. The 1.2-mile loop trail is refreshingly uncrowded—hike the upper trail option for an aerial view over the colorful basin. Across the road from the trailhead is **Elk Park,** where you have a good chance of seeing a large herd of the majestic ungulates.

Norris Geyser Basin

Closest entrances and distances: 28 miles from West Yellowstone (west) entrance; 26 miles from Gardiner (north) entrance

Even if you've visited Yellowstone's oldest, hottest, and most acidic basin before, you haven't really seen it: The volatile **Norris Geyser Basin ★★** changes constantly as old features go dormant, new geysers force their way from the earth, mineral-laden hot springs plug up old tunnels, and earthquakes reroute the underground "pipes." Here, heat-loving microorganisms called thermophiles form intricate mats of yellow, green, red, and black among the superhot features; most of the hot springs and fumaroles (steam vents) have temperatures above the boiling point (199°F/93°C at this elevation). In fact, the park's hottest geothermal temperature ever recorded, a bit more than 1,000 feet underground here, was a blistering 459°F (237°C).

Norris encompasses two loop trails. The shorter one, a .8-mile figure eight through **Porcelain Basin,** starts with a grand overlook across the baked-white landscape of steaming pools and vents. Highlights include the 20- to 30-foot-high Constant Geyser (despite the name, it's not always erupting); pulsing Whirligig Geyser; and the hot spring Congress Pool, which might be a hissing dry vent or a boiling puddle.

Back Basin Loop contains many more features on its 1.5-mile loop trail. The most exciting one is undoubtedly Steamboat Geyser, the world's tallest at more than 300 feet. For years, major eruptions were erratic and rare, but the behemoth woke up in 2018 with 32 different blasts. Since then, it erupts somewhat regularly (though not predictably)—so you could get lucky! Echinus Geyser is the biggest known acidic geyser, with a pH approaching that of vinegar. Lately Echinus's shows have been few and far between. Other geysers, springs, and fumaroles fill out the basin.

When you're through pounding the boardwalks, stop by the stone-and-log **Norris Geyser Basin Museum** (*② 307/ 344-2109*) for exhibits on Yellowstone's thermal features. The building dates to 1929 and also houses a bookstore. A couple of free ranger programs and hikes take off from here in season; check the park newspaper for details. The **Museum of the National Park Ranger** (*② 307/344-2109*) is worth a stop to see historical photos and information on the evolution of the ranger job.

Deadly Misstep

The signs warning against stepping off the boardwalk are no joke—in thermal areas, the ground might be just a thin crust over a boiling spring, and it's far too easy to blunder into an unsafe zone. In 2016, a man died after intentionally venturing off the boardwalk and then (accidentally) falling into one hot spring, and in 2022, a park employee found a human foot in a shoe floating in another pool.

Norris Geyser Basin Museum is open daily from late May to mid-October, weather permitting, 9am to 5pm. The Museum of the National Park Ranger is only open in July and August, daily 10am to 4pm.

The **Norris Campground,** which is just slightly north of Norris Junction, is a very popular campground. Its best attribute just might be that it lets you walk to the geyser basin and skip the parking problems of high summer.

Norris to Mammoth Hot Springs

Closest entrances: Norris is 28 miles from the West Yellowstone (west) entrance; Mammoth Hot Springs is 5 miles from the Gardiner (north) entrance.

Distance: 21 miles from Norris to Mammoth Hot Springs

Driving north from Norris wends you past grassy meadows on one side and jagged cliffs on the other, with plenty of stands of trees and small lakes providing habitat to bison and elk. Pause at the **Nymph Lake Overlook** for a nice vista over the water and several steaming hot springs. The boggy meadow areas just beyond are popular with moose.

Pull over at **Roaring Mountain,** 4 miles north of Norris, to check out a hillside steaming with fumaroles. As steam vents developed here, the ground became hot and acidic, bleaching and crumbling the rock and taking the undergrowth with it. The hill earned its name in the 1880s, when the vents were loud enough to "roar." Today, the sound is more like a hiss.

A half-mile past Beaver Lake, you'll reach **Obsidian Cliff.** Native Americans began collecting chips of this glassy black volcanic rock for tools as long as 11,000 years ago, and pieces from this very cliff were discovered as far away as western Canada and the Midwest, thanks to ancient trade routes.

Continue on as **Willow Park** opens up to the west, an open meadow where you might see beaver, moose, or coyotes. **Indian Creek Campground,** one of the park's choicest places to pitch a tent, lies on the north end of this area. Just up the road, the **Sheepeater Cliff** picnic spot is worth the short detour. The peaceful area sits well off the road along a basalt column cliff that cooled into its present columnar shape from lava 500,000 years ago.

Keep going north to cruise through **Swan Lake Flat,** a wide-open expanse with huge views of the Gallatin Range.

At the northernmost edge of the Yellowstone Plateau, you'll begin a descent through **Golden Gate.** This steep, narrow stretch of road was once a stagecoach route constructed of wooden planks anchored to the mountain near a massive rock called the **Pillar of Hercules,** the largest rock in a pile that sits next to the road.

Beyond Hercules are the **Hoodoos,** an ominous-looking jumble of travertine boulders on the north side of the road, which have tumbled off the mountainside above to create a pile of unusual formations.

One of the best hikes in the area is to 8,564-foot **Bunsen Peak.** The 4.6-mile round-trip travels through grizzly-frequented meadows to a sweeping view over the Blacktail Plateau and Yellowstone River Valley. And though you can't summit the peak on a bike, the old **Bunsen Peak Road** circling the mountain is one of the few off-road spots open to bicycles. Access both trailheads 5 miles south of Mammoth.

Once you head north from Mammoth, you're off the Grand Loop and on the North Entrance Road. The historic flooding of the Gardner River in June 2022 washed out huge sections of this road, forcing the park to quickly transform the single-lane Old Gardiner Road into a steep, winding, paved, two-lane access route between Mammoth and the town of Gardiner. This road will provide full visitor access until park officials settle on a new permanent road plan—a process expected to take years.

Mammoth Hot Springs

Closest entrance and distance: 5 miles from the Gardiner (north) entrance

The northernmost developed area at Yellowstone revolves around the one-of-a-kind travertine terrace features here—one of the planet's best examples of this type of geologic sculpture. Though they're fueled by the same potent combination of heat, geology, and water that power the rest of the park's thermal features, Mammoth's terraces are unlike anything else you'll see here.

Mammoth's signature feature looks like a series of stair steps frosted with a chalky white trimming. Bright greens, oranges, and yellows cover some of the terraces, and intricate ripples of rock glaze others. Steaming pools rise in some areas, and others resemble dry, bare, white fields. In this area, limestone deposited by an ancient sea is common. As in other thermal areas, an underground heat source causes groundwater to rise back to the surface; as it does, the water dissolves the calcium carbonate in the limestone. Once on the surface, the water quickly deposits the mineral to build the terraces at the pace of a ton of limestone every 24 hours. Heat-loving microorganisms called thermophiles create the color swatches in some areas.

This is one of Yellowstone's most dynamic zones. Old hot springs may go dry for days, weeks, or much longer, leaving bare expanses. New springs perpetually seep up in different places, sculpting fresh terraces. Such constant shifting makes Mammoth an especially fascinating stop: Where else can you watch geologic changes practically before your eyes?

A series of interconnected boardwalks, some of which are wheelchair accessible, wind through the active terraces, granting an up-close look. Start with the **Lower Terraces ★★**, where the boardwalk connects you to major features and then climbs 300 feet to an observation deck up top. Walking the whole thing out and back covers about 1.5 miles.

Liberty Cap greets you near the start of the trail: This 37-foot, pointy pillar formed when a high-pressure hot spring steadily deposited minerals over hundreds of years. Next up is **Palette Spring,** a gorgeously furrowed slope painted in broad strokes of orange and brown. **Minerva** and **Cleopatra Terraces** are just beyond. This area changes frequently from active to dry. **Jupiter** and **Mound Terraces** are similarly volatile: Mound has cycled through on-and-off periods for decades, and Jupiter flowed so forcefully in the 1980s that it overtopped the boardwalks a few times. Hoof it up the final staircases to the overlook, where you'll get a top-down view of the terraces and several hot springs.

From here, you can connect to **Upper Terrace Drive** to walk the 1.5-mile loop through more terraces (alternatively, hop back in the car and drive it). Though there's a collection of live and dormant terraces and several nice views from up here, particularly around **Canary Spring,** this loop is skippable unless you're a real terrace fiend.

Back in the main Mammoth Hot Springs area, consider taking the short, self-guided **Fort Yellowstone** tour (from the

Mammoth Hot Springs

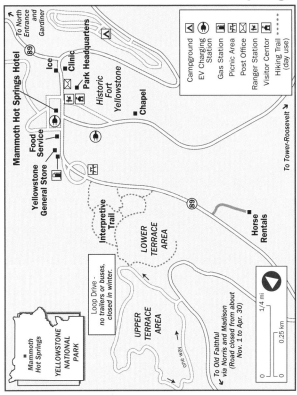

Albright Visitor Center). In Yellowstone's early days, before there was a National Park Service, the U.S. Army played the role of protectors of the park's wildlife and resources. Many structures from that era (1886–1916) still stand; check out the officers' quarters, a chapel, cavalry barracks, and more (although you can't enter most buildings).

Just steps from the lower terrace is the trailhead for the **Beaver Ponds Loop Trail,** a 5-mile jaunt through fir and spruce, then sagebrush and aspen, along a trail that follows **Clematis Gulch.** The ponds are about 2.5 miles from the trailhead, where the toothy beavers are most active in early morning and at night. The area is also a hangout for elk and bears, and may be closed early in the summer season.

Mammoth Hot Springs to Tower Junction

Closest entrance: Mammoth is 5 miles from the Gardiner (north) entrance.

Distance: 18 miles from Mammoth to Tower

The first highlight you'll hit heading east out of Mammoth is a lovely pair of waterfalls. The first, triple-tiered **Undine Falls,** is visible from a road pullout, while seeing the second, **Wraith Falls,** requires an easy 1-mile (round-trip) hike. Also of note: the **Forces of the Northern Range Trail,** 8 miles from Mammoth. This flat, .5-mile loop augmented with interpretive signs delivers a firsthand lesson on fire ecology.

Escape the summer traffic on **Blacktail Plateau Drive,** a 6-mile, scenic alternate route running parallel to Grand Loop Road. The unpaved route (fine for passenger cars, but no trailers or RVs) winds through aspen stands and meadows with excellent views of the Northern Range, and you might spot elk, deer, or bears. The drive essentially follows a route used by the long-vanished Bannock people; scars in the land made by their *travois* (luggage racks made of twin poles tied to a horse) are still evident along the trail.

You'll end up back on the Grand Loop Road a mile west of the **Petrified Tree** turnoff. It's well worth the short detour. Here stand the remains of an ancient redwood that was swiftly buried by volcanic debris and mudflows between 45 and 50 million years ago. Eventually, silica from the eruptions filled in the tree's cells, preserving it to this day.

Tower-Roosevelt

Closest entrances and distances: 23 miles from the Gardiner (north) entrance; 29 miles from the Cooke City (northeast) entrance

Frontiersy **Tower-Roosevelt** is the most relaxed of the major park junctions—a far cry from the hordes that sometimes descend on Old Faithful or the Canyon area. The 26th president really did camp in the area in 1903, and much of the spirit of Teddy Roosevelt's Old West remains here. **Roosevelt Lodge,** a log building dating back to the 1920s, houses a barbeque restaurant and bar, plus a check-in desk for the simple log cabins scattered nearby (see "Where to Stay & Eat in Yellowstone," in chapter 7). A concessionaire-run corral also offers trail rides, stagecoach rides, and a mighty fun cookout accessed on horseback or by wagon.

Like the North Entrance Road, the Northeast Entrance Road between Tower Junction and the Northeast Entrance/ Cooke City suffered substantial damage when June 2022 floods washed out multiple sections of pavement. Park officials swiftly repaired the route, and substantial construction in 2023 further improved the road.

Just east of the junction, the **Yellowstone River Picnic Area** is worth a quick stop to see if the bighorn sheep that frequent the cliffs in this area are out. Continue along the Northeast Entrance Road 4½ miles past the Tower Junction to reach the unmarked trailhead to **Specimen Ridge.** A short (3 miles round-trip) but very steep hike up this hillside leads to a fossilized forest—the largest concentration of petrified trees in the world, in fact. You can still pick out the rings on many of these 50-million-year-old trees, which were buried and subsequently fossilized by a series of volcanic eruptions.

A Detour: The Beartooth Highway

Closest entrance and distance: 29 miles to the Cooke City (northeast) entrance

The dramatic scenery of the park's Northeast Entrance Road remains something of a secret. It's far enough removed from the Grand Loop Road to shake most of the hordes—all the better for those with the time to cruise the area's wildlife-packed valleys, idyllic creeks, and striking peaks. Just beyond the park boundary and the towns of Silver Gate and Cooke City, the high-mountain Beartooth Highway picks up for one of the prettiest drives in the Rockies.

Driving east from **Tower Junction** on the Northeast Entrance Road, you'll quickly enter the **Lamar Valley ★★★**. This grand expanse is one of the park's best zones for wildlife-watching: You might see elk, deer, badgers, bison, osprey, and bears, but the area's real stars are the wolves. Biologists reintroduced this native predator to Yellowstone in 1995 and 1996. Today, about 124 wolves in 10 packs inhabit the park. For your best chance of spotting them, head to the Lamar Valley at dawn and look for the park's wolf-watchers set up at pullouts with large spotting scopes. These volunteers often have the most up-to-date intel on where the wolves are and will usually let you take a peek through their scopes.

Continuing east, you'll pass the turnoff to **Slough Creek Campground** (one of the best in the park) and the historical **Lamar Buffalo Ranch,** where a bison-breeding program ran from 1906 to the 1950s to replenish the dwindled bison population. The scenery grows more striking as you press on along Soda Butte Creek, with views of summits like the 9,583-foot Druid Peak and 10,404-foot Barronette Peak rising before you. **Pebble Creek Campground,** another choice place to pitch a tent, is in this area, as are several lovely hiking trails, such as **Pebble Creek Trail** and the **Thunderer Cutoff Trail** to Chaw Pass. (*Note:* The June 2022 floods also damaged some of the area trails. It's essential that hikers check in with the Backcountry Office for current conditions and closures.) You'll also pass secluded picnic pullouts along Soda Butte Creek, **Soda Butte Picnic Area** and **Warm Springs Picnic Area.** Both are small, lovely places for a bite.

The northeast gateway towns of **Silver Gate** and **Cooke City** don't offer many dining and lodging options, but they're gorgeous, quiet, and make an excellent base for exploring this forgotten area. See chapter 8, "Gateways to Yellowstone & Grand Teton," for details.

Now, begin your climb into the high country on the spectacular **Beartooth Highway ★★**, a 68-mile stretch of U.S. 212 connecting Cooke City to Red Lodge, Montana. The summer-only route delves into a wilderness with views of lakes, flowery alpine meadows, and the Absaroka and Beartooth mountains, hitting its apex on 10,947-foot Beartooth Pass. We'd go at least this far for the best sampling of the highway's charms; then, you can backtrack to the northeast entrance or swing southeast on the **Chief Joseph Scenic Highway ★★** (Wyo. 296), which connects to Wyo. 120 into Cody. This highway, also called the Sunlight Basin Road, offers great opportunities for viewing wildlife.

From Tower Junction to the Grand Canyon of the Yellowstone

Closest entrances: 23 miles from the Gardiner (north) entrance; 29 miles from the Cooke City (northeast) entrance

Distance: 19 miles from Tower Junction to Canyon Village

Grand Loop Road veers south here, cruising up and over Dunraven Pass on one of the park's most beautiful drives.

The first highlight on the way is the **Calcite Springs Overlook,** a vantage point 500 feet above the Yellowstone River. Just north you'll spot a series of hot springs at the foot of a white- and yellow-splotched slope, colored by white calcite crystals and oil deposits brought to the surface by underground heat. Across the canyon stands a cliff of columnar basalt, left behind by a long-ago lava flow. Bighorn sheep or soaring raptors might also add to the view.

Just beyond is a general store and short trail to an overlook of **Tower Fall,** a powerful, 132-foot plume. Unfortunately, you can no longer hike to the base of the falls, but the aerial view is worth catching. **Tower Fall Campground** is across the road, a secluded and rustic option.

The drive gets even more scenic from here, climbing a winding road with sweeping vistas over the Lamar Valley and the **Washburn Range** (where the 1988 wildfires left a visible scar). Look for bighorns and bears as you scale the side of **Mount Washburn ★★★**—grizzlies are frequently spotted up here. The peak itself makes an excellent destination for a day hike; start your trip either on the northwest side, from Old Chittenden Road (another spot where mountain bikes are okay), or from the southwest at 8,859-foot **Dunraven Pass.** See chapter 4, "Getting Outdoors in Yellowstone," for details.

It's all downhill from here. Pause at the **Washburn Hot Springs Overlook,** from which you can spot the rim of the Grand Canyon of the Yellowstone and miles beyond on a clear day. If you need a break, the **Cascade Lake Picnic Area** is a particularly nice, wooded spot with firepits.

Canyon Village

Closest entrances and distances: 40 miles from West Yellowstone (west) entrance; 38 miles from Gardiner (north) entrance; 48 miles from the Cooke City (northeast) entrance; 43 miles from the east entrance

The Canyon area should be on the top of any Yellowstone visitor's to-do list for one simple reason: the **Grand Canyon of the Yellowstone ★★★**. Along with Old Faithful, this is one of the park's marquee destinations. Seen from above, the canyon looks like the Earth itself has a loose seam: A 20-mile-long, sheer-sided gorge plunges more than 1,000 feet to the Yellowstone River, widening up to 4,000 feet across in places. Two thundering waterfalls pour over two immense drops in the river's course, and a palette of bright reds, yellows, oranges, whites, and browns swirls across the rocky walls. In short, it's every bit as impressive as that *other* Grand Canyon, if not quite as big.

The Yellowstone River carved this massive chasm over thousands of years. Volcanic activity deposited rhyolite and tuff over the area, and heat from the geyser basins here weakened the rock, making it soft and easily eroded by the rushing river. Upper and Lower Falls owe their existence to bands of harder volcanic rock, which didn't erode as quickly as the softer stuff; these more resistant spots formed dramatic drops that the river plummets over, to grand effect. And those colors? There's plenty of iron in the rhyolite. As different layers of rock are exposed at different times, varying stages of oxidation turn the cliffs their signature hues.

Canyon Village is the base for exploring the canyon, a sprawling development with lodging, dining options, a general store, **Canyon Campground,** and the **Canyon Visitor Education Center** (© **307/344-2550**). Stop here for a primer on Yellowstone's supervolcano and its effects on the landscape: Exhibits include a floating globe showing the world's volcanic hot spots; a 3D map; video reenactments of the major Yellowstone eruption 640,000 years ago; and blocks of ash illustrating the volcano's destructive power.

Then go see that geology in action. One-way **North Rim Drive** begins 1¼ miles south of the village and cruises past a series of canyon rim overlooks before returning to the village. If you only have time to see the canyon from one side, hit the South Rim—but the north side offers perspectives you can't see across the way, so it's well worth the trip.

First stop: **Brink of Lower Falls Trail,** a .8-mile (round-trip) paved trail that dips 600 feet to a precarious perch above the 308-foot waterfall. It's a steep trip to a gorgeous vantage point and also grants a peek at 109-foot Upper Falls near the top. Next up is **Lookout Point** for a wider perspective on Lower Falls (and an osprey nesting site). If you're feeling energetic, continue down the **Red Rock Trail,** a boardwalk staircase that dives 500 feet deeper into the canyon in .4 mile. The next pullout, **Grand View Overlook,** is unique in that it points not to the waterfalls, but downstream, where you'll see the rich canyon colors and the Yellowstone River below. The final view, **Inspiration Point,** offers another astounding vista of Lower Falls and the canyon downstream.

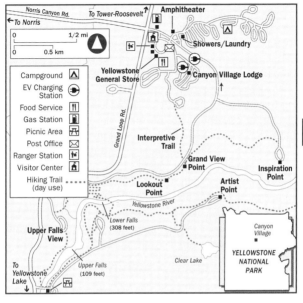

Campground △
EV Charging Station ⊕
Food Service ⑪
Gas Station ⑧
Picnic Area ⊞
Post Office ✉
Ranger Station ⊡
Visitor Center ⊡
Hiking Trail (day use) • • • •

Norris Canyon Rd.
To Tower-Roosevelt↑
← To Norris
Amphitheater
Showers/Laundry
Yellowstone General Store
Canyon Village Lodge
Grand Loop Rd.
Interpretive Trail
Grand View Point
Inspiration Point
Lookout Point
Artist Point
Yellowstone River
Lower Falls (308 feet)
Upper Falls View
Clear Lake
Upper Falls (109 feet)
To Yellowstone Lake ↓
Canyon Village
YELLOWSTONE NATIONAL PARK

0 — 1/2 mi
0 — 0.5 km

3

EXPLORING YELLOWSTONE

Yellowstone: The Extended Tour

You can drive between these major viewpoints, but the better option is hoofing it on the **North Rim Trail ★★** connecting Inspiration Point to the Wapiti Lake Trailhead on the South Rim. This 3-mile (one-way) track links all the North Rim Drive highlights, but you won't have to fight for parking spaces, plus you'll drink in extended views along the chasm's edge. The section between Lookout Point and Grand View is even wheelchair accessible.

Back out on Grand Loop Road, a short spur south of North Rim Drive leads to the **Brink of Upper Falls** viewing platform. Take the .3-mile trail to an overlook so close to the pounding cascade you'll feel the power of this incredible plume.

The turnoff to **South Rim Drive** shoots east off Grand Loop Road 2¼ miles south of Canyon Village. The first stunner here is the **Upper Falls Viewpoint,** which gives a longer view than the up-close-and-personal one you just saw at Brink of Upper Falls. Some maps still show a route called Uncle Tom's Trail a bit farther down, but this "trail"—actually a set of 328 steel steps bolted to the canyon's side—is now closed for safety reasons.

Artist Point ★ is the final stop off South Rim Drive. If this encompassing view of Lower Falls, the Yellowstone River, and the polychrome canyon looks familiar, it's probably because this vista is one of the park's most-photographed spots. Well before it earned that distinction, artist Thomas Moran made Artist Point famous with his landscape painting from this very perspective; you've likely seen a reproduction of it in a gallery or art book. Head this way early in the morning for the best light and to avoid midday crowds. Several hikes take off from here, including the trail to **Lily Pad Lake, Ribbon Lake,** and **Point Sublime.** That last one is especially notable: Hike 3.3 miles (one-way) along the rim to a much more private vista over the canyon.

Just like on the North Rim, hiking all or part of the **South Rim Trail ★★** is the best way to take in the airy views. The 1.8-mile, partially paved path links the Wapiti Lake Trailhead to Artist Point and winds through a high-elevation forest with near-constant peeks into the canyon.

Canyon Village to Fishing Bridge

Closest entrances: 27 miles to the east entrance; 43 miles to the south entrance

Distance: 16 miles from Canyon Village to Fishing Bridge

Heading south from Canyon Village, Grand Loop Road follows the wide Yellowstone River through **Hayden Valley ★★**, the park's largest valley. Glacial till (sediments left behind from an ice sheet that once covered the valley) interferes with water soaking into the ground here, resulting in marshy areas and few trees. The valley is an idyllic place where grizzly bears, bison, wolves, moose, elk, and coyotes roam.

About 12 miles south of Canyon you'll run into the unusual **Mud Volcano/Sulphur Caldron** area. *Fumaroles* (steam vents) and mud pots are the stars here: The area's soil and clay sit over chambers of hydrogen sulfide gas, which forms sulfuric acid as it rises through the ground. That acid dissolves the soil into mud pools, which more rising gases (including steam and carbon dioxide) pass through to delightful effect—roiling, slurping gurgles of mud. If you've ever wondered what boiling mud looks like, well, here's your answer.

The **Mud Volcano** itself was once much more dramatic: In 1870, members of the Washburn Expedition found a looming cone of mud over the feature, and by 1872, a thermal explosion had blasted it away. Today, its burbling mud pools are still fun to watch. A mile-long boardwalk extends through this small thermal zone to more features. At **Dragon's Mouth Spring,** turbulent pulses of water splash out from an underground cavern; tongues of water combined with steady bursts of steam really do call to mind a lurking medieval beast. **Black Dragon's Caldron** emerged from the earth in 1948 in a grand explosion, uprooting nearby trees and spraying the surrounding forest with mud. Since then, seismic activity has moved the feature several hundred feet south.

Just across the street, **Sulphur Caldron**'s yellowish, bubbling waters represent one of the park's most acidic hot springs, with a skin-melting pH similar to battery acid. If you're pressed for time, skip this.

A couple of miles beyond you'll hit **LeHardy Rapids,** the geographic point where Yellowstone Lake technically ends and the Yellowstone River resumes. Topographer Paul LeHardy, a member of the 1873 Jones Expedition, gave the spot its name when he capsized his raft attempting to run the rapids. Watch for cutthroat trout leaping over the drops en route to their springtime spawning grounds at Fishing Bridge.

Fishing Bridge itself spans the Yellowstone River as it flows out of Yellowstone Lake, just off Grand Loop Road on the East Entrance Road. Built in 1937, the bridge once attracted mobs of fishermen eager to dip a line into the trout spawning area directly below; trout populations subsequently dropped, and the park outlawed fishing here in 1973. But it remains a prime spot for watching trout swim, as well as the lake's resident pelicans and Canada geese.

Fishing Bridge Visitor Center (✆ 307/344-2109) is worth a stop to peruse its displays on park bird life. The area also has a general store, along with the **Fishing Bridge RV Park** (p. 141). This is the only campground restricted to hard-sided vehicles (because of the area's abundant grizzlies).

You'll find an excellent hiking trail, **Elephant Back Loop Trail ★**, leading off the road between Fishing Village and the Lake Village area. The 3.5-mile loop leads to an overlook with panoramic views of Yellowstone Lake and its islands, the Absaroka Range, and Pelican Valley to the east. Instead of taking the entire loop around to the overlook, you can shorten the hike a half-mile by taking the left fork approximately 1 mile from the trailhead and doubling back from the overlook.

A Detour: The East Entrance Road

Closest entrance and distance: 27 miles from Fishing Bridge to the east entrance

The mountainous **East Entrance Road** ★★ is second only to the Beartooth Highway in terms of scenically splendid ways to access the park. If you're bound for Cody, Wyoming or want to make the gorgeous loop drive to the Chief Joseph and Beartooth highways and back through the northeast entrance, you'll peel off here from the Grand Loop Road.

Begin by tracing the shores of Yellowstone Lake past **Indian Pond** and the **Pelican Valley Trail.** This trail leads into remote and beautiful country, but this is ground zero for grizzlies, and hiking is restricted to daytime hours only. Continue around **Mary Bay,** the hottest part of the lake at 252°F (122°C) under the lakebed. A hydrothermal explosion formed this bay, and a small thermal area remains today.

Steamboat Point provides a nice vista over the lake, but the **Lake Butte Overlook,** a short spur off the road, is better. Cruise up here for sweeping views over the lakeshore, thermal zones, and an old wildfire burn. Between them you'll find one of the park's best picnic grounds at **Sedge Bay:** a stony beach right along the shore that doubles as a boat launch.

The road climbs into the high country from here, and 10,000-foot peaks crop up on either side of the pavement. After passing the delicate **Sylvan Lake** and **Eleanor Lake** (both dynamite picnic spots), you'll reach 8,530-foot **Sylvan Pass.** This high point flanked by steep, craggy peaks makes a fine turnaround spot. For a serious cardio challenge, don't miss the **Avalanche Peak Trail,** a short but steep grunt to the 10,556-foot summit.

Yellowstone Lake Area

Closest entrances: Approximately 27 miles from Fishing Bridge to the east entrance; 43 miles from Fishing Bridge to the south entrance

Distances: The lakefront from Fishing Bridge to the West Thumb Geyser Basin is 21 miles.

Clear, deep, and expansive **Yellowstone Lake** ★★ dominates the southeastern part of the park. At 132 square miles,

Yellowstone Lake: Fishing Bridge to Bridge Bay

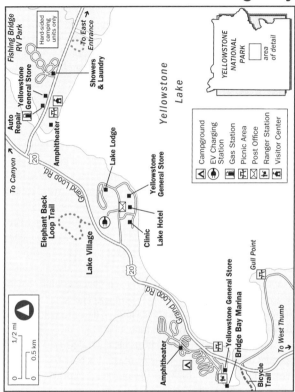

with 141 miles of shoreline, it is North America's largest natural freshwater lake above 7,000 feet. People cruise and paddle its waters, fish, and camp along its rocky shores, while the lake and its beaches provide habitat for grizzlies, moose, golden and bald eagles, pelicans, and cormorants.

A lake this large can act more like a sea, with frequent winds whipping up treacherous waves. Combine that chop with water that averages 41°F (5°C) even in the height of summer, and swimming becomes inadvisable—and boating or paddling are risky endeavors that demand plenty of know-how. Under the surface, Yellowstone Lake is just as turbulent: Researchers have discovered underwater fumaroles, geysers, and hot springs, and canyons plunge to at least 410 feet in depth. In two places, underwater volcanic vents called resurgent domes are rising and falling with an average uplift of an inch a year—lickety-split in geologic time.

The lake, which is roughly shaped like a four-legged octopus, has several distinct zones. Most boating happens in the broad main area, while the West Thumb branch features an active thermal zone. The South and Southeast Arms are much more remote and have more restrictions on motorboats, making them excellent places for kayak or canoe camping.

Lake Village forms the area's primary developed hub, with a couple of lodging and dining options, plus a general store. The canary-yellow **Lake Yellowstone Hotel** is the park's most elegant, while nearby **Lake Lodge** offers rustic cabins and a killer front-porch view. See p. 136 for more details.

Continue south on Grand Loop Road to **Bridge Bay Marina,** the hub for water-based activities. Boat launches grant entry for DIYers, and you can also rent motorboats from park concessionaires in summer. There's also a popular, 1-hour scenic cruise around Stevenson Island complete with historical tales from the boat's skipper. The small general store sells food and fishing permits. The adjacent **Bridge Bay Campground** is Yellowstone's largest.

Although the **Natural Bridge,** near Bridge Bay, is well marked on park maps, it's one of the park's best-kept secrets. The mile-long path down to the bridge, a geologic masterpiece consisting of a massive rock arch spanning Bridge Creek, is also one of the few trails open to bikes.

If you're looking to get off the beaten path, one-way **Gull Point Drive** shoots off the main road just south of Bridge Bay and traces the lakeshore past a lovely picnic spot with great shoreline access. If not, continue west to West Thumb.

So called because it would be the thumb on Yellowstone Lake's "hand," **West Thumb** represents a caldera within the larger Yellowstone caldera, formed by an eruption 174,000 years ago. The heat from underground hydrothermal features here can melt the ice that covers the rest of the lake surface for much of the year. It's a great spot to look for bears and elk (especially in spring), river otters playing in the warm waters in winter, and bald eagles or osprey year-round. The small **West Thumb Information Station** is open 9am to 5pm summer through early fall.

The primary attraction here is **West Thumb Geyser Basin ★**, a unique shoreline thermal area where you can see hot springs pouring into the lake, brightly hued pools, brownish-green paint pots, and shoreline geysers. Although it's less crowded than the bigger basins, it's still advisable to stroll the .25-mile inner loop and .5-mile outer loop early or late in the day to avoid tour bus jams. **Fishing Cone** gained fame in the late 1800s, when anglers would catch trout and then cook them, still on the line, in the spring's hot water (a practice that is decidedly not allowed today, for health reasons).

As you depart the West Thumb area, you have two choices: either to head south, toward Grand Teton National Park, or to head west, across the **Continental Divide** at Craig Pass, en route to Old Faithful.

Grant Village to the South Entrance

Closest entrance and distance: 22 miles from Grant Village to the south entrance

The **Grant Village** complex lines the lakeshore on the south side of West Thumb. It's a convenient home base if you're combining your visit with a trip to Grand Teton National Park, and it boasts stunning sunset views, but the lodging and dining choices are more serviceable than they are inspiring. The **Grant Village** lodges provide motel-style accommodations, **Grant Village Campground** lets you sleep under the stars, and **Grant Village Dining Room** serves upscale dishes. Better bet: **Lake House Restaurant,** a casual eatery on the water, offers unbeatable lake views. For more details about dining and accommodations in the area, see chapter 7. **Grant Village Visitor Center** (*©* **307/242-2109**) has exhibits on the 1988 wildfires and the forest's subsequent recovery, plus animal hides and skulls for kids to touch and a beautiful porch overlooking the lake.

Heading south on the South Entrance Road soon takes you over the **Continental Divide** and on to evergreen-lined **Lewis Lake.** This lake makes for excellent boating, paddling, and fishing. Indeed, one of the park's best paddling trips starts at the boat ramp here: Paddle across Lewis Lake,

Yellowstone Lake: West Thumb to Grant Village

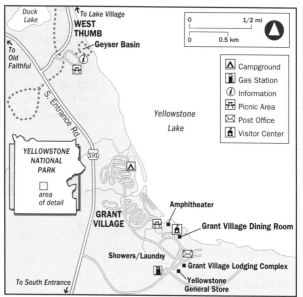

up the **Lewis River,** and into **Shoshone Lake,** a gorgeous backcountry waterway and the park's second-largest lake. The **Lewis Lake Campground** on the southern shore is one of Yellowstone's quietest, most away-from-it-all camps.

Just south of here is **Lewis Falls,** a lacy, 29-foot waterfall pouring right over the lip of the Yellowstone caldera. Then follow the river south through the dramatically plunging **Lewis River Canyon;** don't blow past the pullouts here without getting out to gaze across the chasm at least once.

West Thumb to Old Faithful

Closest entrance: 22 miles from West Thumb to the south entrance

Distance: 17 miles from West Thumb Geyser Basin to Old Faithful

The high-altitude road west of West Thumb crosses the **Continental Divide** twice in this section, the second time at 8,262-foot **Craig Pass.** At both points, precipitation falling on the east side of the divide eventually flows to the Atlantic

Ocean, and anything falling to the west is Pacific Ocean–bound. An interesting phenomenon takes place at **Isa Lake** atop Craig Pass. It has both eastern and western drainages and ends up in both the Pacific Ocean and the Gulf of Mexico. Amazingly, because of a gyroscopic maneuver, the outlet on the *east* curves *west* and drains to the Pacific, and the outlet on the *west* curves *east* and drains to the Gulf.

About 3 miles south of the Old Faithful area, an overlook grants a peek at **Kepler Cascades,** a 150-foot stair-step waterfall on the Firehole River. This is also the trailhead for one of Yellowstone's best easy day hikes, the 4.8-mile (round-trip) hike to **Lone Star Geyser ★★**. The trail winds along the Firehole River to the geyser's cone (bikes are allowed most of the way, and it's also a fun cross-country-ski route), where a 30- to 45-foot plume erupts every 3 hours or so (a logbook on-site should tell you when the last eruption occurred). Wide meadows and sunny riverside basking rocks make waiting for the next spout more than pleasant.

Old Faithful Area

Closest entrance and distances: 16 miles from Old Faithful to Madison Junction, then 14 miles to West Yellowstone (west) entrance

Interested in seeing a few geysers? Boy, have you come to the right place. The Old Faithful area contains the world's largest concentration of these geothermal spouters, including, of course, the most famous example. It's Yellowstone at its best—don't miss it.

Thanks to its marquee attraction, this area is exceedingly popular and offers the widest variety of services in the park. Choose from three different lodging options—**Old Faithful Lodge, Old Faithful Snow Lodge,** and the magnificent **Old Faithful Inn**—and dining options from casual cafeterias and ice-cream stands to the swanky Snow Lodge's **Obsidian Dining Room.** (See chapter 7 for info on lodging and dining here.) This area also has a general store, gas station and EV charger, clinic, backcountry office, and post office.

One must-do stop: the **Old Faithful Visitor Education Center** (✆ **307/344-2750**). It will walk you through the mechanics of all the hydrothermal features waiting outside, and giant picture windows let you see Old Faithful in all its glory. If you can stand to wait, head here first for a primer on Yellowstone's grand plumbing system before exploring the basins; rangers post the next predicted eruption times for several major geysers, so you'll know exactly how much time you have to browse. The **Tribal Heritage Center,** which debuted in 2022, is another worthy stop. From late May through September, the center hosts a rotating art show featuring artists and presenters from one of the 27 tribes with historic ties to Yellowstone. The eclectic mix includes photographers, dancers, painters, jewelers, and storytellers.

And now for the main event. Several distinct basins sit in close proximity here: **Upper Geyser Basin, Black Sand Basin,** and **Biscuit Basin.** Upper Geyser Basin is the star, containing the most interesting features, but all are worth a look. **Old Faithful Geyser ★★★**, around which all the area's buildings cluster, is a fine place to start. It's not the park's largest or most frequent eruptor, but it has remained about as predictable as it was when the 1870 Washburn Expedition named it. Eruptions occur about every 90 minutes, spewing 3,700 to 8,400 gallons of boiling water up to 184 feet. No matter how many times you've seen Old Faithful on postcards or videos, there's nothing like the thrill of seeing the real thing in action.

Views of Old Faithful are excellent from the boardwalk and the second-floor deck of Old Faithful Inn, but an even better vantage point is atop **Observation Point ★★**. The 1.6-mile (round-trip) trail departs from the boardwalk on the way to Geyser Hill, past the Firehole River Bridge, and climbs 160 feet to an eagle's-eye view over the basin. Continuing a bit farther along the trail loops you past frequent eruptor **Solitary Geyser** for the 2.2-mile trip back to the boardwalk.

Begin your geyser gazing with the 1.3-mile boardwalk loop around Geyser Hill. You'll likely catch **Anemone Geyser** in action; the 6-footer goes off every 7 to 10 minutes. **Beehive Geyser** is much less predictable but more impressive, shooting a towering column of water up to 200 feet. The four-geyser **Lion Group** comes next. The largest member, Lion Geyser, announces an impending eruption with steam plumes and a guttural roar. Farther down the path, you'll have to be lucky to glimpse **Giantess Geyser:** This powerhouse shoots water 200 feet high and shakes the ground with

Old Faithful Area

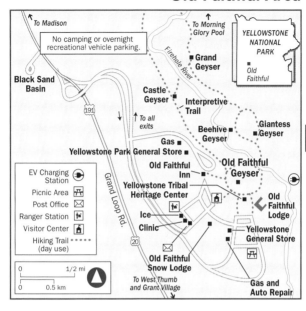

To Madison

No camping or overnight
recreational vehicle parking.

To Morning
Glory Pool

YELLOWSTONE
NATIONAL
PARK

Old
Faithful

Firehole River

■ Grand
Geyser

Black Sand
Basin

191

Castle
Geyser ■

Interpretive
Trail

↑ To all
exits

Beehive ■
Geyser

■ Giantess
■ Geyser

Gas ■

Yellowstone Park General Store ■

Old Faithful
Inn ■

Old Faithful
Geyser

Yellowstone Tribal
Heritage Center

Old
Faithful
Lodge

Ice ■

Clinic ■

■ Yellowstone
General Store

Grand Loop Rd.

EV Charging
Station

Picnic Area

Post Office

Ranger Station

Visitor Center

Hiking Trail
(day use)

0   1/2 mi
0   0.5 km

Old Faithful
Snow Lodge

To West Thumb
and Grant Village

Gas and
Auto Repair

its steam blasts. If it is active (which happens every 2–6 months), eruptions occur as frequently as every 30 minutes.

Plenty more features await along the boardwalk northwest of Geyser Hill. **Castle Geyser** ★★ erupts from a fortress-like sinter cone formed over thousands of years. It's one of six geysers that rangers predict, so check at the visitor center or the hotels for the next show time (about every 14 hr.). **Grand Geyser** ★★, another predicted spouter, lets loose powerful water pulses up to 200 feet high.

Closer to the Firehole River, **Beauty Pool** and adjacent **Chromatic Pool** display brilliant rings of blue, green, yellow, and orange created by thermophile microorganisms. Rangers also predict **Riverside Geyser**'s ★★ eruptions: Every 6 hours or so, the waterfront feature blows water and steam in an arch over the Firehole. The paved trail ends at **Morning Glory Pool,** a once-vibrant blue hot spring now gone yellow and brown thanks to thoughtless visitors tossing trash and rocks into its underground portal over the years.

Continuing to **Biscuit Basin** (a 5.2-mile round-trip from the visitor center) takes you to a smaller collection of geysers and hot springs headlined by deep-blue **Sapphire Pool.** In a dramatic reminder of Yellowstone's dynamic nature, a surprise hydrothermal explosion in Biscuit Basin in 2024 blasted rock and boiling water hundreds of feet in the air, demolishing a section of boardwalk (luckily, no one was hurt). The final basin in this area, **Black Sand Basin,** lies about a mile northwest of Old Faithful and does indeed contain black sand (a derivative of obsidian) as well as bright hot springs and **Cliff Geyser.**

Old Faithful to Madison Junction

Closest entrances: 30 miles from the Old Faithful area to the West Yellowstone (west) entrance; 39 miles to the south entrance

Distance: 16 miles from the Old Faithful area to Madison

The hydrothermal fireworks continue as you move north along Grand Loop Road. At the next major stop, **Midway Geyser Basin ★★**, you'll see two of the largest features of their type in the world. **Excelsior Geyser** used to erupt mightily in the 1880s—its bursts reached 300 feet and were as wide as they were tall. (Perhaps we're lucky it's rather quiet today.) The geyser still issues 5.8 million gallons of water per day into the Firehole River. **Grand Prismatic Spring,** at 370 feet across and 125 feet deep, is the second-largest hot spring on the planet. A boardwalk leads you close to the colorful spring, a bright blue pool ringed by striking bands of yellow, green, and orange thermophiles. But for my money, the best way to see it is from above, on the overlook platform that delivers an encompassing aerial view of the

---

Top 5 Places to Watch Old Faithful Erupt

1. From above, at Observation Point
2. From Old Faithful Inn's second-floor porch
3. Front and center on the boardwalk
4. Through the picture windows in the Old Faithful Lodge lobby
5. Framed in the viewing window at Old Faithful Visitor Education Center

Know Your Bacteria

Even the most casual visitor can do some scientific sleuthing at the **Fountain Paint Pot ★**, learning to identify water temperature by observing the colors in the pots. The colors result from different types of bacteria that survive at specific water temperatures. Some are yellow until temperatures reach 161°F (72°C), above which the yellow bacteria cannot live. As temperatures approach boiling—199°F (93°C) at this elevation—pinks begin to appear.

spring's grandeur. Reach it via a moderate, 1.2-mile (round-trip) hike from the **Fairy Falls Trailhead.**

About 8 miles north of Old Faithful, take the turnoff to **Firehole Lake Drive ★**. This 2-mile, one-way detour winds through another remarkable thermal area—and it's much less crowded than Norris or Old Faithful. **Great Fountain Geyser** is one highlight: One of the six geysers that rangers publish predicted eruption times for, this fountain blows water 100 feet in the air, and the pulsing eruptions last up to an hour. **White Dome Geyser** features a giant sinter cone built up over hundreds of years; watch for its frequent 30-foot eruptions. And at **Firehole Lake,** stroll the boardwalk along a massive hot spring circled with travertine deposits.

Firehole Lake Drive will deposit you at the parking lot for **Lower Geyser Basin ★**, home to **Fountain Paint Pot.** A .5-mile boardwalk loops past the highlights, though what you'll see depends on the season: Early in the year, the bubbling mud will be thin with abundant water, but later in summer it thickens to a muddy paste. Take care here—the reddish paint pots have tossed mud all the way to the boardwalk. Nearby **Red Spouter** sprang to life after the 1959 Hebgen Lake earthquake. It, too, changes seasonally, from a hot spring and small, red-colored geyser in the spring to a mud pot in late summer to a steaming fumarole at year's end.

The boardwalk swings west to a small geyser area with six spouters. Chances are excellent you'll see at least a few go off: **Spasm Geyser** tosses up 20-foot-high spray frequently, and the burbling of **Clepsydra Geyser** is almost constant.

As you continue toward the Madison Junction, consider a detour along **Fountain Flat Drive,** a left turn about 2 miles beyond Fountain Paint Pot. This scenic paved road ends a ¼ mile north of Ojo Caliente, after which it is open only to hikers and bikers. One mile south of the Firehole River Bridge is the **Imperial Meadows Trailhead.** Park the car and head up the 4-mile trail to the 200-foot **Fairy Falls.**

The last side road you'll hit before Madison Junction is also the best: The 2-mile **Firehole Canyon Drive** ★★. You'll have to backtrack a bit after cruising the one-way, south-only road when coming from this direction, but the payoff is worth it. The road winds through a super-sheer gorge along the Firehole River, abutting 7,500-foot National Park Mountain and passing 800-foot-thick lava deposits. Stop for a peek at the tumbling cascade of 40-foot **Firehole Falls** before reaching the cherry on top: a **swimming hole** ★★ near the end of the road. This is one of the only places in the park where it's safe to splash around, and the cool water can't be beat on a sweltering August afternoon (only open when conditions permit; check the park website).

ORGANIZED TOURS

Yellowstone guide services and commercial bus tours abound, based both inside the park and in the gateway towns. The in-park tours are operated by concessionaire **Xanterra** (www.yellowstonenationalparklodges.com; ✆ **307/344-7311**), some of them in a historic yellow bus. The most intensive option whirls you to the major highlights on Grand Loop Road, an all-day affair taking off from Old Faithful,

Mammoth, or Gardiner ($171–$177 adults). Other trips are shorter and more specialized, focusing on wildlife-watching, geyser basins, photography, and more; these range from 90 minutes to 8 hours and cost $40 to $177 for adults. When the snow flies, **snowcoach tours** take over for the buses (p. 92).

Xanterra's tours don't stop at the water's edge, either: You can hop on a **Yellowstone Lake Scenicruise** for a boat trip around Stevenson Island, with historical commentary from the boat's skipper. The cruise lasts an hour and costs $23 for adults. Guides will also take you out on chartered fishing and sightseeing rides on a powerboat ($257/2 hr.).

Several standout tours begin outside the park. **Yellowstone Vacations** (www.yellowstonevacations.com; ✆ **800/426-7669**) is one favorite out of West Yellowstone: Choose from an upper loop or lower loop tour and visit park hot spots with a certified guide. Trips cost $140. **Yellowstone Recreation Co.** (www.yrc.tours; ✆ **406/641-0662**) runs full-day tours of the upper or lower loops, the Hayden and Lamar valleys, and hydrothermal hot spots, all out of Gardiner; tours start at $250 per adult.

One of the best ways to really get to know Yellowstone is through the park's nonprofit partner, **Yellowstone Forever** ★★★ (www.yellowstone.org; ✆ **406/848-2400**), formerly the Yellowstone Association. The group runs a staggering number of day and multiday courses on wildlife, geology, hiking, photography, fishing, and more. Many **Field Seminars** base you out of the Lamar Buffalo Ranch Field Campus in the Lamar Valley or the Yellowstone Overlook Field Campus in Gardiner, both excellent perks of participating. **Lodging & Learning** programs are even more inclusive, including nights in park hotels and most meals. For more information, see "Academic Trips" (p. 28).

RANGER PROGRAMS

Among the national parks' most valuable services are the highly informative, free **ranger programs** ★★★: At Yellowstone and Grand Teton, rangers lead hikes, tell stories around the campfire, help you gaze into the heavens, and educate you on the area's natural wonders and human history. Programs run all year but most occur from late May to early September. Check **www.nps.gov/yell/planyourvisit/ rangerprog.htm** or the park newspaper for places and times. You're also likely to run into a roving ranger happy to answer your questions on geyser basin boardwalks or hiking trails. Just keep an eye peeled for the signature wide-brimmed hat bobbing among the crowds.

You can learn enough for an honorary degree in geyserology on one of the many guided walks through the Old Faithful, Norris, Mud Volcano, West Thumb, and Mammoth areas, where rangers will teach you all about the basins' hydrothermal features. Brush up on basic wildlife safety at talks in several locations or focus on history at Canyon and Mammoth. Guided hikes are great for anyone concerned about exploring on their own in bear country, and rangers might take you along the Grand Canyon of the Yellowstone's rim or to Storm Point on Yellowstone Lake.

Yellowstone offers several fantastic after-dark talks, too. **Evening programs** at some campgrounds or developed area cover topics from biology and geology to human history.

If you have kids (or remain a kid at heart), you won't want to miss the **Junior Ranger Program.** Pick up a free workbook at any visitor center and complete the activities inside—they often include attending a ranger program or going on a hike—then demonstrate your newfound knowledge with a ranger to earn a special badge and sticker. The similar **Young Scientist Program** for kids ages 5 and up guides participants to solve science mysteries through investigating visitor center exhibits and trails. Find a free, self-guiding booklet at Canyon or Old Faithful Visitor Education Centers.

GETTING OUTDOORS IN YELLOWSTONE

T he Great Outdoors: It's why you're here. And Yellowstone's natural wonders are unlike anything you'll see elsewhere on the planet. Roads will take you to only a fraction of the immense wilderness here, but more than 1,200 miles of trails can lead you to peaceful lakes, up airy peaks, and through steaming backcountry geyser basins. Make sure to hike at least one trail while you're here—you haven't really visited the park if you don't.

4

With hikes from short, easy strolls to strenuous, multiday endeavors, Yellowstone has something for everyone. In fact, with so much to see and do here, it's easy to get overwhelmed with the choices. Here is the crème de la crème: Choose any one, or more, and you won't be disappointed.

DAY HIKES

Yellowstone's trails range from flat, easy strolls to extended paths that delve deep into the wilderness. And though you'd need months to explore all the hidden corners here, even a single day hike will reveal a whole new side of the park to you. These selected day hikes from every developed area are the best of the best—you won't regret saving time to make tracks on at least one of them. *Note:* The trails through the geyser basins also make for excellent day hikes. See details on those trips in chapter 3.

Keep in mind that hiking in Yellowstone can be hazardous for the unprepared: Bad weather, river crossings, and wildlife all pose real risks. Check in at a visitor center or ranger station for details on the weather forecast and trail conditions for your hike, and make sure to pack the essentials (see box p. 83).

West Yellowstone to Madison

Purple Mountain ★   You'll truly earn your views on this challenging trail—reaching the summit of the flat-topped mountain requires hoofing it up 1,500 vertical feet in 3 miles—but the eagle's-eye vistas from the top are worth it. Begin hiking through a lodgepole pine forest, then pop out on a plateau with views of the twisty Gibbon and Madison rivers—and all the way to the Tetons on bluebird days.

6 miles round-trip. Difficult. **Access:** Trailhead is at a turnout ¼ mile north of Madison Junction.

Norris Geyser Basin area

Artists' Paintpot ★   This short loop trail between Madison and Norris provides an uncrowded quick fix for geothermal junkies. Stroll the trail/boardwalk combo through a young lodgepole pine forest to see brightly colored hot springs, hissing steam vents, and mud pots tossing mud several feet in the air. A slight climb to the top of the basin gives you a lovely aerial view over the thermal features and a distant peek at 10,336-foot Mount Holmes.

1.2-mile loop. Easy. **Access:** Trailhead is 4½ miles south of Norris Junction.

Mammoth Hot Springs Area

Beaver Ponds Loop Trail ★   Start at Clematis Gulch and hike through sage-filled meadows and Douglas fir/aspen forest to a series of beaver ponds. Your best chance of seeing the big-tailed beasts is early morning or late afternoon, and you might spot a moose, pronghorn, or elk on the way. Some of the splendid views from this trail take in Mount Everts.

5 miles round-trip. Moderate. **Access:** Trailhead is located at Mammoth Hot Springs Terrace.

Bunsen Peak Trail ★★   Climb an 8,564-foot mountain to big views of the Absaroka Range to the northeast and

Mammoth Area Trails

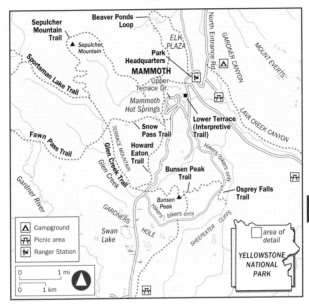

10,969-foot Electric Peak to the north on this moderate outing. You'll switchback 1,300 feet up the peak's northwest ridge, gaining better vistas with each step, before reaching the summit. Continue down the other side of the peak toward Sheepeater Cliffs, then loop back to the trailhead on Bunsen Peak Road. Tack on the 2.4-mile (round-trip) out-and-back spur trail that picks up near the road junction to see Osprey Falls. The steep, rocky trail into Sheepeater Canyon leads to the multitiered waterfall, which drops 150 feet into the Gardner River.

4.6 miles round-trip. Moderate. **Access:** Trailhead is across the road from the Glen Creek Trailhead, 5 miles south of Mammoth.

Sepulcher Mountain Trail ★★ There are several ways to approach this broad-sided, 9,652-foot peak just west of Mammoth Hot Springs, but the top route begins on the Sepulcher Mountain Trail at Mammoth, ascends the summit, loops back on the Glen Creek Trail, and crosses Snow Pass to return to the trailhead. Hike west across an old burn area now strewn with wildflowers in summer, then begin gaining for a total of 3,400 feet. You'll get views across the Absaroka-Beartooth Wilderness and Custer Gallatin National Forest, and down into Mammoth and Gardiner. A 360-degree panorama opens at the summit. Switchback your way down the peak's southeast ridge and swing east to approach Snow Pass and your route back to the trailhead. Look out for moose, bighorn sheep, mountain goats—and grizzlies. This is a favorite habitat for bears, so be loud and hike in a group.

11-mile loop. Moderate to difficult. **Access:** Sepulcher Mountain Trailhead at Mammoth Hot Springs Terrace.

Tower-Roosevelt Area

Hellroaring Trail ★   An ideal early-season hike because the snow melts here sooner than in other areas, the Hellroaring Trail drops you down to a sage-filled plateau where bison often gather. Traipse across the open field to reach an impressive suspension bridge that spans a steep, roiling section of the Yellowstone River. (The bridge also makes a good turnaround point if you prefer a shorter hike.) Continue to the banks of Hellroaring Creek and trace it to its confluence with the Yellowstone (both waterways are great for fishing). The trail goes on much farther into the backcountry, but you can turn around here for a manageable day hike.

6.2 miles round-trip. Moderate to difficult. **Access:** Trailhead is 3½ miles west of Tower Junction.

Petrified Trees of Specimen Ridge ★★   This shuttle hike packs a whole lotta geologic marvels into a few beautiful miles: petrified trees, basalt columns, and plunging canyon cliffs, to name a few. Start by dropping a car or bike at the Yellowstone River Picnic Area, then proceed to the trailhead for the unnamed but official trail (not to be confused with the Specimen Ridge Trail). From here, you'll climb steeply to excellent views over the Lamar Valley and Absarokas until you reach a rocky outcrop with fossilized, 50-million-year-old sequoias, firs, and other trees. Take care in this area because it's steep, and resist the temptation to take a fossil home—not only does that damage a precious resource, it's also illegal. Continue west across a sage-filled meadow on the Specimen Ridge Trail (the path is faint up here) to the east rim of a narrow canyon on the Yellowstone River; trace the rim northwest on the Yellowstone River Picnic Trail, looking out for ospreys, peregrine falcons, bighorn sheep, and the distinctive volcanic basalt columns across the river. The trail will take you back down to the picnic area.

6-mile shuttle. Difficult. **Access:** Trailhead is 4½ miles east of Tower Junction, in a striped pullout marked "trailhead." Ending trailhead is Yellowstone River Picnic Area, 1¼ miles east of Tower Junction.

Lamar Valley Area

Slough Creek Trail ★★   Anglers and wildlife-watchers, this one's for you. Pretty Slough Creek is revered for its cutthroat-trout fishing, and bears, moose, and bison are frequently spotted in the meadows along its banks. For a day-sized chunk, follow the Slough Creek Trail up a short, steep section of Douglas firs, then descend to First Meadow. This grassy expanse features rocky outcroppings, peak views, and easy access to fishing holes. Extending your hike along the creek to Second Meadow adds another 5.2 miles round-trip.

3.4 miles round-trip. Easy to moderate. **Access:** Trailhead is on dirt road to Slough Creek Campground; park where the road curves left.

Trout Lake Trail ★   A short, somewhat steep hike through spruce and fir, this trail's destination is small Trout Lake, encircled by a footpath. The lake, nestled between dramatic cliffs and Druid and Barronette Peaks, is a favorite fishing hole and one of the best places in the park to witness the fascinating cutthroat spawn. Because of the density of the fish, the lake once served as a major source of food for Cooke City and still attracts otters, beavers, and bears.

1.3 miles round-trip. Easy. **Access:** 10 miles west of the northeast entrance, at the trailhead 1 mile west of Pebble Creek campground.

Upper Pebble Creek ★★   The lesser-traveled region off the Northeast Entrance Road holds some of the most dramatic scenery in the park, including this gorgeous ramble in a remote valley. Even better, abundant wildflowers decorate the meadows in July. The first mile climbs fairly steeply to views of the cliffs along Soda Butte Creek and the area's imposing stone buttes, then flattens to an easy meadow stroll. Turn around at the first backcountry campsite along Pebble

Creek, where you'll spy still more giant summits. Alternately, you can park a shuttle car at the Pebble Creek Trailhead and hike all the way there for a 12-mile day.

4 miles round-trip. Moderate. **Access:** Warm Springs Trailhead is 8 miles east of Pebble Creek Campground.

Grand Canyon of the Yellowstone River Area

Clear Lake and Ribbon Lake Loop ★ A relatively easy loop hike combines a trio of backcountry lakes with a stroll along the canyon rim. You can start from several spots, but we like beginning at the Clear Lake Trailhead. After less than a mile, turn left to reach tree-ringed Clear Lake. Lily Pad Lake is just beyond, and peaceful Ribbon Lake is about a mile past that. Retrace your steps to Lily Pad Lake, then turn north, then west, to approach the knockout vista of the Lower Falls at Artist Point. The rest of the loop follows the South Rim Trail along the canyon's edge, offering views of thundering waterfalls and brightly colored rock walls.

5.8-mile loop. Easy to moderate. **Access:** Clear Lake Trailhead is 2¼ miles south of Canyon Junction on South Rim Dr.

Mount Washburn ★★★ This is one of Yellowstone's most popular day hikes for good reason. The climb up to 10,243 feet is challenging but gradual, the peak's slopes are known for a rainbow of wildflowers in summer, and the view from the summit is practically unmatched. You might spot bighorn sheep, black bears, or grizzlies up here—in fact, grizzlies tend to congregate on the slopes in fall to munch on whitebark pine nuts. The best approach begins from Dunraven Pass and follows a wide trail up above the tree line with ever-expanding views. From the top, you'll see the Grand Canyon of the Yellowstone, the Hayden Valley, Specimen Ridge, Slough Creek, and even the Tetons on a clear day. A lookout on the summit provides welcome shelter from the often-whipping winds. You can also hike it from the Old Chittenden Road, a slightly shorter (5 miles round-trip) but steeper trail. *Note:* Much of this hike is exposed to the elements, so don't attempt it if there's a chance of lightning.

6 miles round-trip. Moderate. **Access:** Trailheads are at Dunraven Pass and the end of Old Chittenden Rd.

Grand Canyon Area Trails

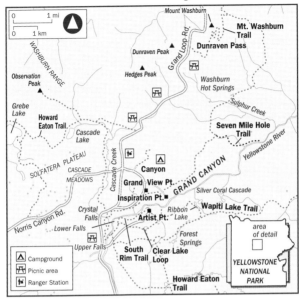

North Rim Trail ★ The trail skirting the north rim, which is described more fully under "Canyon Village" in chapter 3, offers better views of the falls and the river than you'll get from the parking areas. It's a nice way to see a longer stretch of the canyon.

6 miles round-trip. Easy. **Access:** Trailheads are at Wapiti Lake Trailhead and Inspiration Point.

Observation Peak ★★ Climb past a riot of purple and pink wildflowers in summer en route to 360-degree views on this classic summit hike. The trail begins by crossing patches of forest and meadows to Cascade Lake, a great spot for fishing or even swimming on hot days. Then hoof it 1,400 vertical feet in 2.6 miles through a whitebark pine forest to the Observation Peak summit. There's an old wooden fire tower up here, but you'll be more interested in the encompassing views of the Gallatins, Absarokas, and the Grand Canyon of the Yellowstone.

9.6 miles round-trip. Difficult. **Access:** Cascade Lake Trailhead, 1¼ miles north of Canyon Junction.

Seven Mile Hole ★   The only way to reach the Yellowstone River in the Grand Canyon area, Seven Mile Hole Trail is a doozy: You'll drop more than 1,000 feet in just 2.3 miles going from rim to river. But first, the trail wanders along the north rim, stopping at overlooks with views of 1,200-foot Silver Cord Cascade across the canyon. Soon you'll graduate from gazing as you hike into the canyon and pass dormant and active hot springs on the way to the wide Yellowstone River. This exposed hike can be hot, and don't underestimate the challenge of climbing back out of the canyon.

10 miles round-trip. Moderate to difficult. **Access:** Trailhead is at Glacial Boulder pullout on the road to Inspiration Point.

South Rim Trail ★   As with the North Rim Trail, this hike has more and better views of the canyon and river than you can see from a vehicle. It's easy and not long, yet you'll have it mainly to yourself because most folks are hopping in and out of the bus at the parking lots.

7 miles round-trip. Easy. **Access:** Trailheads are Wapiti Lake Trailhead and Artist Point.

Yellowstone Lake Area

Avalanche Peak ★★   Looking for the best bang for your buck? It's tough to beat this peak, which delivers fantastic panoramas of the park's remote corners in just 2.1 miles. Of course, you'll have to work for it—the trail rises a vertiginous 2,100 feet in that distance—but keep your eyes on the prize: the 10,566-foot summit, in view for most of the climb up talus slopes and narrow ridgelines. At the top, you'll have unimpeded views over Yellowstone Lake and across to many of the park's craggiest peaks, such as Hoyt Peak, Mount Sheridan, Mount Stevenson, and Top Notch. The window to ascend to these heights is narrow: The trail is often snow-covered into July and increased grizzly bear activity makes fall a dicey proposition. Be alert for lightning risks anytime.

4.2 miles round-trip. Difficult. **Access:** Trailhead is 8 miles west of the east entrance.

Elephant Back Loop Trail ★   Here's an opportunity to look down (literally!) on the island-dotted expanse of Yellowstone Lake, the Absaroka Range, and the Pelican

Valley. This is a great photo opportunity and a fairly easy hike for a novice.

3.5 miles round-trip. Moderate. **Access:** From the east, the trailhead is on the right side of the road, just before the turnoff for the Lake Yellowstone Hotel.

Pelican Valley Trail ★   This trip across marshy meadows and alongside a peaceful creek could be either a hiker's dream or a nightmare—depending on how you feel about grizzly bears. The remote Pelican Valley is some of the best grizzly habitat in the continental U.S., and as such, the park restricts hiking to daytime, and only after July 4. If that excites rather than terrifies you, get a group of at least four and strike out into the wide-open valley. The trail wanders through meadows and traces the meandering Pelican Creek, where you might also see bison, wolves, elk, and eagles. The washed-out bridge across the creek at mile 3.1 makes a good turnaround point, but the trail extends all the way into the Lamar Valley for multiday excursions.

6.2 miles round-trip. Easy. **Access:** Trailhead is 3 miles east of Fishing Bridge, just past Storm Point/Indian Pond Trail.

Storm Point Loop ★   One of the park's nicest lakeside rambles, this trail begins at Indian Pond and passes through a pine forest before popping out at Storm Point, the rocky western corner hemming in Mary Bay. You'll gaze across the lake to views of Stevenson Island, distant Mount Sheridan, and the Tetons. *Bonus:* Marmot sightings are practically guaranteed on a stony outcrop near the shore. Grizzlies frequent the area in spring and early summer, so check with rangers to make sure the trail is open to hikers.

2.3 miles round-trip. Easy. **Access:** Trailhead is 3 miles east of Fishing Bridge, across from the Pelican Valley Trailhead (on the lake side of the road).

West Thumb/Grant Village Area

DeLacy Creek Trail ★★   Yellowstone's largest and most impressive backcountry lake, Shoshone Lake, requires a significant haul on foot or kayak to reach—except by this quick, sneaky route. Head south along DeLacy Creek, passing open meadows that make wonderful habitat for moose and sandhill cranes, to Shoshone's northern shores. Bask by the rocky beaches or explore farther down the lakeshore.

5.8 miles round-trip. Easy. **Access:** Trailhead is 8¾ miles west of West Thumb Junction.

Yellowstone Lake Overlook ★ Earn big views in record time on this short lollipop loop that gets you out of the forest and up to lovely vistas over Yellowstone Lake in less than a mile. The trail begins in lodgepole pine forest but quickly ascends a few hundred feet to an open, grassy hillside. A few minor thermal features are near the trail's top, but the real star is the perspective of Yellowstone Lake from on high, framed by the Absaroka Range on the lake's eastern shore.

1.7 miles round-trip. Moderate. **Access:** Trailhead is in West Thumb Geyser Basin parking lot.

Old Faithful Area

Lone Star Geyser ★★ Front-country geysers are spectacular, but there's something extra-special about a backcountry spouter you have all to yourself (or more likely, yourself and a few other hikers). Lone Star Geyser is one of the easiest ones to reach, and it's predictable enough (eruptions happen every 3 hr. or so) to make catching its show likely: The 12-foot-high cone sprays water 45 feet into the air. Getting here means tracing the Firehole River on an old service road, passing intermittent meadows along the way; bikes can follow it almost all the way to the geyser. Check the register near the geyser to estimate the next eruption time.

4.8 miles round-trip. Easy. **Access:** Trailhead is at the parking lot opposite Kepler Cascades.

Mystic Falls ★★ Appreciate Yellowstone's multitiered architecture firsthand on this loop past a booming cascade. From Biscuit Basin, trace the Little Firehole River, ascending gradually through an evergreen forest until you reach 70-foot Mystic Falls pouring off the lip of the Madison Plateau. This is a fine turnaround point for a 2.4-mile round-trip, but it's worth the sweat equity to continue higher, grunting 500 feet uphill in the half-mile to the plateau's top. Turn right on Fairy Creek Trail and continue to a lookout: Upper Geyser Basin

Old Faithful Area Trails

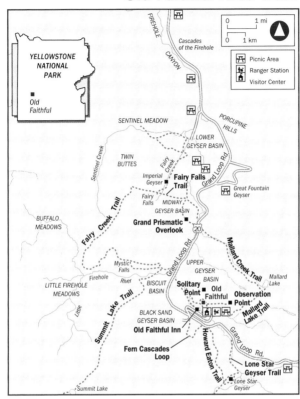

spreads out below, dotted with steaming hydrothermals. Switchback down to close the loop.

3 miles round-trip. Moderate to difficult. **Access:** Trailheads are on the far side of the Biscuit Basin Boardwalk (shortest option) and a quarter-mile south of Biscuit Basin (Upper Geyser Basin–Biscuit Basin Trail; add .5 mile).

Observation Point & Solitary Geyser Loop ★★

An alternate look at Old Faithful's famous eruption—with a grander scope, no less—is just a short climb away from the busy Upper Geyser Basin. From the boardwalk, ascend 160 feet in .8 mile up to the natural viewing platform of Observation Point, then enjoy the geyser doing its thing. Backtrack to the trail junction and turn west to hike through forest to Solitary Geyser. This frequent spouter steams in the middle of a wide, white circle, and its runoff has created a colorful, mineral-laden slope streaked with thermophile bacteria. Heading south down the hill takes you back to the boardwalk.

2.2-mile loop. Easy to moderate. **Access:** Trailhead is at the Old Faithful boardwalk.

Sentinel Meadows & Imperial Geyser Loop ★★

See backcountry hot springs and geysers, a National Historic Site, and Fairy Falls on this loop. Begin with a hike to Sentinel Meadows, a grassy area with thermal features, and the Queen's Laundry Bathhouse, an unfinished building from 1881 that has been preserved by thermal minerals. Swing around to the south to follow Fairy Creek through lush meadows. You'll pass Spray Geyser and Imperial Geyser (the latter can erupt up to 60 ft.) before reaching 200-foot Fairy Falls. Reconnect with Fountain Freight Road and return to your trailhead. This area can be boggy and buggy in early summer, so pack insect repellent.

10.5-mile loop. Easy. **Access:** Trailhead is at the end of Fountain Flat Drive.

EXPLORING THE BACKCOUNTRY

The backcountry of Yellowstone is the real deal: a domain of free-roaming wildlife and natural treasures. The U.S. National Park Service, through its system of permits, designated camping areas, and rules, has managed to protect this special wilderness. Yellowstone has more than 1,200 miles of trails (mostly in the backcountry) and 293 backcountry campsites.

For information on backpacking and safety, see chapter 10.

INFORMATION BEFORE YOU GO Contact the **Yellowstone Backcountry Office** (www.nps.gov/yell/planyourvisit/backcountryhiking.htm; ✆ **307/344-2160**) with questions about campsites, permits, and reservations. The website above has links to all kinds of useful info, including a detailed map showing where the campsites are and tips on preparation.

BACKCOUNTRY PERMITS Backcountry permits are required for any overnight trips on foot, horseback, or by boat, and cost $5 per person per night, plus a $10 reservation fee. You have several different ways to get one. For first dibs on reserving campsites during the peak season (May 15–Oct 31), apply for the Early Access Lottery via **www.recreation.gov** from March 1 to 20 ($10 application fee). If selected, you'll be able to secure reservations in April, before most other applicants. Anyone can make reservations for the remaining permits during the general on-sale period beginning in late April on www.recreation.gov; but you must book the permit at least 3 days before your trip ($10 plus $5 per person per night). Last-minute campers can try their luck with a walk-up permit up to 2 days before their start date at one of the park's backcountry offices (available in person only). For winter and early spring (Apr 1–May 14) trips, book a permit on www.recreation.gov, then contact the Yellowstone Backcountry Office (see above) so it can be officially issued to you. Camping is allowed only in designated campsites, many of which are equipped with food storage poles to keep wildlife out of your stores (BYO rope). Some are also equipped with pit toilets.

Pick up your peak-season permit in the park within 48 hours of your departure at one of the following stations any day of the week: Bechler, Bridge Bay, Old Faithful, and South Entrance Ranger Stations; Grant Village, Mammoth, and West Yellowstone visitor centers; or Tower Backcountry Office.

WHEN TO GO Many trails into the park backcountry remain covered with snow and become muddy in the first weeks of melt, well into June. At the higher elevations, over 9,000 feet, summer doesn't truly begin until early July. Even then, the weather is unpredictable at best. Creeks and streams described as "intermittent" during summer might be filled with snowmelt that transforms them into impassable, swiftly

---

Bear Safety

Grizzly bear attacks in the park are incredibly rare, but possible. Reduce your chances of an encounter by respecting seasonal bear closures, hiking in groups of four or more, not hiking off-trail, and making noise by talking loudly, singing, or clapping your hands. Always carry bear spray, a very effective deterrent to a charging bear, and know how to use it.

running rivers that often drench trails and convert them to mud. Generally, the best backpacking weather is from mid-July through mid-September. Look on **www.nps.gov/yell/planyourvisit/backcountryhiking.htm** for the latest trail and campsite conditions.

MAPS A good topographic map is essential for backcountry trips. GPS units and smartphone mapping apps can be very useful, but always carry a paper map as backup. Park rangers suggest using maps from the Trails Illustrated Map series, published by National Geographic Maps. These maps are printed on durable, tear-resistant paper and also show backcountry campsite locations. For more information, contact **National Geographic Maps** (www.natgeomaps.com) or **Yellowstone Forever** (www.yellowstone.org; ✆ **406/848-2400**).

OUTFITTERS An alternative to venturing into the backcountry on your own is to go with an outfitter. Outfitters usually arrange for backcountry permits and provide most equipment, which can offset the cost of their services. Some offer an even more catered experience, setting up tents and preparing meals.

Check **www.nps.gov/yell/planyourvisit/guidedtours.htm** for a list of companies with permits to operate inside the park.

The Yellowstone Backcountry

Auto touring is great, and day hiking is grand—but if you *really* want to experience Yellowstone, spending a night or more in the wilderness is the way to go. With its vast and varied terrain, this park has something to satisfy everyone, from the novice camper to the backpacking junkie. Trip options range from short, easy overnights to multiday excursions spanning dozens of miles. Peruse the park's backcountry web pages, call the park backcountry office, and check out these top trips to find your ideal escape.

SHOSHONE LAKE ★★

Gorgeous, expansive, and quiet, Shoshone Lake is the largest backcountry lake (that is, you can't drive to it) in the lower 48. Motorized boating is not allowed, making the scenic campsites on its shoreline especially peaceful. Add to that good trout fishing and a notable backcountry geyser basin, and it's no wonder Shoshone Lake is such a beloved destination. Camping is best starting in July, when spring flooding has usually eased up.

THE 10 essentials + 1

Though hiking is a very safe activity and most visitors run into no problems while exploring the park, don't forget that you're entering a true wilderness. It's vital to be prepared for changing weather conditions, rugged trails, and wildlife encounters. Experienced backcountry travelers swear by carrying the "10 Essentials," or a must-pack list of comfort and safety gear to stash in your daypack. Make sure you have the following items with you before any hike, even if you're only going a short distance.

1. **Navigation:** Always carry a map and compass. GPS units and smartphone apps are helpful—until they run out of power or malfunction. That's why they shouldn't replace a paper map and compass. The maps you get at the parks' entrance stations are not detailed enough for true navigation, so pick up a topographic map that shows terrain details.

2. **Sun protection:** Everyone in your party should have a hat (wide-brimmed sun hats are best), sunglasses, and sunscreen with an SPF of at least 30.

3. **Extra clothing:** This should include both warm layers (such as fleece or down jackets) and waterproof rain gear.

4. **Light:** Pack a headlamp or flashlight in case you're unexpectedly caught out on the trail after dark.

5. **First-aid kit:** You can buy compact, ready-made wilderness kits or assemble your own. Carry pain relievers, bandages, and blister treatments.

6. **Fire-starting materials:** Waterproof matches and/or a lighter, plus tinder, can be the difference between life and death if you're lost in bad weather.

7. **Repair kit:** A knife or multi-tool plus duct tape can temporarily fix a surprising number of gear malfunctions.

8. **Food:** Trail mix, trail bars, dried fruit, jerky, and peanut butter are all calorically dense, long-lasting foods for extra energy.

9. **Water:** Prevent dehydration by making sure everyone in your group has a sizable water bottle or hydration bladder.

10. **Emergency shelter:** A space blanket is small and light, but even a large garbage bag can add essential warmth and weather protection.

And, at Yellowstone, there's an 11th Essential:

11 **Bear spray:** Don't be caught without this highly effective deterrent against a charging bear.

The quickest way here is via the **DeLacy Creek Trail** (see p. 77), which begins 8 miles east of Old Faithful. A 2.9-mile (one-way) hike takes you to the northern shore, with a couple of campsites just west. For a longer trip, you can either hike southwest along the **North Shoshone Trail** or southeast on DeLacy Creek Trail. The **Shoshone Lake Trail** connects the two, enabling a multiday trip circling the lake. The highlight of any trip in this area is a visit to **Shoshone Geyser Basin ★★**, a thermal area with hundreds of features. A trail winds through the hot springs, vents, and geysers—stick to it, as no boardwalks protect you from the steaming water just under the thin earth here. If you're heading straight for the basin, the shortest route is the Shoshone Lake Trail via the Lone Star Trailhead; you'll pass Lone Star Geyser and cross **Grants Pass** on the way.

For a shorter overnight, make for the southeastern corner of Shoshone Lake on the **Channel Trail** following the Lewis River Channel. You might spy eagles and ospreys near the water's edge before reaching the lake. Some of the campsites in this area are for boaters only, so you might need to hike a bit farther to spend the night along **Moose Creek.** Return on the **Dogshead Trail** for a 10.8-mile loop.

This is also the place for one of the park's classic paddling trips. Launch at Lewis Lake and canoe or kayak up the Lewis Channel (wind can make this a real workout). You'll have to drag your boat the final mile before reaching Shoshone Lake, but then the enormous lake's shoreline will be yours to explore. Many beach sites are reserved for paddlers only.

THE BECHLER REGION

This area in the park's southwest section is often referred to as Cascade Corner because it contains most of the park's waterfalls. It escaped the fires of 1988 and offers great opportunities to view thermal features. Backpacking options abound here. Mid- to late summer is the best time to travel, as early-season runoff makes the creek crossings dangerous.

To reach the **Bechler Ranger Station,** a primary jumping-off point for exploring the region, drive in from Ashton, Idaho. Take Cave Falls Road 17 miles, then turn north on Bechler Ranger Station Road and go another 1½ miles.

The **Bechler River Trail ★★** starts here and leads to one of Yellowstone's coolest spots: the soakable backcountry hot spring called **Mr. Bubbles ★★**. It's one of the only places where getting into a spring is safe (or permitted), and the area's remoteness means you probably won't have to share (much). Follow the Bechler River 13.5 miles up to the Ferris Fork Campsite; Mr. Bubbles, a large pool deep enough to submerge yourself and splash around, lies .25 mile beyond.

The **Bechler Meadows Trail ★★** also departs from the ranger station, but heads into waterfall-rich country northwest of the River Trail. About 6 miles into the journey, the trail fords the river several times as it enters Bechler Canyon, where it passes Colonnade and Iris Falls. Along this trail, you can view the Tetons in the distance and the hot springs that warm the creeks. You can cover a good 30 miles in 3 or 4 days, depending on what turns you take. For a shorter trip, hike 3.5 miles along the Bechler River Trail to the **Boundary Creek Trail,** and then return to the station via the **Bechler Meadows Trail,** a round-trip of 7 miles.

Another knockout waterfall hike begins off Grassy Lake Road to the east on the **Cascade Creek Trail.** Link the **Mountain Ash Creek** and **Union Falls trails,** braving several creek fords along the way, for a 15.6-mile round-trip to **Union Falls ★★**. Two creeks merge at the top to form a 260-foot cascade resembling a frothy white volcano, and you'll also find a fine swimming hole off a short spur trail in the area. Choose from several campsites lining the route.

The Bechler River Trail extends all the way to the Old Faithful area for an epic, 32-mile shuttle hike. Beyond Iris Falls and then Ragged Falls, you'll reach a patrol cabin at Three Rivers Junction at the 13-mile mark, a popular camping area. If you continue toward Old Faithful, you'll intersect the **Shoshone Lake Trail** and exit 6.5 miles later.

HEART LAKE AREA

This (somewhat) heart-shaped lake in south-central Yellowstone makes for another popular destination for backcountry travelers: It's relatively easy to get to, cutthroat trout swim its waters, and it offers the chance to summit one of the park's iconic peaks. You can do it as an overnight by taking the 7.5-mile (one-way) **Heart Lake Trail ★** out and back; this section of trail overlaps with the 3,100-mile **Continental Divide Trail** that follows the spine of the continent from Mexico to Canada. You'll hike through small thermal areas on the lake's northwestern shore and catch dreamy sunrises on 10,308-foot Mount Sheridan, which looms just to the west. Or make it a 3- or 4-day excursion by continuing around the lake to the **Heart River Trail,** a loop with stretches in an old burn area. It also involves several challenging river crossings. Don't miss the excellent peak-bagging detour on the **Mount Sheridan Trail,** a steep, 7-mile round-trip across alpine tundra to huge views.

THOROFARE AREA

Serious about getting away from it all? This is your trip. The vast meadows, remote peaks, massive plateaus, and abundant wildlife of Yellowstone's southeastern corner—a zone known as the Thorofare—is as off the grid as it gets. You can't get farther from a road anywhere else in the lower 48. Throughout the area, tepee rings and lean-tos are reminders that Native Americans once used this trail as the main route between Jackson Hole and points north. Because it's such a far-flung destination, you're far more likely to see bears, moose, elk, river otters, and loons than other backpackers. But if you're experienced enough to handle a week or more in the backcountry, you'll find that the relatively flat terrain of the Thorofare makes for a thoroughly enjoyable trip. Seasonal bear closures and high water in early summer mean mid-July to early September is prime time in these parts.

The 68-mile point-to-point hike on the **Thorofare Trail ★★** and **South Boundary Trail ★★** takes you deep into the heart of this wild area. Start by tracing the eastern shoreline of Yellowstone Lake (waterfront campsites included) and then the Yellowstone River, traversing grassy meadows in the shadow of 11,000-foot peaks. You'll reach the out-there Thorofare Ranger Station at mile 32, near the horizon-dominating Trident Plateau, then turn west to cross Two Ocean Plateau. The trail briefly dips out of the park and into the Teton Wilderness before following the Snake River en route to the South Entrance Road. Backcountry junkies can also turn the trip into a lollipop loop by connecting to the **Trail Creek Trail** and hiking back to the start for an 80-miler. The **Mountain Creek Trail** grants slightly shorter access into the Thorofare from the east, but there's no quick fix for getting here—all part of this wilderness's charm.

BLACK CANYON OF THE YELLOWSTONE

One of the earliest backpacking routes to melt out in the spring, the shuttle hike linking Hellroaring Creek, Yellowstone River, and Blacktail Deer Creek between Mammoth and Tower-Roosevelt travels through some of northern Yellowstone's prettiest river country. The 2- or 3-day trip crosses a pair of suspension bridges, hugs the banks of the mighty Yellowstone, and passes beneath craggy Hellroaring Mountain and through the steep, thickly forested Black Canyon. Wildflowers like golden arrowleaf balsamroot bloom in spring and summer, and there's a good chance of spotting bison, elk, and pronghorn around here. Begin on the **Hellroaring Trail ★** (see p. 72 earlier in this chapter) and turn west on the **Yellowstone River Trail ★★**. This stretch features excellent fishing, blufftop views over the waterway, and basalt columns high on the cliffs. Finish by turning south on **Blacktail Creek Trail** and climbing back to the road. Camp along the Yellowstone and/or Hellroaring Creek. Early fall is the best time to hike the canyon, but it's usually passable by mid-May (just watch for high water and ticks). Avoid the dog days of summer—this area can get hot.

OTHER ACTIVITIES

BIKING You'd think Yellowstone would be a primo spot for road cycling, what with its hundreds of miles of paved roads through spectacular scenery. But while bikes (including e-bikes and pedal-assist bikes) are allowed on all public roads, cycling here isn't exactly a Sunday cruise. Roads tend to be narrow and twisty and often lack a shoulder. Traffic can be heavy. Count on dealing with enormous RVs and trailers if you go. Still, well-prepared cyclists can have a great time; make sure to ride cautiously and use reflectors and lights for visibility. E-bikes have been getting more popular lately, and several outfitters rent them or offer guided tours. In Gardiner, **Big Sky Ebike Tours,** 405 Scott St. West (www.bigskyebiketours.com; © **406/223-8139**), can set you up with a rental or take you cruising in or near the park; trips start at $200.

The happy exception to the status quo here is during early spring (typically late Mar and early Apr) and fall (typically Nov), when the park opens roads to cyclists before and after visitors' cars are allowed. You'll have the pavement nearly to yourself, but the weather can be brutally cold.

Mountain bikers have better luck. Though you can't bike on most backcountry trails, a handful of old dirt or gravel roads are open to cycling. Those with quads of steel can pedal 3 miles uphill to the Mount Washburn summit via **Chittenden Road** or circle Bunsen Peak on the 10-mile **Bunsen Peak Loop. Fountain Freight Road** follows Fairy Creek near Midway Geyser Basin for 5.5 miles and makes the trip to Fairy Falls much faster, and cyclists can also zip along the Firehole River most of the way to **Lone Star Geyser.**

Bike rentals are available inside the park at **Old Faithful Snow Lodge** (www.yellowstonenationalparklodges.com; ✆ **307/344-7311;** $40/day) and in the gateway town of West Yellowstone at **Freeheel and Wheel** (www.freeheeland wheel.com; ✆ **406/646-7744;** $50/day).

BOATING Powerboats are permitted on most of **Yellowstone Lake** (which has the most services and panoramic views) and on **Lewis Lake.** Park concessionaire Xanterra rents motorboats out of **Bridge Bay Marina:** An 18-foot motorboat will run you $68/hour.

Canoeists, kayakers, and paddleboarders can paddle on these lakes and most other park lakes; the **Lewis River Channel** between **Lewis** and **Shoshone lakes** is the only river that's open to paddling. Many boat-only campsites along Yellowstone and Shoshone lakes enable fantastic multiday trips, but be aware that high winds and very cold water can make paddling dangerous. Both motorized and nonmotorized boaters need permits, available at the Lewis Lake Ranger Station, Grant Ranger Station, and Bridge Bay Ranger Station. A number of other spots issue permits for angler float tubes only; check **www.nps.gov/yell/planyour visit/boating.htm** for a list. The cost is $20/week for nonmotorized and $40/week for motorized, which includes inspection for aquatic invasives.

FISHING Seven varieties of game fish live in the parks: cutthroat trout, rainbow trout, brown trout, brook trout, lake trout, Arctic grayling, and mountain whitefish. Cutthroat trout were the dominant species here before European settlers arrived; Arctic grayling and mountain whitefish are also native. The rest of the trout are nonnative species that have been introduced to the ecosystem along the way, threatening the native varieties. The park works with anglers to help restore balance: Most of the park has been designated a Native Trout Conservation Area, with no fishing limit on nonnative species. In fact, in certain waterways, you *must* kill rainbow, brook, lake, and cutthroat/rainbow hybrids, as well as smallmouth bass. Limits do exist within the Nonnative Trout Tolerance Area on the western side of the park. Everywhere in Yellowstone, you must release native fish species unharmed. You'll find the Yellowstone Fishing Regulations at www.nps.gov/yell/planyourvisit/fishing.htm.

The Yellowstone season opens on the Saturday of Memorial Day weekend and ends on October 31. Starting in 2024, the park also opened sections of the Madison and the Gardner rivers to year-round fishing. Note that many rivers and streams have seasonal closures due to heavy grizzly bear activity; check dates at www.nps.gov/yell/planyourvisit/conditions.htm.

Many fine anglers come to Yellowstone, and they are well informed about which seasons are best on which stretches of river. In June, try the **Yellowstone River** downstream of Yellowstone Lake, where the cutthroat trout spawn. Fish the **Madison River** near the west entrance in July, and fish again in late fall for rainbow and some brown trout. In late summer, you can try to hook the cutthroats that thin out by September on the **Lamar River,** in the park's beautiful northeast corner.

Fishing on **Yellowstone Lake** was popular until recent years, when regulations designed to bring back the waning population of cutthroat trout began to send some of the trolling powerboats elsewhere. Certain areas of the lake, such as the southeast arm, are closed to motorized boats; this makes the Yellowstone River inlet a lovely area to canoe, camp, and fish.

You can fish the **Yellowstone River** below the Grand Canyon by hiking down into **Seven Mile Hole,** a great place to cast (not much vegetation to snag on) for cutthroat trout from July to September. You'll have the best luck around Sulphur Creek. Other good fishing stretches include the **Gibbon** and **Firehole rivers,** which merge to form the Madison River on the park's west side, and the 3-mile **Lewis River Channel** between Shoshone and Lewis lakes during the fall spawning run of brown trout.

Access on the **Madison River** for anglers with disabilities is 3½ miles west of Madison Junction at the Haynes Overlook, where you'll find an accessible fishing platform over the river's edge along 70 feet of the bank.

Permits   Park permits (not state fishing permits) are required for Yellowstone anglers ages 16 and older; the permit costs $40 for 3 days, $55 for 7 days, and $75 for the season. Children 15 and under don't need a permit if they are fishing with an adult who has one, but they need to pick up a free permit if they're fishing without supervision. Rangers strongly encourage buying your permit ahead of time at **www.recreation.gov**, but you can also buy them at ranger stations, visitor centers, Yellowstone General Stores, and most fishing shops in the gateways.

Supplies & Fishing Guides   If you need supplies or a guide in Gardiner, stop at **Parks' Fly Shop,** 202 Second St. South (www.parksflyshop.com; ℂ **406/848-7314**). In West Yellowstone, check out **Big Sky Anglers,** 39 Madison Ave. (www.bigskyanglers.com; ℂ **406/646-7801**). Full-day trips typically cost about $700 for two people in high summer.

Several Jackson, Wyoming–based fishing guides also lead trips into Yellowstone. See "Fishing," in the "Other Activities" section of chapter 6 (p. 127), and the Jackson "Essentials" section, in chapter 8 (p. 174).

HORSEBACK RIDING   You can BYO horse (or llama or mule) to the park for day rides or horse-packing trips; all overnight outings require a backcountry permit. If you're more in the market for a catered day ride, concessionaire **Xanterra** (www.yellowstonenationalparklodges.com; ℂ **307/344-7311**) offers mellow 1- and 2-hour horseback trips out of Tower-Roosevelt on well-mannered horses ($94 or $142 for riders ages 8 and up).

Many outfitters have permits to run horse-packing trips to a variety of destinations inside the park (go to **www.nps.gov/yell/planyourvisit/guidedtours.htm** for a full list). Saddling up with one of them typically means horses, gear, meals, camping equipment, and permits are all included. Prices vary widely according to trip length and number of people, so contact individual outfitters for your options.

4

Other Activities

GETTING OUTDOORS IN YELLOWSTONE

WINTER SPORTS & ACTIVITIES

Nope, the park doesn't shut down in the winter. Instead, an entirely new Yellowstone emerges when the snow—all 150 annual inches of it, or 300 inches in the high country—starts flying. Why is a winter trip a great idea? Let us count the ways. One, the crowds melt away, leaving visitors who do venture out into the cold with a shockingly quiet, solitude-filled landscape. Two, snow makes park wildlife easier to spot and track. Winter is an especially exciting time to look for wolves, which hunt bison slowed down by deep drifts (the bears, however, will be hibernating—which could be a plus, depending on your perspective). Three, snow and ice create a whole new feel: Waterfalls freeze into ripply ice sculptures, geysers and hot springs spew and steam over whitewa-shed basins, frozen thermal vapors transform trees into "snow ghosts," and thick ice blankets Yellowstone Lake. And four, winter opens up a slew of new outdoor activities, from skiing and snowshoeing to zipping along in a snowmobile.

Naturally, you'll want to be ready for Yellowstone's winter conditions. Daytime highs might be anywhere from 0°F (–18°C) to the 30s (–1°C to 4°C), and nighttime lows can reach –20°F (–29°C). The coldest temperature ever recorded here was a frostbite-inducing –66°F (–54°C)! Dress in warm layers and make sure to both eat and drink frequently to stay energized and hydrated.

Only two park hotels open for a December-to-March winter season after a brief shutdown in the fall: **Mammoth Hot Springs Hotel** (p. 134) and the **Old Faithful Snow Lodge** (p. 138). And the Northeast Entrance Road between Mammoth and Cooke City is the only one that's cleared for cars in winter; traveling anywhere else requires a snowcoach or snowmobile.

All in-park amenities—including lodging, dining, ski shops, ski shuttles, and snowcoach tours—are handled by concessionaire **Xanterra** (www.yellowstonenationalpark lodges.com; © **307/344-7311**). Several other outfitters and gear shops in the gateway towns can also set you up for

4

Winter Sports & Activities

winter fun. If you're looking to combine recreation with education, the **winter courses** offered by **Yellowstone Forever** (www.yellowstone.org; © **406/848-2400**) can't be beat. Seasonal field seminars focus heavily on wildlife, particularly wolves, and also incorporate geology and the natural and cultural history of the area.

CROSS-COUNTRY SKIING Yellowstone is an amazing place to be on skinny skis. The park grooms ski trails at Mammoth, Old Faithful, and Tower; many other ungroomed, marked ski trails are available in those places too, as well as in the park's northeast corner and at Canyon. Skiers also have free rein over any unplowed road or trail, though you'll want heavy-duty skis to break trail in powder.

Gliding among the geysers is one of Yellowstone's most unique winter activities, making Old Faithful a top spot to explore. You can ski 4.5 miles (one-way) on the groomed **Lone Star Geyser Trail** for a backcountry water show (return via the **Howard Eaton Trail** for a more challenging loop) or circle past geysers and hot springs on the **Biscuit Basin** and **Black Sand Basin trails.** At Mammoth, the groomed **Upper Terrace Loop** tours around steaming travertine terraces, and the untracked **Bighorn Loop** traces Indian Creek up to expansive views over the Gallatin Range.

The **Bear Den Ski Shops** at Mammoth and Old Faithful rent ski packages ($17/half-day, $26/day) and offer group and private ski lessons ($37 or $45/hour). Xanterra's ski shuttles will drop you off at Indian Creek, Bunsen Peak, several stops along the Divide Route, and two stops on the Fairy Falls route ($17–$31). Ski back to the hotels or catch the return shuttle after exploring each area. You can also hop on guided ski tours of places like Canyon ($292) or Mammoth (prices vary), which include transportation to the trailheads and lunch.

ICE-SKATING Both the **Old Faithful Snow Lodge** and **Mammoth Hot Springs Hotel** maintain ice-skating rinks (weather permitting) with free skate rentals.

SNOWCOACH TOURS What, exactly, is a snowcoach? Picture a midsize van or bus with heavy-duty tank treads

winter **ROAD CONDITIONS**

Due to the high elevation and the abundance of snow, most roads in Yellowstone are closed to all wheeled vehicles in winter. The only major park area that is typically accessible by car is Mammoth Hot Springs; cars are allowed to drive in the village there. Signs will alert you as to how far south into the park you can go (usually to Tower Junction, 18 miles away). From Tower Junction, it's another 29 miles to the northeast entrance. This entrance is open but not accessible from Red Lodge, Montana, and points east (because the Beartooth Hwy. is closed in winter). You can go only as far as Cooke City, Montana, and the roads are only kept open so that the folks in Cooke City aren't stranded during the long winters. **Snowmobiles, snowcoaches,** and **cross-country skiers,** however, use park roads regularly throughout the winter season. For up-to-the-minute information on weather and road conditions, call ⓒ **307/344-2117.**

Basing yourself in **West Yellowstone** is another winter option. From the West Yellowstone entrance, it's only 14 miles to Madison Junction, which presents opportunities to head south to Old Faithful or north to the Grand Canyon and Mammoth Hot Springs. Because this is the most popular way to access the park, plan on making reservations early.

instead of tires, plus big windows and a toasty heating system, and you get the idea. These lumbering vehicles are one of the primary ways that travelers access Yellowstone when snow blankets the landscape, and they're a lot of fun. If you're bound for Old Faithful Snow Lodge, this is probably how you'll get there. Xanterra's shuttle from Mammoth costs $168 for adults and $84 for children each way, and you're allowed two pieces of luggage; you can also find private outfitters out of West Yellowstone or Jackson.

Snowcoaches do more than shuttle you from place to place: You can also sign up to tour the park in one. It's a much warmer way to see the winter sights than a snowmobile, though you'll want to bundle up for the many stops along the way. Xanterra's options range from half-day or full-day scenic routes to tours focused on wildlife-watching or photography, and cost $80 to $351 for adults. Private outfitters also run a variety of group and custom tours.

For info on Xanterra's tours, call ☏ **307/344-7311** or go to www.yellowstonenationalparklodges.com. **Backcountry Adventures** (www.backcountry-adventures.com; ☏ **406/646-9317**) offers tours to Old Faithful and Canyon out of West Yellowstone. On the south side, Jackson's **Scenic Safaris** (www.scenic-safaris.com; ☏ **307/734-8898**) can get you to Old Faithful.

SNOWMOBILING   For a faster and more thrilling way to see the park, a snowmobile is the way to go. Suit up (mind that windchill) and take off over the park's oversnow routes, connecting top destinations and scoping for wildlife along the way. **Warming huts** at West Thumb, Old Faithful, Madison, Indian Creek, Canyon, and Fishing Bridge provide welcome respite from the bitter cold en route.

Winter access rules designed to protect Yellowstone's resources from both noise and emissions pollution make it challenging to plan private snowmobiling trips. Hopefuls can apply for a permit ($40/day plus $6 application fee) to the **Non-Commercially Guided Snowmobile Access Program** through a lottery open August 1 through 31 for the following winter: Four snowmobiling groups (maximum five snowmobiles per group) are allowed to enter the park each day, one at each oversnow entrance. Permittees must also complete an online snowmobile education course, and their vehicles must meet certain standards for noise and emissions. For more, see **www.nps.gov/yell/planyourvisit/ncgsap.htm**.

If you haven't planned ahead or didn't get lucky in the lottery, guided snowmobile trips can get you cruising in the park without the paperwork. Several outfitters operate in the gateway towns, with West Yellowstone boasting the most options. **Backcountry Adventures** (www.backcountry-adventures. com; ☏ **406/646-9317**) runs several daily or weekly tours to different park highlights for $279 per snowmobile. **Two Top Snowmobile Rental** (www.yellowstonevacations.com; ☏ **406/646-7802**) is also popular for its tours to Old Faithful and Canyon ($340–$370/snowmobile), as well as private options. The only option near the East Entrance, **Gary Fales Outfitting** (www.garyfalesoutfitting.com; ☏ **307/587-3970**) has trips that take you over Sylvan Pass on an all-day circle tour for $400 per double snowmobile.

SNOWSHOEING The winter travel method with the lowest learning curve—just strap on snowshoes and walk—is an excellent way to soak in the snowy landscape. Explore along any of the park's marked ski trails (just don't step in the ski track; these are groomed for skiers) or unplowed roads; at Old Faithful, the loop up to Observation Point and Solitary Geyser is snowshoe-only. Park rangers sometimes lead free snowshoe walks (BYO snowshoes) at Mammoth and West Yellowstone, and Xanterra runs guided trips to Canyon and the Old Faithful area ($32–$394 adults). The **Bear Den Ski Shops** at Mammoth and Old Faithful Snow Lodge rent snowshoes ($14/half-day, $21/full day).

Winter Sports & Activities

EXPLORING GRAND TETON

Grand Teton is a bit like Yellowstone's kid brother—a much smaller slice of a similar ecosystem populated by similar wildlife. It's also a premier national park in its own right: Few, if any, other parks can claim such a stunning mountain skyline, and the Tetons' backcountry is the stuff of legend for hikers and river rafters. You could blaze through the park roads in a day, but you'd merely be scratching the surface of this fascinating combination of geologic artistry and ecological diversity.

One more bonus Grand Teton has on its northern neighbor: The park's proximity to Jackson, Wyoming, means you can easily combine the alpine wilderness with an A-list travel destination. Where else can you hike in the shadow of 13,000-plus-foot peaks by day, then sit down to a perfectly prepared steak and dance the two-step by night?

ESSENTIALS

ACCESS/ENTRY POINTS Grand Teton National Park runs along a north-south axis, bordered on the west by the Teton Range. **Teton Park Road** skirts along the lakes at the mountains' base. From the **north,** you can enter the park from Yellowstone National Park, which is linked to Grand Teton by an 8-mile stretch of highway (U.S. 89/191/287) running through the **John D. Rockefeller Jr. Memorial Parkway,** along which you might see some bare and blackened trees from the 1988 and 2016 fires. If you enter this way, you can stop at the park information center at Flagg Ranch, just outside Yellowstone, to get Grand Teton information. From mid-December to mid-March, Yellowstone's south entrance is open only to snowmobiles and snowcoaches.

You can also approach the park from the **east,** via U.S. 26/287. This route comes from Dubois, 55 miles east on the other side of the Absaroka and Wind River ranges, and crosses **Togwotee Pass,** where you'll get your first views of the Tetons towering over the valley. Travelers who come this way can continue south on U.S. 26/89/191 to Jackson and enjoy spectacular mountain and Snake River views.

Finally, you can enter Grand Teton from Jackson in the **south,** driving about 12 miles north on U.S. 26/89/191 to the Moose Junction turnoff and the park's south entrance. Here you'll find the park headquarters and the Craig Thomas Discovery and Visitor Center, plus a small, developed area that includes restaurants and shops.

VISITOR CENTERS & INFORMATION Grand Teton National Park (www.nps.gov/grte) has three visitor centers, plus a couple of smaller information centers. The **Craig Thomas Discovery & Visitor Center** (© **307/739-3399**) is a half-mile west of Moose Junction and jam-packed with info and exhibits about the park's natural and human history. Here you'll find displays on glaciation and park ecosystems, old wagons, Native American artifacts, and a wall on the history of mountaineering in the area. In summer, it's open daily 8am to 5pm; hours change to 9am to 5pm daily in May and October. **Colter Bay Visitor Center** (© **307/739-3594**), the northernmost option, features a visiting Indigenous artist program and a big porch with Jackson Lake views; it's open daily 8am to 5pm in summer and 9am to 5pm in May. The **Jenny Lake Visitor Center,** at the southern end of Jenny Lake, is open daily 9am to 5pm mid-May to September.

On the Moose-Wilson Road is the **Laurance S. Rockefeller Preserve Center** (© **307/739-3654**), open summer daily 9am to 5pm. Finally, an information station is at the **Flagg Ranch** complex (© **307/543-2372**), approximately 5 miles north of the park's northern boundary; it's open daily 9am to 3:30pm in summer.

FEES With no park gates on U.S. 26/89/191 coming south from Yellowstone, you can get a free ride through the park

Grand Teton National Park

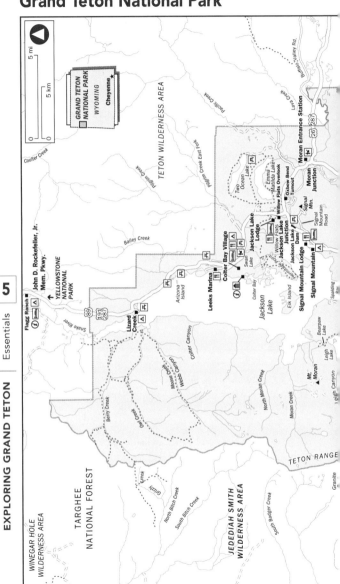

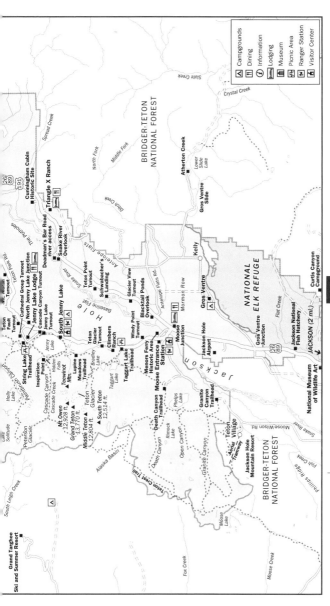

from that entrance; otherwise, you'll pay $35 per automobile for a 7-day pass ($30 for motorcycles and $20 for hikers/cyclists). If you expect to visit the park more than once in a year, buy an annual pass for $70. And if you plan to visit parks and national monuments around the country, purchase an **America the Beautiful Annual Pass** for $80 (good for 365 days from the date of purchase at nearly all federal preserves). Anyone ages 62 and older can get a **Lifetime Senior Pass** for a one-time fee of $80, and people who are blind or who have a permanent disability can obtain an **Access Pass,** which is free. All passes are available at any entrance point to the parks. Most of the money from entrance fees goes back into the park where it was collected, so consider it a contribution worth making.

Fees for **tent camping** are between $49 and $79 at all six park campgrounds. For more information on camping, see "Where to Camp in Grand Teton" in chapter 7. Reservations are required and go quickly; get them up to 6 months in advance at www.recreation.gov.

SPECIAL REGULATIONS & WARNINGS   See chapter 3 (p. 30) for a summary of the major park regulations, which are nearly identical in both parks.

THE HIGHLIGHTS

You can't miss the centerpiece of Grand Teton's natural wonders: The stunning, craggy peaks lining the western skyline of the park dominate pretty much every view. But tear your eyes away from them and you'll find gorgeous lakes, wildflower-lined trails, and a mighty river, too.

THE PEAKS   Each of the park's signature peaks has its own personality. The **Cathedral Group** ★★★ encompasses a series of the tallest peaks in the Teton Range, all clustered between Death Canyon to the south and Cascade Canyon to the north. The big daddy is 13,775-foot **Grand Teton,** one of the mountaineering world's prized summits, but **Mount Owen** (12,933 ft.) and **Teewinot** (12,330 ft.) are equally impressive. Nearby peaks like **Middle Teton** (12,809 ft.), **South Teton** (12,519 ft.), and **Mount Moran** (12,610 ft.) make for spectacular bookends. The Teton Range was uplifted along the Teton fault starting 10 million years ago, and the magic of wind, water, and ice has been carving the peaks into their jagged shapes ever since. The Teton peaks tower about 7,000 feet higher than the surrounding valley, making them some of North America's most dramatic mountain vistas.

JACKSON LAKE ★   Grand Teton's largest lake is a natural one, even if it was raised 39 feet by the addition of a dam. Its expansive shoreline holds several visitor facilities, marinas, boat launches, hiking trails, and campgrounds (including **Lizard Creek, Colter Bay,** and **Signal Mountain Campgrounds**). **Colter Bay Village** forms the northernmost visitor hub, complete with a visitor center, swimming beach, restaurants, lodging, and a general store. A bit farther south, the swanky **Jackson Lake Lodge** sits alongside primo moose habitat, and the **Willow Flats Overlook** grants views across a marshland and over to Mount Moran. **Chapel of the Sacred Heart,** a beautiful old Catholic church, is just beyond that. The Signal Mountain area is the southernmost development on Jackson Lake and includes **Signal Mountain Lodge** and the winding **Signal Mountain Road** leading to a summit with amazing Teton Range views.

JENNY LAKE ★★   Much smaller than Jackson Lake but charming in its own right, glacially carved Jenny Lake is a favorite place to soak in the views or set out on a trail. The south end of the lake—where you'll find popular **Jenny Lake Campground,** the visitor center, and trailheads to **Jenny Lake Overlook** and **Hidden Falls/Inspiration Point** ★★—tends to get crowded in the summer. You can swim or boat here, or hop on the **Jenny Lake Boating shuttle** to the **Cascade Canyon Trail** ★★★. Don't miss the one-way scenic drive from North Jenny Lake Junction, which passes several excellent vistas and the luxe **Jenny Lake Lodge.**

MOOSE ★   The first developed area you'll hit if you're coming in from Jackson, the Moose District features a snazzy visitor center and dining, lodging, and shopping options in the tiny **Dornans** complex. **Menors Ferry Historic District** preserves a late-19th-century homestead and general store, and the peaceful, 1925-era **Chapel of the Transfiguration** is a lovely spot for contemplation. Excellent hiking trails lead to **Taggart Lake, Bradley Lake,** and

Death Canyon, and you can pitch a tent at **Gros Ventre Campground.**

SNAKE RIVER ★★ The mighty Snake flows out of Jackson Lake and south through the park, providing fantastic opportunities for floating, rafting, fishing, and scoping for wildlife. One of the prettiest river views awaits at **Oxbow Bend,** a riverbend pullout with expansive views of Mount Moran and frequent moose and trumpeter swan sightings; reach it on U.S. 89/191 just east of Jackson Lake Junction.

IF YOU HAVE ONLY 1 DAY

Unlike Yellowstone, Grand Teton is small enough to make touring it in a single day reasonable. You'll be able to hit most of its main attractions, and a loop road means you won't have to retrace all your steps. This itinerary assumes you'll be coming in from Yellowstone to the north, but you can just as easily follow it starting in Jackson.

From Yellowstone's south entrance, take U.S. 26/89/191 south 8 miles through the **John D. Rockefeller Jr. Memorial Parkway,** passing **Flagg Ranch**'s information center and lodging/dining. Once inside Grand Teton National Park, the road quickly sticks to **Jackson Lake**'s eastern shore, giving you windshield-wide views of **Mount Moran** and the **Cathedral Group.** Skip **Leeks Marina** and continue south.

First stop: **Colter Bay Village.** Take a spin around the visitor center here and check out the visiting Indigenous artist program inside. This is also a great spot for a quick swim or paddling trip; you can launch your own boat or rent a kayak or canoe from **Colter Bay Village Marina.** If you'd rather go hiking, keep driving south for the park's best quick-fix trails.

Continue about 5 miles down to the road to **Jackson Lake Lodge** and hop out to see the commanding peak view from the hotel's impressive lobby. A stone's throw farther, **Willow Flats Overlook** is also worth a stop for its vantage point on the Teton Range (and to look for moose). At **Jackson Lake Junction,** turn right to follow **Teton Park Road,** the park's inner route, where the peaks are front and center in your view.

Turn left to follow **Signal Mountain Road** to its 7,727-foot summit. From here, you'll get a spin-around view of the Cathedral Group, Mount Moran, Jackson Lake, and Jackson

Hole. Come back down and press on to **North Jenny Lake Junction,** then turn right to drive the one-way loop to Jenny Lake's northern end. Must-stop pullout: **Cathedral Group Turnout.** You can also access a couple of short day hikes here, like the 3.7-mile loop around **String Lake** or the lakeshore **Jenny Lake Trail.** Exploring the north end of Jenny Lake also means you'll avoid some of the visitor hordes that congregate at the south end.

Rejoin Teton Park Road and continue south (you'll pass one more excellent hike, the 3.9-mile **Taggart Lake Loop**). Take a break at **Menors Ferry Historic District** and peek into a preserved late-1800s homestead, smokehouse, icehouse, and general store, then visit perhaps the most scenically blessed church in the country, **Chapel of the Transfiguration.** Get back in the car for the short jaunt over to **Craig Thomas Discovery & Visitor Center** to learn more about the geology and ecology behind the park sights.

From **Moose Junction,** take the park's outer road, U.S. 26/89/191, north. You'll be treated to constant wide-angle views of the Teton peaks with several strategically placed pullouts. Turn left at **Moran Junction** and swing over to **Oxbow Bend** for the chance to see waterfowl or moose. From here, you could head back up to Yellowstone, set up camp in Grand Teton (reserve a campsite online well ahead of time), or head south to the lights of Jackson.

TOURING GRAND TETON

Grand Teton is much more amenable to auto touring than Yellowstone: Park roads connect many attractions, and it's a far more manageable size. But as jaw-dropping as the views of the Teton peaks are from the roads, the park's most stunning scenery is in its backcountry. Sticking to the car would mean missing out on that unique Teton magic. You need 2 days, and preferably 3, to do this park up right. Save 1 day for a longer hike, 1 for swimming, kayaking, or paddleboarding one of the park's lakes, and 1 for checking out visitor centers, off-the-beaten-path historic sites, and viewpoints.

This section kicks off at the northern end of the park, but you could just as easily start exploring from the southern end near Jackson. From Jackson, it's about 13 miles to the Moose Entrance Station, then another 8 miles to the Jenny Lake

Visitor Center, another 12 miles to the Jackson Lake Junction, and 5 more miles to Colter Bay.

Jackson Lake & the North End of the Park

Technically, Yellowstone and Grand Teton don't border each other; they're separated by a sliver of federal land called the **John D. Rockefeller Jr. Memorial Parkway.** As you head south from Yellowstone, you'll cover 8 miles of this forested preserve—watch for blackened trunks from the Berry Fire, which forced the evacuation of **Flagg Ranch** in 2016 but thankfully didn't damage the structures. The Flagg Ranch hub has lodging, dining, camping, gas, and a general store. The other important feature here is **Grassy Lake Road,** a remote road granting access to some of the wildest, least crowded canyons and free primitive campsites in both the Tetons and Yellowstone.

The parkway crosses into Grand Teton National Park and quickly hugs the eastern shoreline of **Jackson Lake ★**. Glaciers gouged out its 400-foot-deep lakebed 10,000 years ago, and melting glacial ice filled it to form the park's largest lake. Though it is a natural waterway, the construction of Jackson Lake Dam (finished in 1916, before Grand Teton was a protected park) to provide irrigation for farmers in Idaho's Snake River Valley raised the lake 39 feet. The Snake River pours into its northern tip, then exits east of the dam. Today, Jackson Lake is the place for sailing, powerboating, windsurfing, waterskiing, and paddling—and swimming, if you're brave enough to face the, er, brisk water.

After passing **Lizard Creek Campground,** a few pullouts, and picnic areas (**Lakeview Picnic Area** is especially nice, with its sandy beach and aspen groves), you'll come to **Leeks Marina,** a place to launch your own boat; no rentals are available. A casual pizza and ice cream joint is open in summer.

The busiest outpost on the north side, **Colter Bay Village,** is just south. Get oriented at the **Colter Bay Visitor Center** (✆ **307/739-3594**), where visiting Native American artists display and sell their work in summer. You'll also find an auditorium showing park programs, an info desk, and a bookstore. Water lovers will appreciate the swimming beach

Jackson Lake: Colter Bay Area

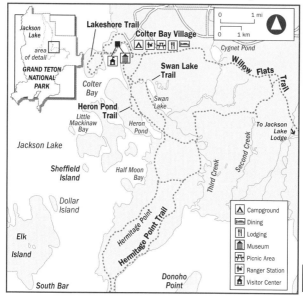

and marina; rent a kayak, canoe, or powerboat or sign up for a boat cruise or guided fishing outing. (*Note:* Check lake conditions before you go. Low water levels on Jackson Lake forced the marina to shut down in summer 2022.) A general store stocks groceries. On the hiking front, **Hermitage Point Trail** connects Colter Bay to a network of trails through sagebrush meadows and lodgepole forests near the lakeshore. Looking to stay the night? Your options include cabins, an RV park, and **Colter Bay Campground** (see chapter 7).

Continuing south, the next major attraction is the stately **Jackson Lake Lodge,** a National Historic Landmark with a picture-perfect view of Jackson Lake and the Teton peaks. Even if you're not staying here, swing by to check it out. The upscale lobby, with its fireplaces and 60-foot windows framing Mount Moran and the Cathedral Group, makes a wonderful spot for coffee or a cocktail. Several restaurants line the lobby, including the fancy **Mural Room** with its historic namesake paintings, and boutiques round out the offerings.

Jackson Lake: Signal Mountain Area

Legend:
- △ Campground
- 🏠 Ranger Station

Two Ocean Lake Trail

Two Ocean Lake

Grand View Point

Emma Matilda Lake Trail

Two Ocean Lake Rd.

Emma Matilda Lake

Lozier Hill ▲

Christian Pond Trail

Christian Pond

Lunch Tree Hill

Willow Flats Overlook

Jackson Lake Lodge

OXBOW BEND

To Moran →

Christian Creek

Spring Creek

WILLOW FLATS

Jackson Lake Junction

Raft Launch

Emma Matilda Overlook

Jackson Lake Dam

Signal Mountain Rd.

SIGNAL MOUNTAIN

Jackson Lake

area of detail

GRAND TETON NATIONAL PARK

Cow Lake

Signal Mountain Lodge

Signal Summit Mountain Trail

Snake River

Teton Park Rd.

To Jenny Lake ↓

0 — 1 mi
0 — 1 km

This area is also the jumping-off point for some excellent, lesser-traveled trails in the park's northeast region. Circle **Christian Pond** on an easy, 3.3-mile loop, or connect to the longer trails around **Emma Matilda** and **Two Ocean Lakes.** You can also hike (or drive) to the **Willow Flats Overlook,** a beautiful spot to scope for moose—especially in fall, when the willow bushes turn gold.

Just beyond, you'll hit **Jackson Lake Junction.** Turning east brings you to the Moran entrance and an alternate access point to Emma Matilda and Two Ocean Lakes. Going south from there traces the Snake River along U.S. 26/89/191 on the eastern edge of the park. But doing so would skip far too many inner-park sights, so turn right to follow **Teton Park Road** instead. You'll cross **Jackson Lake Dam** and soon reach the resplendent log church, **Chapel of the Sacred Heart ★**. The 1930s-era Catholic chapel holds services from June to September. Its rustic architecture is worth a look, and this is a peaceful place for a lakeside picnic.

Press on south to reach the hub of Jackson Lake's south side, **Signal Mountain.** The lake side of this junction holds a lodge, a couple of restaurants, a gas station and EV charger, a general store with surprisingly healthy snack options, and the **Signal Mountain Campground.** Park concessionaire Aramark also runs guided fishing trips and rents powerboats, pontoons, and kayaks from the marina here. Across the street, **Signal Mountain Road** winds up the side of 7,727-foot **Signal Mountain ★**. Don't miss this short detour to drink in views of the lake and the shockingly vertical Tetons to the distant Absarokas, Gros Ventre, and Yellowstone Plateau, all the way across Jackson Hole. About 3 miles from the base of the hill, before you reach the summit, a paved path leads to **Jackson Point Overlook,** the spot where photographer William Henry Jackson shot his famous landscapes of Jackson Lake and the Tetons in the 1870s.

Looking for a hideaway? On the right (west) side of the road between Signal Mountain and North Jenny Lake Junction, about 2 miles south of the Mount Moran turnout, an unmarked, unpaved road leads to **Spalding Bay,** a sheltered little backcountry camping area and boat launch area with a primitive restroom. It's a great place to be alone with spectacular views of the lake and mountains. If you decide to camp, a permit is required (even though it's accessible by road). Reserving the site in advance is your best bet, but you might get lucky and score a walk-in permit, too. An automobile or SUV will have no problem with this road, but speed had better not be important to you. Passing through brush and forest, you might just spot a moose.

Jenny Lake & the South End of the Park

Driving in the Tetons is like starring in your own car commercial—all winding roads looping beneath super-scenic peaks—and the Jenny Lake area is your picture-perfect setting. At **North Jenny Lake Junction,** turn right to access a drive skirting the trailheads for **Leigh** and **String lakes,** two mountain-ringed lakes that make top-notch day hikes. Continue past **Jenny Lake Lodge** to trace the northeast shore of **Jenny Lake ★★**. Named for a Shoshone woman married to a prominent 1870s mountain guide, this bucolic lake tucked between Teewinot and Rockchuck Peak has been a favorite travelers' destination since the early 1900s.

The scenic drive pops you back out on Teton Park Road just north of the bustling **South Jenny Lake Junction.** The **Jenny Lake Visitor Center** is housed in Harrison Crandall's 1920s photography studio and features a three-dimensional park map, a small gift shop, and antlers and skulls to touch. You'll also find a general store, a ranger station—and a competitive parking scene. The park's best campground, **Jenny Lake Campground,** is also here, a spot for (somewhat polar bear) swimming, boating, fishing, and hiking. The flat, 6.8-mile **Jenny Lake Trail** circles the lake, or you can hike it partway to reach **Hidden Falls** and **Inspiration Point.** Or take the **Jenny Lake Boating** (www.jennylakeboating.com; ℂ **307/734-9227;** round-trip $20 adults, $12 children) shuttle across the lake to the **Cascade Canyon** trailhead.

Farther south, the **Teton Glacier Turnout** gives you a peek at one of the few park glaciers visible from the road. Teton Glacier grew for several hundred years until, pressured by the increasing summer temperatures of the past century, it reversed course and began retreating. Just beyond that is the turnoff to **Climber's Ranch,** a dorm-style lodge run by the

Jenny Lake Area & Trails

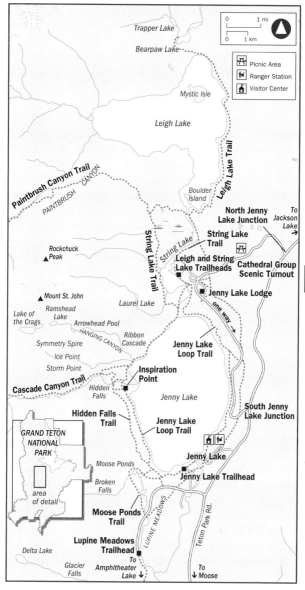

American Alpine Club (www.americanalpineclub.org/grand-teton-climbers-ranch; ✆ 307/733-7271). It caters to climbers staging attempts on the Teton's most prized peaks, but anyone can bunk here for $35/night ($25 club members); it's one of the best lodging deals for miles around. Another stone's throw beyond that, the **Taggart Lake Trail** leads to a beautiful tarn at the foot of Avalanche Canyon.

If you're curious about what life was like in Jackson Hole before it became a recreation mecca/glitterati hot spot, stop at the next attraction down the road: **Menors Ferry Historic District ★**. Homesteader Bill Menor operated a simple ferry across the Snake River and a general store here in the 1890s and early 1900s, and today you can see reconstructed versions of both. The general store is half historic exhibit, half actual store selling local honey and jam; there's also a smokehouse, icehouse, and 1917 cabin furnished in pioneer style. Nearby, the 1925 log **Chapel of the Transfiguration ★** is a sought-after wedding venue; Episcopal services are still held on summer Sundays.

By now you've reached **Moose,** the southernmost entrance to the park. The **Craig Thomas Discovery & Visitor Center** offers a treasure trove of info on the area's human history, ecology, wildlife, and geology: Check out historic wagons and Native American arrows, watch the park movie, and peruse the wall dedicated to the development of modern mountaineering, or just pick up maps. Just down the road you'll find **Dornans** (www.dornans.com), a complex with lodging, restaurants, grocery store, gift shop, wine shop, gas station, and an outfitter that rents kayaks, canoes, paddleboards, and bikes.

The East Side of the Park

The 18-mile outer park road, U.S. 26/89/191, is usually a faster trip through the park, and it grants panoramic views of the Tetons from its more removed vantage point. But if you're coming up to the park from Jackson, consider turning east at **Gros Ventre Junction,** just south of the airport, instead of beelining north. The less-busy **Gros Ventre Campground**'s sites line the river of the same name; just north of that is **Mormon Row ★**. Mormon settlers from Utah homesteaded here in the 1890s, and a couple of quaint old barns still stand imposingly in front of the Teton tableau.

For an interesting side trip, continue east on Gros Ventre Road past the tiny town of **Kelly** into the **Bridger-Teton National Forest.** In 1925, a mile-wide slab of Sheep Mountain that broke free and poured into the canyon, blocking the Gros Ventre River with 50 million cubic yards of rock and debris. The landslide dammed the river and formed Lower Slide Lake, but the dam failed in spring rains 2 years later and flooded Kelly almost into nonexistence. Interpretive signs at the site point out remnants of these geologic events.

Otherwise, **Antelope Flats Road** will take you back to the highway. Less than a mile down U.S. 26/89/191, on the left, **Blacktail Ponds Overlook** offers an opportunity to see how beavers build dams and the effect these hard-working creatures have on the flow of park streams. Two miles farther along U.S. 26/89/191, the **Glacier View Turnout** has views of an area that 140,000 to 160,000 years ago was filled with a 4,000-foot-thick glacier. Then **Schwabacher Road** gives you your first access to the Snake River: Drive the 1-mile dirt road to **Schwabacher Landing** to enjoy the view of the peaks reflected in a channel of the Snake. Keep your eyes peeled for bald eagles, ospreys, moose, river otters, and beavers (a large dam is just north).

The **Snake River Overlook** ★, approximately 4 miles beyond the Glacier View Turnout, is the most famous view of the Teton Range and the Snake River, immortalized by photographer Ansel Adams. From this overlook, you'll also see at least three separate, distinctive 200-foot-high plateaus that roll from the riverbed to the valley floor, a vivid portrayal of the power of the glaciers and ice floes that sculpted this area. In the early 1800s, this was a prime hunting ground for John Jacob Astor's Pacific Fur Company and a certain David E. Jackson, for whom the lake and valley are named. By 1840, the popularity of silk hats had put an end to fur trapping, and the hunters disappeared. Good thing—the beaver population was almost decimated.

A half-mile north of the Snake River Overlook is the steep paved road (a 19% grade) to **Deadmans Bar,** a peaceful clearing on the river and popular boat launch site. The unsolved murders of three gold miners in 1886 gave this spot its morbid name.

History lovers will also appreciate **Cunningham Cabin Historic Site** just up the road. The 1888 cabin built by ranchers John and Margaret Cunningham is fairly nondescript, but it's one of the few remaining buildings left from the homesteading era, and the .8-mile (one-way) hike across sage flats to reach it gives excellent Teton peak views and a great shot at seeing bison.

Once you hit **Moran Junction,** turn west to rejoin the inner park road. You'll pass **Pacific Creek Road,** an alternate access point to trails to Emma Matilda and Two Ocean Lakes, and the **Oxbow Bend Turnout ★**, a gorgeous, marshy site along the Snake River where moose and waterfowl roam.

ORGANIZED TOURS

If you'd rather hand over the wheel to someone else and concentrate on the scenery, park concessionaire **Grand Teton Lodge Company** (www.gtlc.com; ℰ **307/543-3100**) offers 4-hour bus tours of the park, with an emphasis on ecology and wildlife. Adult tickets cost $130, and kids' tickets (ages 0–11) are $85; tours run mid-May to early October.

Several companies out of Jackson also offer small-group tours of the park. **Brushbuck Tours** (www.brushbucktours. com; ℰ **307/699-2999**) is one of the best: Sign up for halfday, full-day, or multiday tours built around wildlife-watching and photography. Prices start at $139 for a 4-hour group tour and $1,080 for a full-day private tour for one or two people. **Jackson Hole Wildlife Safaris** (www.jackson holewildlifesafaris.com; ℰ **307/690-6402**) is popular for its half-day to 3-day wildlife-centered tours. Tours cost $305 per person for single-day summer trips and $995 per person for tours guided by pro photographers. Both outfitters also offer winter tours.

The excellent **Teton Science Schools ★★**, 700 Coyote Canyon Rd., Jackson (www.tetonscience.org; ℰ **307/733-1313**), runs immersive all-ages programs on several different campuses, plus inside both parks. Travelers can sign up for popular biologist-led Wildlife Expeditions, half- to full-day sojourns designed to be crash courses on the parks' wildlife. One option includes hiking, and another is tailored for families with kids.

Organized Tours

EXPLORING GRAND TETON

RANGER PROGRAMS

Like Yellowstone, Grand Teton offers topnotch, free **ranger programs** ★★★ throughout the park. The widest variety happen June through early September. You might hike with a ranger on the Lakeshore Trail, explore the park's past through both a natural history and human (especially Native American) lens, or learn about wildlife.

And, just like at Yellowstone, Grand Teton offers the **Junior Ranger Program** for kids (and adults, for that matter). Grab a copy of *The Grand Adventure* workbook at any visitor center and complete the educational activities therein—including attending a ranger program and going on a hike—to earn an official Junior Ranger badge.

Check the park newspaper for details or visit **www.nps. gov/grte/planyourvisit/ranger-programs.htm**.

6

GETTING OUT-DOORS IN GRAND TETON

Grand Teton may be a smaller park than Yellowstone, but its hiking is every bit as stellar. Backcountry trails skirt placid lakes, delve into wildflower-filled canyons, and even scurry straight up the tallest peaks. With some of the most dramatic wilderness scenery in the country just a hike away, the Tetons are bound to amaze anyone who steps off the beaten track.

If you have limited time to explore, choose your hiking destinations based on your favorite ecosystems. Looking for a lakefront hike? Try the shoreline trails at Phelps, Two Ocean, or Jenny Lake. Challenging climbs with great views? Head up one of the canyons. Trying to get away from it all? Hit the Teton Crest Trail. This selection of top trails will help you decide.

DAY HIKES

The park's many trails vary greatly in length and level of difficulty, so you'll want to consult with rangers before tackling them. Rangers can suggest hikes suited to your ability and update you on everything from bear activity to trail conditions to weather concerns. They also conduct guided walks. *Remember:* If you are planning to hike for more than 30 minutes, carry a supply of water and some rain gear.

Colter Bay Area

For a **map** showing the trails in this area, see chapter 5.

Lakeshore Trail ★   Trace both sides of a Jackson Lake peninsula on this figure-eight loop (one circle is .9 mile, the other 1.1 miles) with slap-in-the-face views of Mount Moran, Grand Teton, Teewinot, and other marquee Teton peaks. You'll follow a wide, tree-lined footpath to pebbly beaches with vistas across the lake to the peaks beyond. This hike is easy and has a big payoff, making it good for families.

2.2 miles round-trip. Easy. **Access:** Trailhead is at the Marina entrance.

TRAILS FROM THE HERMITAGE POINT TRAILHEAD

The **Hermitage Point Trailhead,** near the marina, leads to a series of connecting loops that lead past tranquil ponds, head out on a scenic peninsula, and extend to **Jackson Lake Lodge.** Make sure you have a good map when planning your hike in this area—options abound, and it can be easy to take a wrong turn if you don't know where you want to go.

Hermitage Point Loop ★   This long loop out to Hermitage Point and back crosses through forest, rolling meadows, and wetlands out to the shore of Jackson Lake, making it an excellent opportunity to spot a variety of wildlife, such as bears, moose, elk, beavers, ospreys, and herons. Stay close to the lakeshore on your way out, passing ponds and tracing Half Moon Bay before hiking out to the end of Hermitage Point, where the Teton peaks loom large across the lake. Follow Third Creek on your way back to the trailhead.

9.5 miles round-trip. Moderate. **Access:** Trailhead is just south of the Colter Bay Ranger Station.

Heron Pond/Swan Lake Loop ★   A shorter route through the Hermitage Point area, this easy loop cruises past

---

A Blooming Photo Op

Not far from the trailhead, the **Hermitage Point Loop ★** opens to a broad, sagebrush-carpeted meadow. In the summer, the area blooms with wildflowers, offering one of the most spectacular views of colossal **Mount Moran,** which is as impressive in its own way as the Grand Teton. To avoid retracing your steps past Heron Pond, bear right at the third creek intersection and continue straight ahead to the corrals at Colter Bay—this route adds no distance to the hike.

Heron Pond and Swan Lake. You'll still explore a variety of habitats, so keep your eyes peeled for wildlife and summer wildflowers. From the Hermitage Point Trailhead, trace Jackson Lake's shoreline to Heron Pond, a small, lily pad–speckled lake that grants views of the big peaks. This is an excellent spot to scope for moose or beavers. Follow the eastern shore, then turn left at the next junction to head toward Swan Lake. And yes, you might spot trumpeter swans—North America's largest native waterfowl—nesting on this grassy lake. From here, it's a short walk back to the trailhead.

3.1 miles round-trip. Easy. **Access:** Trailhead is at Hermitage Point Trailhead, Colter Bay.

Willow Flats Trail ★   What's better than the lovely view from Willow Flats Overlook? This hike takes you right into the middle of that idyllic scene. From Colter Bay, head east to Cygnet Lake, then cross Pilgrim Creek to access the marshy, willow-filled wetlands. The mountain views are expansive, and you might spot moose grazing on the abundant greenery. The trail leads to Jackson Lake Lodge, a nice excuse to treat yourself to lunch. Retrace your steps for a longer trip or drop a car here ahead of time to cut the hike in half.

10.6 miles round-trip. Easy. **Access:** Horse corrals at Colter Bay.

Jackson Lake Lodge Area

For a **map** showing the trails in this area, see chapter 5.

Christian Pond to Grand View Point ★   This easy-access hike from Jackson Lake Lodge circles a pleasant pond before climbing to standout views of the Teton Range at 7,286-foot Grand View Point. Head east from the lodge to reach pint-size Christian Pond in just .2 mile. Follow its western shore to a hilltop vista on its southern side, then circle southeast, then north through sagebrush flats where elk, pronghorn, or coyotes might be roaming. After the junction leading to Grand View Point, continue north for the moderate climb to the point. Soak in views of Grand Teton, Mount Moran, and all the rest, plus Two Ocean and Emma Matilda lakes. Backtrack, then go west to return to the lodge.

5.8 miles round-trip. Easy to moderate. **Access:** Trailhead is near Jackson Lake Lodge corrals.

A wide-open meadow near the summit of Signal Mountain presents an excellent opportunity to look to the west for photos of both **Mount Moran** and the **Teton Range.** The best time to take those photos is before 11am, when the sun will be mostly at your back, or in the early evening, when the sun is lower in the sky to the west.

Signal Mountain Trail ★★   Why drive up a mountain when you can hike it? Hoofing it up the peak offers a chance to spot wildlife like bears and mule deer and wander among summer wildflowers—plus bragging rights over everyone who merely motored up. Hike through a combo of evergreen forest and meadows to a junction at one end of a loop: Take the southern leg on the way up to pass ponds and good wild-life habitat. Press on to Jackson Point Overlook (the trail stops short of the summit) for picture-perfect views of Mount Moran and the rest of the Tetons, Jackson Lake, and the Snake River. Hike the northern leg of the loop on the way back for mountain views along the ridge.

6.8 miles round-trip. Moderate. **Access:** Trailhead is near the entrance to Signal Mountain Lodge.

Two Ocean & Emma Matilda Lake Trails

You can arrive at these lakes from the east or west: From the west, you begin at the Grand View Point Trailhead, 1 mile north of Jackson Lake Lodge, or at the Christian Pond Trail-head, just east of Jackson Lake Lodge. From the east, go up Pacific Creek Road, 4 miles east of Jackson Lake Junction on the road to the Moran entrance. A pullout for Emma Matilda Lake is 2 miles up this road, or you can go a half-mile farther, take a left on Two Ocean Lake Road, and go to the Two Ocean Lake Trailhead parking lot, from which trails lead to both lakes.

Emma Matilda Lake ★   The larger of the two lakes tucked into this northeastern corner of the park, Emma Matilda Lake offers excellent wildlife habitat, rolling terrain, and a splendid backcountry waterfront. We like starting from the trailhead on Pacific Creek Road. Head for the north shore first to hike it counterclockwise, looking out for ripe thimble-berries in high summer—but be aware that bears love them too, so practice good bear safety. Hike through aspen groves and up a steep ridgeline with bird's-eye views over the lake, then swing south through sagebrush meadows. The southern shore is primarily a thick spruce/fir forest, save for the sweeping vantage point of Lookout Rock. You can also combine this loop with a circumnavigation of Two Ocean Lake for a much longer trip.

9.9-mile loop. Easy to moderate. **Access:** Emma Matilda Lake Trailhead on Pacific Creek Rd.

Two Ocean Lake ★★ The hike around this lake is shorter and easier than Emma Matilda's trail, but you still get the same wildlife-scoping, wildflowers, and lake views—plus a chance to ascend to awe-inspiring views at Grand View Point. From the Two Ocean Trailhead, hike counter-clockwise through meadows and aspen groves with peeka-boo views of Two Ocean Lake and the Teton summits. Look out for waterfowl such as ducks, trumpeter swans, grebes, and loons. Once you start curving around the western edge of the lake, you can add on the 1-mile (one-way) spur up Grand View Point (see the Christian Pond to Grand View Point hike, p. 116) for the best vistas of the day. Huckleberries and

---

GRAND TETON FOR kids

Children of all ages visiting the park are encouraged to explore and experience Grand Teton as members of the **Junior Ranger** program. To participate, pick up a copy of the Junior Ranger activity brochure at any visitor center, and then complete the projects outlined in the booklet during your stay. When you present a completed project to a ranger at the Moose, Jenny Lake, or Colter Bay visitor centers, you'll be awarded a Junior Ranger badge.

Two trails within Grand Teton are especially kid-friendly. At 7 miles round-trip, the entire Jenny Lake Loop Trail is a bit long for kids, but take the boat shuttle across Jenny Lake to the **Inspiration Point Trail ★★** portion, which is less than a mile long. The **Christian Pond Trail,** a level, 1-mile round-trip from the corrals at Jackson Lake Lodge, is also a nice diversion, offering great views and a chance to see myriad waterfowl.

thimbleberries are plentiful along the southern shore, so enjoy a foraged snack—just be very mindful of bears. This trail links up with Emma Matilda Lake Trail for a longer trip.

6.4-mile loop, or 8.6 miles round-trip with the Grand View Point side trek. Easy to moderate. **Access:** Two Ocean Lake Trailhead on Two Ocean Lake Rd.

Jenny Lake Area

A **map** showing the trails in this area is in chapter 5.

Amphitheater Lake ★★★ Beeline from the valley floor to the park's stunning subalpine zone in 1 day on this exceptional (if quite steep—elevation gain is nearly 3,000 ft.) hike. Your views of Grand Teton, Mount Owen, and Jackson get better with every step, and soon you'll ascend to vistas over Bradley and Taggart lakes, too. You know you're almost there when you reach Surprise Lake; press on to the stony cirque cradling Amphitheater Lake, topped off by Disappointment Peak lording over the water to the west. Not only is the trail blessed with views, glacial moraine features, and wildflower meadows, but you might see black or grizzly bears, moose, or grouse—making it one of the finest day hikes in the entire park. As an additional or alternate destination, spire-riddled Garnet Canyon awaits just south on a spur branching off the main trail at mile 3.

9.8 miles round-trip. Difficult. **Access:** Lupine Meadows Trailhead.

Forks of Cascade Canyon ★★★ One of the park's absolute stunners, Cascade Canyon is a U-shaped glacial valley surrounded by skyscraping peaks. Up here, incredibly jagged mountains fill the horizon, marmots and pikas scamper among boulders, and black and grizzly bears feast on abundant trailside berries. Cascade Canyon is a popular entry point for backpackers seeking to explore the Tetons' remote wilderness, but this stretch is doable in a day for fit hikers. Catch the shuttle across Jenny Lake to shave a few miles off the trip, then start with a short, steep climb up to Inspiration Point (see "Hidden Falls and Inspiration Point Trail," below). Most people turn around here, but press on to climb up this narrowing valley, where Mount Owen dominates the view. You'll also skirt under Table Mountain and the Wigwams, two peaks straddling the western border of the canyon. Turn around at the Forks, the point where the canyon (and trail) split in two: North will take you to Lake Solitude, and south heads for Hurricane Pass, both top-shelf backpacking trips.

9.6 miles round-trip via the Jenny Lake shuttle; 13.3 miles round-trip from Jenny Lake Trailhead. Moderate to difficult. **Access:** Inspiration Point.

Hidden Falls & Inspiration Point Trail ★★   It's easy to see why this short, beautiful hike is one of the park's most popular: You can get a taste of the wildlife, views, and water features that make the Tetons so special. The shortest route to **Hidden Falls** starts from the boat dock after taking the Jenny Lake shuttle; from there, you'll cross Cascade Creek and hike through huckleberry patches to the dramatic, 200-foot cascade (via a short spur trail). But don't stop there: The .5-mile (one-way) climb up to **Inspiration Point** is worth it. Tiptoe along a rocky trail cut into a cliff face to reach this, well, inspirational view across Jenny Lake to Jackson and the Gros Ventre Wilderness. For a longer trip, skip the boat and hike the long way on the Jenny Lake Loop, a move that extends the out-and-back hike to 5.7 miles.

1.8 miles round-trip from boat dock; 5.7 miles round-trip from Jenny Lake Trailhead. Moderate. **Access:** Trailheads are at the east or west shore boat docks of Jenny Lake (if you take the boat shuttle).

Jenny Lake Loop ★★   Circling the park's second-largest lake makes for a mellow, view-packed trip. You can hike it in either direction, but hugging the eastern shore earlier in the day means you'll escape more of the road noise from the Jenny Lake scenic drive. From the east side, the park's biggest peaks rise across the lake—behemoths like Grand Teton as well as Rockchuck and Baxter Pinnacle. On the west, wildfire-burned areas alternate with thimbleberry bushes and forest; from here, you can tack on the out-and-back to Hidden Falls and Inspiration Point (see above). A trail to **Moose Ponds** heads south around the southern tip of Jenny Lake (stop here to look for the namesake beasts), then circles back to the start.

7.1 miles round-trip. Easy to moderate. **Access:** Trailhead is at the east shore boat dock.

Leigh Lake ★★   Mount Moran looms large in this hike along a large lake just north of Jenny Lake, especially at the start—but you'll also earn a front-row view of Teewinot,

Rockchuck, and Mount Woodring, and probably shake many of the Jenny Lake crowds. The trail starts at the midpoint of String Lake, then traces the eastern shore of Leigh Lake through woods with frequent openings to gaze at the peaks. The beaches you'll pass provide the best uninterrupted views. Once you've hit the northern tip of Leigh, you can also continue another .9 mile to **Bearpaw** and **Trapper lakes,** two smaller, picturesque lakes with even more solitude.

7.4 miles round-trip; 9.2 miles round-trip to Trapper Lake. Easy to moderate. **Access:** Trailhead is at the end of a spur road off the Jenny Lake scenic drive, ½ mile past the String Lake Trailhead.

Paintbrush Canyon to Holly Lake ★★★
Gorgeous Paintbrush Canyon is a popular backpacking destination, but strong day hikers can get a taste of the magic on this trip up to Holly Lake. You'll climb to views over Leigh Lake and wander through a colorful canyon blanketed with paintbrush, gentian, and columbine blossoms—not to mention dip a toe in glacial Holly Lake, a high-country tarn at the base of 11,590-foot Mount Woodring. The trail starts on the String Lake Loop, then ascends through the rocky, rough terrain of Paintbrush Canyon to your turnaround point at the lake.

12.8 miles round-trip. Difficult. **Access:** Leigh Lake Trailhead.

String Lake Loop ★★
Easy hiking and excellent views are what you get with this pleasant trip circumnavigating String Lake. The trail clings to the eastern shore, with views of Mount Moran and the Cathedral Group. Cross the Leigh Lake outlet and head into the forest, then traverse an open slope that provides a nice look back at String Lake. Ambitious hikers can combine this loop with the Leigh Lake hike, above.

3.7 miles round-trip. Easy. **Access:** String Lake Trailhead.

Taggart and Bradley Lakes ★★
The effort-to-reward ratio is stacked in your favor on this loop to a pair of super-scenic backcountry lakes. Views of major peaks like Grand Teton, Middle Teton, Teewinot, and Mount Owen await almost from the start, and the peaks look even more impressive rising behind the green-blue lake waters. Head straight for Bradley Lake, passing through a conifer-aspen forest on the way, then turn southwest on the Valley Trail to drop down to Taggart Lake. Both are fine places to unpack a picnic and

stay awhile. Finish by hiking another 1.5 miles back on the Taggart Lake Trail.

5.6-mile loop. Moderate. **Access:** Trailhead is on Teton Park Rd., approximately 6 miles south of Jenny Lake.

Laurance S. Rockefeller Preserve

Phelps Lake Loop ★★ The Laurance S. Rockefeller Preserve sits in the southern part of the park, encapsulating beautiful and lesser-traveled backcountry. For a quick taste of the area's trails, loop around peak-ringed Phelps Lake: You'll get views of the mouth of Death Canyon, 10,551-foot Albright Peak, and 11,241-foot Prospectors Mountain, plus a bounty of summer wildflowers and the chance to see bears and moose. Take the Woodland Trail to the lake, then hike around the eastern shore first for the best mountain-lake vistas. You'll pass a few sandy beach rest stops, then swing around to the western shore to stroll through blooming fireweed, asters, and coneflowers. The trail also connects to the ominously named Death Canyon, another lovely chasm leading into the Teton high country.

6.9-mile loop. Moderate. **Access:** Laurance S. Rockefeller Preserve Center, 3½ miles southwest of Moose Junction off Moose-Wilson Rd.

EXPLORING THE BACKCOUNTRY

The Tetons are impressive enough from the roads—so just imagine how magnificent the park is once you hike into the deep wilderness. As in Yellowstone, a permit is required for camping in the backcountry; some sites can be reserved, but the majority are set aside for walk-in campers. You can request a permit for a designated campsite or a camping "zone," where you'll have a choice of sites within the zone boundaries.

For general information on backpacking and safety, see chapter 10, plus p. 83 for a list of essential backpacking gear.

INFORMATION BEFORE YOU GO For background information, check out the backcountry camping information at **www.nps.gov/grte/planyourvisit/back.htm**. For questions, call ✆ **307/739-3309.**

BACKCOUNTRY PERMITS All backcountry campers need a permit. To reserve one for peak season (May–Oct) in advance, request a permit via **www.recreation.gov**. The reservation period opens in January for the following summer. You can also try for a walk-in permit the day before you intend to set out at the Craig Thomas and Colter Bay visitor centers or the Jenny Lake Ranger Station. In both cases, permits cost $20 plus $7 per person per night.

Note: A reservation is just that, a reservation; upon your arrival at the park, you'll need to secure the permit. Permits are issued at the Craig Thomas and Colter Bay visitor centers and at the Jenny Lake Ranger Station.

WHEN TO GO Remember that this region has a short summer and virtually no spring. While the valley floor is usually clear in May, some of the high-country trails might not be free of snow or high water until early July. Check with rangers to find out when specific campsites are usually open.

MAPS Topographic maps of Grand Teton are available from the U.S. Geological Survey and National Geographic's *Trails Illustrated* map series (www.natgeomaps.com; ✆ **800/962-1643**). You can buy the latter, as well as maps for nearby national forests, from the **Grand Teton Association** (www.grandtetonassociation.org; ✆ **307/739-3606**).

The Backcountry in Grand Teton

Just like at Yellowstone, backpacking in the Tetons is the premier way to experience the park. But here you have another option you don't have in Yellowstone: **mountaineering** the area's classic peaks. For more details on trips and outfitters, see "Climbing & Mountaineering" in the "Other Activities" section below.

The most coveted overnight backpacking trip in the park is the 19-mile **Cascade Canyon–Paintbrush Canyon Loop** ★★★. This route takes you through two of the park's most scenically blessed canyons, rife with multicolored wildflowers, jewel-like alpine lakes, incredible mountain views, and a chance to spot moose, bears, and harlequin ducks. Starting from the **Cascade Canyon Trail** west of Jenny Lake, climb to expanding views en route to the North Fork of Cascade Canyon. You can camp here or continue past Lake Solitude and the Paintbrush Divide to Holly Lake, another lovely tent spot in the cirque rounding Mount Woodring. Finish by descending on the **Paintbrush Canyon Trail** back down to Jenny Lake. Considering its strenuous elevation gain, loose scree, and the possibility of snow lingering in the high country well into the summer, this trip is best for backpackers with some mountain experience.

This route also links up with the all-star **Teton Crest Trail,** a high-altitude trail that runs roughly north-south through the Teton peaks. If you have more time, you can expand your loop by hiking out through one of the park's southern canyons. Some of the best views in the Tetons—and truly, in the entire continental U.S.—await on this stunning trail. If you swing south from the top of Cascade Canyon, you'll skirt behind Mount Owen, the Grand Teton, and the Middle Teton to reach **Schoolroom Glacier,** a remnant ice field beside a bright blue tarn, and then 10,400-foot **Hurricane Pass.** Pressing on takes you into the **Caribou-Targhee National Forest**'s **Jedediah Smith Wilderness** and **Alaska Basin,** a wideopen, high-altitude zone dotted with lakes and wildflowers.

Another stellar—and less crowded—trip circles through the southern Tetons via the **Death Canyon Loop ★★★**. This 27-miler takes you to the renowned **Death Canyon Shelf,** a narrow plateau with cliffside campsites and phenomenal mountain vistas. To get there, hike up **Death Canyon** and camp in the shadow of vertiginous granite rock walls. From here you'll cross 9,600-foot **Fox Creek Pass** and reach the shelf, night two's destination. Wrap up the trip by crossing 9,725-foot **Mount Meek Pass,** skirting the southern edge of Alaska Basin, chugging up 10,790-foot **Static Peak Divide,** and looping back to the start.

The park's proximity to Jackson Hole Mountain Resort has a hidden perk for backpackers: You can take the aerial tram up **Rendezvous Mountain ★**, which gives you a fast track into the high country. The tram enables quicker trips north toward **Marion Lake** or south to **Moose Lake** (in the Jedediah Smith Wilderness) or connects to loops through **Granite Canyon ★★** or **Open Canyon ★**.

OTHER ACTIVITIES

In addition to the activities listed here, check out some of the other options in the Jackson area, listed in chapter 8.

BIKING Cycling, including on e-bikes, is allowed on all paved and unpaved roads that also permit cars (but not trails), but you'll want to be choosy about your destination—in some spots, park roads are narrow, winding, and choked with traffic, which makes for less-than-satisfying cycling. Fortunately, an off-road, paved multiuse path extending from Jackson all the way to Jenny Lake makes bike trips much safer and more enjoyable. Road cyclists can also link the Teton Park Road with the one-way **Jenny Lake Scenic Loop** for a 7-mile ride that's partially on a multiuse path. Another option: Ride the path to **Antelope Flats Road** and south along (unpaved) **Mormon Row** to see pioneer-era homesteads and big views of the Gros Ventre. Iron-lunged road riders might also try the steep climb up **Signal Mountain Road** to the 7,727-foot summit (best in the early morning, before traffic picks up).

For mountain or gravel bikers, **Two Ocean Lake Road** is a 6-mile out-and-back over a rolling landscape. For a bike-packing trip, 49-mile **Grassy Lake Road** crosses the John D. Rockefeller Jr. Memorial Parkway past backcountry campsites and serene lakes between Flagg Ranch and Ashton, Idaho.

Look for maps and brochures with bike routes at visitor centers. **Adventure Sports** at Dornans (www.dornans.com; ☏ 307/733-3307), inside the park boundaries at Moose Junction, rents adult and child bikes (complete with helmets and repair kits) as well as bike trailers. **E-Bikes of Jackson Hole,** 150 Scott Lane, Unit C (https://ebikejacksonhole.com; ☏ 307/733-7375), in Jackson is the closest place to the park to rent an e-bike ($70–$100/day).

BOATING & PADDLING Watersports aficionados have plenty of opportunities for fun at Grand Teton, in large part thanks to Jackson Lake. There, you can cruise around in a motorboat, waterski, windsurf, sail, or paddle your own kayak, canoe, or stand-up paddleboard (SUP). Jenny Lake is also open to powerboats (maximum 10hp) as well as human-powered watercraft. Paddlers alone have access to most other park lakes: Phelps, Emma Matilda, Two Ocean, Taggart, Bradley, String, Leigh, and Bearpaw lakes all allow canoes, kayaks, and SUPs.

You'll need a permit to launch your own watercraft, which costs $75 for motorized boats and $25 for nonmotorized craft (good for a calendar year). Buy one online at www.recreation.gov, or pick one up at the Craig Thomas or Colter Bay visitor center. You can rent motorboats from the **Grand Teton Lodge Company** at **Colter Bay Village Marina** (www.gtlc.com; ✆ **307/543-3100**) for $60 an hour. **Signal Mountain Lodge** (www.signalmountainlodge.com; ✆ **307/543-2831**) also rents pontoons, runabout boats, and fishing boats for $55 to $130 per hour or $275 to $599 per day, depending on boat type. Both outfitters rent kayaks and canoes ($30–$45 per hour at Colter Bay Village, $29–$39 per hour at Signal Mountain Lodge), as does **Jenny Lake Boating** (www.jennylakeboating.com; ✆ **307/734-9227**) for $35 per hour.

If you want someone else to handle all the logistics, outfitter **Rendezvous River Sports** (www.jacksonholekayak.com; ✆ **307/733-2471**) offers 1- to 3-night kayak-camping trips on Jackson Lake that include rafting the Snake River ($1,025–$1,850 per person).

Scenic cruises ★ are a popular way to get out on the water. **Jenny Lake Boating** (www.jennylakeboating.com; ✆ **307/734-9227**) offers hour-long cruises on Jenny Lake for $30 ($27 for seniors, $25 for kids 2–11).

CLIMBING & MOUNTAINEERING   Few other destinations offer the combination of so many classic climbing routes, superlative peaks, a long history of mountaineering, and easy access—here, you can bag an iconic summit in just a day or two. But don't let those so-close-you-can-almost-touch-'em peaks fool you: Mountaineering here is a serious endeavor demanding skill and experience. The park's rock, ice, and mixed routes are very strenuous and can be dangerous, even for the pros, thanks to unpredictable mountain weather. If you decide to tackle them on your own, make sure you know how to use an ice axe and crampons, and travel with experienced partners. Skills not so sharp, but still want to make a go of it? Sign up for lessons or a guided trip with the well-regarded climbing outfitters below.

You don't need a special climbing permit to take to the slopes, but you will need a backcountry camping permit if you'll be out overnight (see "Backcountry Permits," p. 123). **Jenny Lake Ranger Station** (✆ **307/739-3343**) is the base for the park's climbing rangers and the best place to get info on current conditions. Climbers often launch their trips from the **American Alpine Club**'s iconic **Grand Teton Climbers' Ranch** (www.americanalpineclub.org/grand-teton-climbers-ranch; ℂ **307/733-7271**). You don't have to be a climber to reserve one of the $25 bunks ($35 for non-club members), but the rustic accommodations cater to those with summit hopes.

If you're looking for guidance, two renowned outfitters offer both guided climbs and lessons: **Exum Mountain Guides** (www.exumguides.com; ℂ **307/733-2297**) offers group climbing classes for $260 and guided trips up any Teton peak (prices vary; call for specifics). **The Mountain Guides** (www.themountainguides.com; ℂ **800/239-7642**) teaches climbing courses starting at $180, leads multiday group trips up the Grand Teton for $2,100, and can also take you up a number of other Teton routes.

FISHING Plentiful fish and beautiful scenery make Grand Teton beloved among anglers. You can cast or troll the lakes and crystal-clear streams for brook, brown, lake, rainbow, and cutthroat trout, plus mountain whitefish; Jackson Lake, Jenny Lake, and the Snake River are all popular destinations, but most waterways in the park are open for fishing. Many anglers prefer fishing from a boat in Jackson and Jenny lakes, but you can also stake out spots along the shorelines of either. The Snake River is a biggie for fly-fishing, particularly the first few miles below the Jackson Lake Dam. Blacktail Ponds and Schwabacher's Landing also draw in hopeful anglers.

You'll need a Wyoming fishing license to ply the waters here ($14/day and $102/year for nonresidents, plus a $21.50 Conservation Stamp for all but 1- or 5-day passes; residents get discounted rates). Nonresidents age 14 and under can fish for free with a licensed adult. Pick up a license at Signal Mountain Lodge, Colter Bay Marina, or Headwaters Lodge at Flagg Ranch. Pick up a copy of the park's fishing brochure to learn rules and regulations, such as seasonal closures. Jackson Lake, for example, closes to fishing in October, and anglers must release all cutthroat trout caught in the Snake River between November 1 and March 31.

Several outfitters based in the park and in Jackson run guided fishing trips. In the park, **Grand Teton Lodge Company** (www.gtlc.com; ℂ **307/543-3100**) will take you out on a private boat in Jackson Lake (if water levels permit) or along the Snake River; lake trip rates are $180 per hour, and fly-fishing the Snake is $825 (both for up to 2 people). The Jackson Lake boat trips offered by **Signal Mountain Lodge** (www.signalmountainlodge.com; ☏ **307/543-2831**) cost $169 per hour or $529 for a half-day for up to two people. Go to **www.nps.gov/grte/planyourvisit/fish.htm** for a full list of fishing concessionaires.

FLOATING & RAFTING Getting the duck's-eye view of the park from the Snake River is alternately thrilling and idyllic, depending on where you are in the 27 miles that wind through the Tetons. Some sections are tranquil, with lots of time to scope for moose, bald eagles, and other animals that frequently visit the river's edge; others are turbulent and challenging, for experienced rafters only. Obstacles such as swift currents, confusing braided channels, shifting logjams, and strong upstream winds can make paddling difficult. Proceed with caution if you'd like to float on your own, and check with rangers for up-to-date information on flow and conditions. The easiest stretch of the Snake is the 5-mile segment from Jackson Lake Dam to Pacific Creek. North of Jackson Lake and south of Pacific Creek, swifter water and route-finding challenges make rafting a skilled boater's game.

If you're not an advanced boater, never fear: Quite a few outfitters will guide you. Mellow 10-mile floats on the Snake River are offered by both **Grand Teton Lodge Company** (www.gtlc.com; ☏ **307/543-3100;** $120 adults, $72 kids 6–11) and **Signal Mountain Lodge** (www.signalmountainlodge.com; ☏ **307/543-2831;** $99 adults, $85 kids 6–12). For a list of other rafting concessionaires operating trips in the park, see **www.nps.gov/grte/planyourvisit/concessions.htm**.

HORSEBACK RIDING Horses are allowed on most park trails; five backcountry camping sites also allow stock. The most popular trailheads for BYO horse rides are Cathedral Group Turnout, Poker Flats, and Taggart Lake. A few outfitters also offer guided horseback rides in the park: **Grand Teton Lodge Company** (www.gtlc.com; ☏ **307/543-3100**) has 1- and 2-hour rides out of Jackson Lake Lodge, Colter Bay Village, and Headwaters Lodge at Flagg Ranch ($68–$100). Guests at the nearby **Lost Creek Ranch & Spa** (www.lost creek.com; ☏ **307/733-3435**) and **Jenny Lake Lodge** (www.gtlc.com; ☏ **307/543-3100**) also enjoy horseback riding options. For the names of several other companies that organize horseback trips in Jackson Hole, see "Jackson, Wyoming," in chapter 8.

WINTER SPORTS & ACTIVITIES

Park facilities pretty much shut down during the winter, and the park shows no signs of becoming a winter magnet, a la Yellowstone. That may be just as well—you can enjoy some quiet, fun times in the park without the crowds.

WINTER ROAD CONDITIONS The park's primary roads, U.S. 26/89/191 and U.S. 26/287, remain open and plowed all winter from Jackson to Flagg Ranch. **Teton Park Road** and **Moose-Wilson Road** close to cars on November 1 until the end of April (Teton Park Road) or mid-May (Moose-Wilson). Note that the 14-mile section of Teton Park Road between Taggart Lake Trailhead and Signal Mountain Lodge is open and groomed for **cross-country skiing and snowshoeing** from mid-December to mid-March.

SPORTING GOODS & EQUIPMENT RENTALS Jackson has enough sporting equipment places to keep all of Wyoming outfitted. **Skinny Skis,** 65 W. Deloney Ave. (www.skinnyskis.com; ✆ **307/733-6094**), is an outdoors shop with a focus on Nordic skiing and touring skis, skate skis, and snowshoes for sale and rent. **Teton Mountaineering,** 170 N. Cache St. (www.tetonmtn.com; ✆ **307/733-3595**), also rents all the gear for backcountry ski touring, splitboarding, and mountaineering, plus tents and backpacks. **Teton Backcountry Rentals,** 565 N. Cache St. (www.tetonbcrentals.com; ✆ **307/828-1885**), offers everything from splitboards to avalanche safety gear to ice axes; they'll even deliver to your hotel.

BACKCOUNTRY SKIING Adventurous and experienced skiers flock to the park to earn their turns, preferring the wilderness slopes to the inbound skiing at the nearby resorts. The peaks have excellent skiing, but fierce weather and significant avalanche risk make this suitable for advanced-level skiers only. For a safe introduction to backcountry skiing, go guided with **Exum Mountain Guides** or

The Mountain Guides (see "Climbing & Mountaineering," above).

CROSS-COUNTRY SKIING   Kicking and gliding under the snowcapped Teton Range makes for an unforgettable day in the snow, and Nordic skiers have plenty of options in the park. The park grooms 14 miles of the closed **Teton Park Road** (btw. Taggart Lake Trailhead and Signal Mountain Lodge) for classic and skate skiing. Other winter routes are ungroomed and unmarked, so plan to use burlier touring skis. For an easier day, try the 8-mile, mostly flat loop that takes off from the Taggart Lake Trailhead and follows an ungroomed winter trail along Cottonwood Creek, then returns on Teton Park Road. The 3-mile **Swan Lake/Heron Pond Loop** from Colter Bay is just as lovely in winter as it is in summer, and the 4.2-mile **South Flagg Canyon Trail** from Flagg Ranch is another easy outing. For something more challenging, ski up the **Signal Mountain Summit Road,** a 12-mile round-trip with a fun downhill return.

SNOWMOBILING   Snowmobiling is a popular winter option in the area. Snowmobiling is allowed on the frozen surface of Jackson Lake for ice fishing only; on Grassy Lake Road; and in nearby Bridger-Teton National Forest, immediately east of the park.

SNOWSHOEING   You can snowshoe pretty much anywhere you can cross-country ski in the park. Plus, rangers lead snowshoe trips weekly, late December to mid-March. Call ⓒ **307/739-3399** to make reservations. Snowshoes and poles are included.

WHERE TO STAY & EAT IN THE PARKS

D o all you can to stay inside park borders at least one night. It's not that the gateway towns around the parks don't have excellent lodging options. But there's something absolutely magical about bunking right where the action is. You'll be treated to a quieter, wilder park after the day-trippers depart, and without the light pollution from civilization, a dazzling night sky awaits. You'll also be inside the park during the prime wildlife-watching times of dawn and dusk: It's quite something to be able to roll out of bed and spy elk, bison, and even bears and wolves just steps away. What's more, you'll skip the sometimes-lengthy drive into the heart of the parks from the gateway towns, maximizing your time.

Carefully consider your choices before you book. Yellowstone is a vast park, and you might spend several hours driving between its top attractions even when you start inside—so where you sleep can have a big impact on what and how much you'll be able to see in a day. Grand Teton is more manageable, but staying at the southern versus northern end can determine whether you can venture into Yellowstone the same day. If you're most interested in geysers, shoot for a room at Old Faithful; if you want to join the dawn wolf-watching patrol, grab a cabin at Roosevelt Lodge or a campsite in the Lamar Valley; go for Lake Yellowstone

Hotel, Colter Bay Village, or Jackson Lake Lodge if you're into water activities. That said: Take advantage of any park lodging you can. Hotels and campsites are in high demand, and each one offers its own incredible experience.

WHERE TO STAY IN YELLOWSTONE

Yellowstone hosts more than 4 million visitors each year, so in-park rooms are at an absolute premium. That's doubly true for summer, but demand is also high in spring and fall. Solution: Book your rooms *early*—a year or even more in advance is not too soon. Make reservations directly with **Yellowstone National Park Lodges,** run by concessionaire Xanterra Travel Collection (www.yellowstonenationalpark lodges.com; ⓒ **307/344-7311**). But don't despair if you're late to the party: Cancelations mean that scattered rooms open up almost daily, even in high summer. To snag one, check online several times a day for new openings, and snap up anything that pops up.

Most of Yellowstone's lodges are open from early May to October. A few open their doors as soon as late April or as late as early June; some close in November. **Mammoth Hot Springs Hotel & Cabins** (p. 134) and **Old Faithful Snow Lodge** (p. 138) are the only options that remain open in winter for the cross-country skiing and snowmobile/snowcoach crowd. Both reopen in mid-December and shut down again in early March. All park lodges are typically fully booked for most of the summer/fall season; it's easier to land a room in the first few weeks of May or later in October. While visitation used to slow down after Labor Day, lately things have remained humming, so don't count on an easy fall getaway.

The park lodges have been lovingly maintained in the historic style in which most of them were built—meaning you won't find in-room TVs or Wi-Fi, pools, or continental breakfasts. Rooms have heat (sometimes from a woodstove, as at Roosevelt Lodge) but no air-conditioning, which is usually not a problem in Yellowstone's cool climate. If you must have cable TV and Wi-Fi, stay in one of the more modern hotels in a gateway town (see chapter 8).

WHAT YOU'LL REALLY pay

The prices quoted here are rack rates, the maximum that the hotels charge; it is likely that you'll end up paying these rates in Yellowstone and Grand Teton unless you arrive in spring or fall. The concessionaires do not offer many discounts, thanks to the short summer season in both parks and the fact that occupancy is near 100% all summer long. During slower times, however, it's possible to obtain a room at an expensive property for the same rate as at a more moderate one.

In both parks, April/May and October are the bargain months, but the sheer number of visitors the rest of the year overwhelms the capacity. If you're looking for a bargain, your best bets are the gateway cities of Cooke City and Gardiner, Montana (see chapter 8). In Cody, Wyoming, you'll be lucky to get a room for less than $200 per night in peak season; in Jackson, Wyoming, $300 is a more realistic baseline for in-town lodgings. You'll want to shop online for deals, but I tend to look hard in Teton Village in summer: You still have easy access to Jackson (and better access to Grand Teton National Park), but the rooms here are intended for the winter ski crowd, and summer vacancies are the norm. In winter, save money by staying in Jackson and taking the free shuttle to the slopes at Jackson Hole Mountain Resort.

Note: Quoted rates almost never include **breakfast, hotel tax, or facility fees.** Many hotels and resorts now tack on these extra facility fees (aka "resort fee," "service fee," "destination fee," "residential fee") to each night's room rates, ostensibly to cover things like Wi-Fi and the use of on-site facilities, like fitness centers. In the Yellowstone and Grand Teton gateway towns, facility fees are all over the map, ranging from $25 to three figures a night for multi-bedroom resort suites. These fees are annoying but mandatory and inflate the quoted room rate; ask about any extra daily fees before booking. You might also run into mandatory daily **"community fees,"** which are surcharges that fund various local causes, from local nonprofits to hotel sustainability programs.

Mammoth Hot Springs Area

5 miles from the Gardiner (north) entrance to Yellowstone

If you're traveling to the park from points north, Mammoth Hot Springs is the first hub you'll hit—and it's a fine base of operations for history buffs, wildlife-watchers, and geology fans. Besides the historic Mammoth Hotel, the complex also features Fort Yellowstone, where rangers from the U.S. Army lived from the 1890s to 1918. Elk frequently graze the hotel lawn, and the area's top attraction—Mammoth's sculpted travertine terraces—should be on everyone's to-do list.

Mammoth Hot Springs Hotel & Cabins ★★ A stone's throw from the stair-step Mammoth terrace formations, this complex's historic buildings (the oldest date to 1911) take you back to the era when cars were new inside the park. Historic touches—like the lounge's elaborate wooden U.S. map—extend inside the hotel as well, but rooms are generally updated and streamlined, with simple wooden furniture and accents. The 1930s-style **Map Room** offers a classy place to congregate, with a coffee/alcohol bar and live piano music most evenings. Cottage-style cabins with small patios cluster behind the hotel; four come with private outdoor hot tubs, while others have communal bathrooms. Since a 2019 renovation, all hotel rooms boast a private bathroom. The hotel sits somewhere between the show-stopping appeal of Old Faithful Inn and Lake Yellowstone Hotel and the no-nonsense lodging at Grant Village, but its proximity to attractions, trailheads, and guided tours makes it a worthwhile base for a night or two. Plus, it's one of two park properties open in the winter.

At Mammoth Hot Springs. www.yellowstonenationalparklodges. com. ☎ **307/344-7311.** 167 units. $399 double; $163–$312 cabin; $392 hot tub cabin; $755 suite. Late Apr to mid-Oct and mid-Dec to early Mar. **Amenities:** Restaurant; cafeteria; lounge; free Wi-Fi.

Canyon Village Area

40 miles from the West Yellowstone (west) entrance; 38 miles from the Gardiner (north) entrance

The Grand Canyon of the Yellowstone, with its two astonishing waterfalls, is one of the park's superstar attractions. Canyon Village serves as its bustling jumping-off point, where hordes of travelers come for food, souvenir shopping, or a stop at one of the park's most impressive visitor centers. Ranger programs and activities give you plenty to do.

Canyon Lodge & Cabins ★ Canyon Lodge's five buildings, which all have eco-friendly LEED Gold or Silver certifications, have the feel of a contemporary resort, with touches like subway-tiled bathrooms and sleek black wooden headboards. The fanciest rooms have porches or decks, and suites offer a little more space with separate bedrooms. The cabins are even more spacious, and though their log cabin–style furnishings are a bit dated, I find them charming. The lodge is also a jumping-off point for several group tours. Don't expect canyon views: The complex sits a half-mile from the rest of the village in a nondescript lodgepole pine forest, and you must hike or drive to the canyon itself. The sheer number of rooms and the super-busy village area mean Canyon isn't the place for a quiet, off-the-grid vibe.

In Canyon Village. www.yellowstonenationalparklodges.com. ⓒ **307/344-7311.** 590 units. $308–$524 double; $401 cabin; $1,010–$1,041 suite. Mid-May to late Oct. **Amenities:** Cafeteria; lounge; 2 delis; free Wi-Fi.

Tower-Roosevelt Area

23 miles from the Gardiner (north) entrance; 29 miles from the northeast entrance

This small development in north-central Yellowstone takes half its name from the fact that Teddy Roosevelt once camped in the area (the other half comes from nearby Tower Fall). The junction sits at the doorstep of the wildlife-packed Lamar Valley, making early-morning wolf- and bear-spotting expeditions easy. It's far enough off the beaten path to feel like a throwback to a simpler time; you won't have to jostle with crowds of travelers as you will at Old Faithful and Canyon.

Roosevelt Lodge Cabins ★★ Yellowstone's simplest lodging is also one of its coolest—a collection of tiny, ultra-rustic cabins, most of which are heated by woodstove (a few have electric heat). What the cabins lack in elbow room and modern hotel amenities they make up for in pioneer ambience, and you're at Yellowstone—you'll be outside all day, anyway. Frontier cabins have bathrooms, while Roughrider cabins share campground-style communal facilities with showers. Guests gather in the log-and-wicker rocking chairs on the main lodge's front porch for sunrise and sunset views over the Lamar Valley. "Rosie" is a great spot for families, thanks to its access to horseback riding and stagecoach rides at the adjacent corral, and kiddos love the Old West Cookout ride (on horseback or wagon) to an alfresco cowboy-style dinner. With these amenities (and the fact that the lodge has the most affordable rooms in the park), cabins at Roosevelt are in high demand, so book ahead.

At Tower Junction. www.yellowstonenationalparklodges.com. ☏ **307/344-7311.** 80 cabins, 14 w/private bathroom. $135 cabin w/ shared bathroom; $208 cabin w/private bathroom. Early June to early Sept. **Amenities:** Restaurant; lounge; no Wi-Fi.

Lake Village Area

27 miles from the east entrance; 56 miles from the West Yellowstone (west) entrance; 43 miles from the south entrance

This complex on the northern shore of enormous Yellowstone Lake is *the* spot for an old-fashioned waterfront getaway. Trails, scenic lake cruises, guided fishing trips, and boat rentals are all on offer in the area, but no one would blame you if you simply whiled away the hours staring at the lake, either. You'll also find several dining options, gift shops, and a nearby visitor center at Fishing Bridge.

Lake Lodge Cabins ★   These cabins along Yellowstone Lake are the *I Love Lucy* of park lodging: a bit outdated, perhaps, but still charming. And they're the way to go if you're looking for lakefront lodging without breaking the bank. The cabins are basic, with log furniture and fishing-themed quilts, plus private bathrooms (some with tubs, others just showers). The main lodge offers a much nicer place to hang out: Curl up by the giant stone fireplace or nab one of the rocking chairs on the wide front porch for an unforgettable sunset. Also on-site are a gift shop, bar, and a fast-casual cafeteria-style restaurant called **Wylie's Canteen.**

On Yellowstone Lake. www.yellowstonenationalparklodges.com. ☏ **307/344-7311.** 186 cabins. $135–$331. Mid-June to early Oct. **Amenities:** Cafeteria; lounge; no Wi-Fi.

Lake Yellowstone Hotel and Cabins ★★★   The park's most upscale lodging, this creamy-yellow National Historic Landmark channels the *Downton Abbey* spirit: From the elegant sunroom with views of the lake to the fancy cocktails to the live string quartet most evenings, you may almost believe you've gone back in time to a more genteel era. Built in 1891 and renovated in 2014, the hotel has hung on to its Colonial Revival charm. Rooms are beautifully furnished, with large tile bathrooms; some have a lake view (although you'll pay more for it). You'll find older, more standard amenities in the standalone Sandpiper Lodge and cabins, but their proximity to the hotel's glamorous common spaces makes them a worthy way to save cash without missing out on the scene.

Yellowstone Lake. www.yellowstonenationalparklodges.com. © **307/ 344-7311.** 300 units. $370–$690 double; $318 cottage; $978–$1,185 suite. Mid-May to early Oct. **Amenities:** Restaurant; lounge; deli; business center; free wired Internet in some rooms.

Grant Village Area

22 miles from the south entrance; 47 miles from the West Yellowstone (west) entrance

The first developed area you'll hit coming from the park's south entrance, Grant is a sprawling collection of lodge rooms, restaurants, a giant campground, visitor center, and general store.

Grant Village ★   The rooms in these six lodge buildings, all dating back to the early 1980s and renovated in 2016, are nothing to write home about—many large tours base themselves out of Grant, which perhaps explains the one-size-fits-all feel. But the motel-style accommodations have much nicer furnishings than your standard roadside stop, plus you're only a short stroll from Yellowstone Lake, and West Thumb Geyser Basin is a 5-minute drive away. There's no grand lobby, but all buildings have common rooms with couches and tables. Some rooms have lake views. You can also pick up the all-day guided "Circle of Fire" tour from concessionaire Xanterra here.

On the West Thumb of Yellowstone Lake. www.yellowstonenational parklodges.com. © **307/344-7311.** 300 units. $312 double. Late May to early Oct. **Amenities:** 2 restaurants; lounge; no Wi-Fi.

Old Faithful Area

30 miles from the West Yellowstone (west) entrance; 39 miles from the south entrance

If there's a single can't-miss spot in this gigantic park, it's the Old Faithful area. Upper Geyser Basin, home to the world's densest concentration of geysers, is the centerpiece of this hub, but you'll find plenty of manmade attractions, too: three lodging options, five restaurants, a top-notch visitor center, and a general store. And Old Faithful Snow Lodge is one of two park hotels open in winter.

Old Faithful Inn ★★★ The Old Faithful Inn, built between 1903 and 1904, is Yellowstone's most-requested hotel—and it deserves every bit of attention it gets. From its steep, wooden-shingled roof to its 76-foot-tall, log-walled lobby to its towering stone fireplace, you've never seen anything like it. Stay in the Old House if you can: Although its rooms are rustic, with log or wood-paneled walls and shared (but quite nice) bathrooms, they offer the best, most historic vibe. The crème de la crème rooms are the dormers on the front-center side of the building, with three queen beds and views over Upper Geyser Basin. The East and West Wing rooms are larger but more basic, though they have private bathrooms. Suites come with couches and a stocked mini fridge. If you can tear yourself away from gazing at the stunning architecture, activities abound: Photo safaris, several guided park tours, and a fascinating hotel tour all jump off from here.

At Old Faithful. www.yellowstonenationalparklodges.com. © **307/ 344-7311.** 329 units. $246–$435 Old House room; $473–$638 double; $1,164–$1,329 suite. Early May to early Oct. **Amenities:** Restaurant; lounge; deli; no Wi-Fi.

Old Faithful Lodge Cabins ★★ The cluster of cabins east of the geyser basin are typical Yellowstone fare: basic furniture accentuated with pinecones, plaid blankets, and tiny bathrooms or shared bathhouse space. But the location elevates these bargain cabins to the next level. They're tucked away in a young lodgepole pine forest and offer a surprisingly peaceful escape from the madness around Old Faithful, just steps away. Some even have views of the famous spouter, but my money is on the cabins that border a back meadow with a stream and several small, unnamed thermal features, where guests often spot bears passing through. The main lodge houses a cafeteria, bakery/ice cream shop, and gift shop, plus a cozy lobby with a huge window framing Old Faithful.

At Old Faithful. www.yellowstonenationalparklodges.com. © **307/ 344-7311.** 161 units. $137 cabin w/shared bathroom; $229 cabin w/ private bathroom. Mid-May to early Oct. **Amenities:** Cafeteria; snack bar; free Wi-Fi in lobby and cafeteria only.

Old Faithful Snow Lodge & Cabins ★★ Here's Yellowstone's answer to the modern ski resort. The lodge's contemporary style features exposed beams, wrought-iron accents, and lots of blond wood, and the lobby fireplace and enclosed sitting porch offer plenty of spaces to curl up with a hot toddy. The high-end feel extends to the spacious lodge rooms, which have wood shutters, evergreen-shaped lamps, and beds with high wooden headboards; some rooms have cozy window seats, and all have private bathrooms with tubs. The cabins out back are more affordable and less flashy: Western cabins have run-of-the-mill furnishings and closet-size private bathrooms, while Frontier cabins are much smaller, with wood-paneled walls and shower-only bathrooms.

At Old Faithful. www.yellowstonenationalparklodges.com. ⟨ 307/344-7311. 134 units. $444–$476 double; $174–$320 cabin. Late Apr to late Oct and mid-Dec to early Mar. **Amenities:** 2 restaurants; lounge; free Wi-Fi.

WHERE TO CAMP IN YELLOWSTONE

Nothing compares to a night under the stars at Yellowstone. If you're remotely interested in camping, this is a phenomenal place to do it—and an excellent way to stay inside the park without maxing out your vacation budget. You have two options: staying in one of the 12 developed, drive-in campgrounds or backpacking into the wilderness. If the latter is more up your alley, check out rules, regulations, and info on getting a permit at **www.nps.gov/yell/planyourvisit/backcountryhiking.htm** or call the **Backcountry Office** at ⟨ **307/344-2160.**

GETTING A CAMPSITE Advance reservations are required at all 12 developed campgrounds (except for Mammoth Campground in the off-season from mid-Oct to early Apr). The park operates seven of the campgrounds—Indian Creek, Lewis Lake, Mammoth, Norris, Pebble Creek, Slough Creek, and Tower Fall—and you can book sites at **www.recreation.gov**. Concessionaire **Xanterra** runs the other five; reserve these sites at www.yellowstonenational parklodges.com.

Camping is hugely popular in the park, and campgrounds often fill up every night in summer and early fall. Make reservations well ahead of time—as with hotels, a year in advance is not too early for the Xanterra campgrounds. The park-run campgrounds typically open reservations 6 months ahead of time, with a portion of sites released 2 weeks in advance for those who can't plan ahead quite that far.

CAMPGROUNDS Yellowstone's campgrounds range from enormous tent-and-RV villages with hundreds of sites to intimate, back-of-beyond outposts. The larger, more developed options have showers, laundry, flush toilets, and RV dump stations, while the more rustic ones have pit toilets and more limited spaces for RVs. Most campgrounds have picnic tables, campfire rings, and running water. For details on specific amenities, prices, and opening dates for each campground, see the chart on p. 142.

NORTH

Mammoth ★ The first campground you'll hit coming in from the north entrance, Mammoth is the only year-round camping facility. Sites are clumped among the sagebrush, with a few trees for shade. A short trail connects to the Mammoth Hot Springs attractions. This is a good pick for larger RVs, though it does not have RV hookups.

Tower Fall ★★ Set off a bit from Grand Loop Road in an evergreen forest, Tower Fall is a small, quiet (no generators) campground at the west end of the Lamar Valley. A general store and the overlook to the Tower Fall waterfall are a stroll away.

Slough Creek ★★★ Located creekside in the Lamar Valley, this 16-site, generator-free campground is a popular base for anglers and wildlife-watchers—and my favorite in the park, thanks to its out-there feel, small size, and lovely setting.

Pebble Creek ★★★ The park's most far-flung option, this small, primitive campground deep in the Lamar Valley is a great site for spotting wildlife and fishing. *Note:* Devastating floods in 2022 closed Pebble Creek for several seasons, and at press time the site was still undergoing flood-recovery repair; check the park website for reopening updates.

Indian Creek ★★ This primitive campground just west of Sheepeater Cliff between Mammoth and Norris campgrounds sits in an evergreen forest at 7,300 feet, close to the Gallatin Mountains. Its mountain views, fishing ops, and remote vibe make it one of the park's best camps.

CENTRAL

Norris ★   This midsize campground on a hill features shady sites (a few near the Gibbon River), the Museum of the National Park Ranger, and frequent bison visits. But the best reason to pitch a tent here? Its proximity to Norris Geyser Basin, so you can walk right over and skip the parking hassles.

Madison ★★   A sprawling camp (nearly 300 sites) near where the Firehole and Gibbon rivers join to form the Madison, Madison Campground is about halfway between Old Faithful and West Yellowstone. It's a good bet for bison- and elk-watching and fly-fishing.

Canyon ★   Big and busy, Canyon (elevation 7,900 ft.) sits in a lodgepole pine forest a short walk from the restaurants and other facilities at Canyon Village. Here you'll find laundry, showers, and evening ranger programs.

Fishing Bridge RV Park ★   This huge campground on the north side of Yellowstone Lake is essentially a large parking lot for RVs—as this is the heart of grizzly country, tents aren't allowed. Though it's a bit short on charm, the RV park comes with an amphitheater with ranger programs, the Fishing Bridge Museum and Visitor Center, and a general store, and it's the only one with full RV hookups.

Bridge Bay ★   The park's largest campground with 432 sites, Bridge Bay is the best option if you're looking to get out on the water. It's very close to the Yellowstone Lake shoreline and walking distance from Bridge Bay Marina. Sites are hit or miss: Some bake in full sun, while others are tucked in the trees. The campground also has a general store.

SOUTH

Grant Village ★   This mega-campground on Yellowstone Lake's West Thumb is fully loaded with laundry facilities, showers, dump stations, and a boat launch. It's very close to the restaurants, general stores, and visitor center at Grant Village, and also offers evening ranger programs.

Lewis Lake ★★ Shaded and remote, the sites at the midsize Lewis Lake Campground are very private and all a short stroll from the lakeshore and its boat ramp. This generator-free camp, 8 miles north of the south entrance, is also a great spot to scope for moose.

WHERE TO CAMP NEAR YELLOWSTONE

The Custer Gallatin and Shoshone national forests run several wonderful primitive campgrounds near the north, northeast, east, and west entrances to the park. You won't find space for hundreds of campers, full RV hookups, or flush toilets, but you will enjoy amenities like trout streams, lakeside sites, and quiet nights around the campfire. Most campgrounds are first-come, first-served and some fill quickly in the summer. Sites cost $15 or $20 per night unless otherwise noted.

Three developed campgrounds cluster just north of Gardiner, near the north entrance. **Eagle Creek** is the closest, just 2 miles northeast of town on the Yellowstone River, and can be booked ahead of time at www.recreation.gov. Next

Amenities for Each Campground: Yellowstone National Park

CAMPGROUND	TOTAL SITES	RV HOOKUPS	
Bridge Bay*	432	No	
Canyon*	273	No	
Fishing Bridge RV Park*	310	Yes	
Grant Village*	430	No	
Indian Creek	70	No	
Lewis Lake	85	No	
Madison*	278	No	
Mammoth	85	No	
Norris	112	No	
Pebble Creek	27	No	
Slough Creek	16	No	
Tower Fall	31	No	

* Reserve through Xanterra; Fishing Bridge RV Park accepts only hard-sided vehicles.

come **Timber Camp** and **Bear Creek** (both free). The latter have no vehicle access, so you'll have to walk in a short distance from your car.

You'll find four nearby developed campgrounds on the Beartooth Highway outside Cooke City, starting with **Soda Butte** and **Colter;** both are for hard-sided campers only (because of frequent bear activity in the area). **Chief Joseph** ($8) is a very small option just east of Colter Pass, 4 miles from Cooke City; continue down the road to reach **Fox Creek** ($30; electric hookups available), a remodeled campground in Wyoming's Shoshone National Forest.

Two popular campgrounds just past the east entrance offer riverside camping along the North Fork of the Shoshone River for hard-sided campers only. **Threemile** is 3 miles east of the park entrance and can be reserved ahead of time at www.recreation.gov. Continue east another 5 miles to reach **Eagle Creek** ($25).

The national forest lands west of West Yellowstone offer a slew of options, and the closest ones to the park boundary are especially desirable for anglers. **Baker's Hole** ($26), 3 miles northwest of town, lies on the Madison River; **Rainbow Point** ($26) is 5 miles from West Yellowstone on Hebgen

DUMP STATION	FLUSH TOILETS	DRINKING WATER	SHOWERS	FIRE PITS/ GRILLS	LAUNDRY	FEES	OPEN
Yes	Yes	Yes	No	Yes	No	$38	Mid-May to early Sept
Yes	Yes	Yes	Yes	Yes	Yes	$45	Late May to mid-Sept
Yes	Yes	Yes	Yes	No	Yes	$95	Mid-May to mid-Oct
Yes	Yes	Yes	Yes	Yes	Yes	$45	Early June to early Sept
No	No	Yes	No	Yes	No	$20	Early June to early Sept
No	No	Yes	No	Yes	No	$20	Mid-June to mid-Oct
Yes	Yes	Yes	No	Yes	No	$38	Early May to mid-Oct
No	Yes	Yes	No	Yes	No	$25	Year-round
No	Yes	Yes	No	Yes	No	$25	Mid-May to late Sept
No	No	Yes	No	Yes	No	$20	Mid-June to late Sept
No	No	Yes	No	Yes	No	$20	Mid-June to mid-Oct
No	No	Yes	No	Yes	No	$20	Late May to late Sept

Lake (reservations accepted for both; www.recreation.gov). Both have some electric hookups. Among private options, **Madison Arm Resort** stands out for its lakefront campsites, free showers, full RV hookups, and marina with boat rentals (www.madisonarmresort.com; $60–$65 tent site, $85 full hookup site).

WHERE TO EAT IN YELLOWSTONE

Given the park's size and the distances between its developed hubs and the gateway towns, you're something of a captive audience when it comes to dining at Yellowstone: You'll likely find yourself lining up for a seat at the concessionaire-run restaurants at least a few times—it's that or stick to your camp stove. Generally, prices are high and the food ranges from adequate to pretty good—these outfits serve millions of people a year, and it shows. Still, the higher-end restaurants can offer up a memorable experience, and many menus prioritize local, sustainable, and/or organic ingredients.

Mammoth Hot Springs

You have three options for grub near the Mammoth terraces—deli sandwiches and ice cream at the general store, quick cafeteria food at **Terrace Grill,** and sit-down meals at the Mammoth Hotel Dining Room.

Mammoth Hotel Dining Room ★ SEAFOOD/STEAKS For a meal that pairs an Art Deco–inspired space with relatively casual food, head over to Mammoth's flagship restaurant. The chefs emphasize sustainable options with a distinctively Montana flavor, such as local Wagyu beef sliders and bison carpaccio. There are also burgers and salads, though starters/small plates get a bit more creative. The dining room's expansive mirrors once hung in the 1883 National Hotel, the first lodging on this site.

Mammoth Hot Springs Hotel & Cabins. www.yellowstonenational parklodges.com. ℂ **307/344-7311.** Dinner reservations required in winter. Main courses $6–$18.25 breakfast, $17–$20 lunch, $17–$49 dinner. Late Apr to mid-Oct daily 6:30–10am, 11:30am–2:30pm, and 4:30–10pm (5–9pm late Apr to mid-May); late Dec to early Mar daily 6–10am, 11:30am–2:30pm, and 5–9pm (8pm Jan–Mar). Closed mid-Oct to mid-Dec and early Mar to late Apr.

Canyon Village Area

Canyon's cafeteria-style dining options are a cut above. The funky 1960s, astro-themed complex hosts two quick-bite restaurants: **Slow Food Fast** ★ offers up comfort food like rotisserie chicken and beef short ribs with mashed potatoes, while **Fresh Woks** ★ features design-your-own noodle or rice bowls with veggies and flavorful sauces. Also in the village is **Falls Café,** with espresso and to-go breakfast and lunch, and **The Ice Creamery,** which scoops Montana-made flavors. Over on the other end of the village, **Canyon Soda Fountain** inside the Canyon General Store serves sit-down and to-go burgers and sandwiches.

M66 Lounge ★ AMERICAN   Canyon's swingin' cocktail lounge gets its name from the National Park Service's Mission 66 program, which aimed to expand visitor services by the NPS's 50th anniversary in 1966—and true to concept, you'll sip beneath mod, star-shaped light fixtures and geometric art. Cocktails and local drafts dominate here, plus a few wines by the glass, but you can also snack on apps like pretzel bites or chicken wings.

At Canyon Village. www.yellowstonenationalparklodges.com. © **307/ 344-7311.** Appetizers $10–$21. Mid-May to mid-Oct daily 3–11pm.

Tower-Roosevelt Area

Roosevelt Lodge Dining Room ★ BARBECUE   The park's most rustic lodge pairs its rough-log decor with a cowboy menu: burgers, pulled pork, bison brats, and ribs (this is not the place for inspired vegetarian dishes). It's fairly standard fare, but portions are hearty and there are a few surprises (such as bison taco nachos). For a more memorable meal, sign up for the Old West Dinner Cookout: You'll hop on horseback (or jump in a wagon) for an alfresco supper of 12-ounce steak, baked beans, potato salad, and cobbler. The price sounds steep ($88–$122 adults, $68–$105 kids), but considering you get a full meal for a little more than a stand-alone horseback ride, it's a pretty good deal.

At Tower Junction. www.yellowstonenationalparklodges.com. © **307/ 344-7311.** Reservations not accepted for the dining room; required for Old West cookouts. Main courses $9–$16 breakfast, $17–$34 lunch and dinner. Early June to early Sept daily 7–10am, 11:30am– 3pm, and 4:30–9:30pm.

Yellowstone Lake

The options here range from pretty good and more affordable to date-night good (with a price tag to match). The casual **Wylie's Canteen** at Lake Lodge offers local burgers and hot dogs with cafeteria-style seating. One step down are the basic sandwiches, salads, and soups at the general stores (one near Lake Lodge and one at Fishing Bridge) or **Lake Hotel Deli.**

Lake Yellowstone Hotel Dining Room ★★ FRENCH

This upscale restaurant in the park's fanciest hotel delivers the most refined dining experience at Yellowstone. Though the food is quite good—think cassoulet, coq au vin, and steak au poivre, prepared with an eye toward sustainable and organic ingredients—it's only half the appeal. Spending an hour or two sipping wine in the sophisticated dining room, gazing out at front-row views of Yellowstone Lake, is itself worth the bill. Make reservations well ahead of time, or at least a day or two in advance.

Yellowstone Lake. www.yellowstonenationalparklodges.com. ℰ **307/ 344-7311.** Dinner reservations required. Main courses $6–$20 breakfast, $18–$24 lunch, $23–$49 dinner. Mid-May to early Sept daily 6:30–10am, 11:30am–2:30pm, and 4:30–10pm.

Grant Village

Like many of the park's developed areas, Grant Village features a few casual establishments and one higher-end dining room. But one of Grant's quick-service restaurants comes with a truly killer view and fantastic wildlife-watching. At **Lake House Restaurant,** dine on street tacos with a vista that's as lakefront as you can get—the building extends over the water on a pier. Wildlife fans may spot pelicans and grizzly bears on the adjacent sandbars, especially in spring. **Grant General Store** offers fast-food burgers and sandwiches.

Grant Village Dining Room ★ AMERICAN

Like the nearby Lake House Restaurant, Grant's dining room offers a lovely lakefront view (if not quite the on-the-water feel). Main courses fit right in with the waterfront theme: Look for a raw bar with oysters and tuna, plus salmon, trout, and crab cakes, many of which are sustainably sourced. Lunch options range from a chicken banh mi to burgers and tacos.

At Grant Village. www.yellowstonenationalparklodges.com. ℂ **307/ 344-7311.** Dinner reservations required. Main courses $6–$18 breakfast, $17–$23 lunch, $19–$32 dinner. Late May to early Oct daily 6:30–10am, 11:30am–2:30pm, and 5–10pm.

Old Faithful Area

The bustling Old Faithful zone boasts more dining options than anywhere else in the park, including two upscale dining rooms and an array of casual joints. Grab sandwiches and local Montana ice cream at the Old Faithful Inn's **Bear Paw Deli;** for a hot lunch or dinner, the Snow Lodge's **Geyser Grill** slings burgers, hot dogs, and cheesesteaks. The **Old Faithful Lodge Cafeteria** offers a varied menu ranging from chicken tikka masala to lamb gyros to hot dogs. You'll find sandwiches and salads at the adjacent **Bake Shop,** plus soft-serve ice cream. The **general store** and **Old Faithful Basin Store** serve burgers, sandwiches, and other quick choices.

Old Faithful Inn Dining Room ★★ SEAFOOD/ STEAKS   Along with the Lake Yellowstone Hotel Dining Room, this is one of the park's quintessential dining experiences. Just like the rest of the storied inn, the atmosphere can't be beat: Giant log beams, chandeliers, and a huge stone fireplace dominate the room. The nightly dinner buffet features such menu highlights as prime rib and chicken skewers, but the a la carte options are tasty, too—including gnocchi, fried chicken, and pork *osso buco.*

At the Old Faithful Inn. www.yellowstonenationalparklodges.com. ℂ **307/344-7311.** Dinner reservations required. Main courses $6–$18 breakfast, $17–$19 lunch, $23–$48 dinner. Early May to mid-Oct daily 6:30–10am, 11:30am–2:30pm, and 4:30–10pm.

Old Faithful Snow Lodge Obsidian Dining Room ★ SEAFOOD/WILD GAME   Wild boar, bison, and elk, oh my! Wild game plays a starring role on this menu, in dishes such as fried elk ravioli, game sausage charcuterie, and bison short ribs. More traditional fare—burgers, trout, chicken breast—rounds out the choices, and there are typically a few tasty vegetarian or vegan options. The dining room is sleek and cozy, with wrought-iron mountain scenes on the lamps and bear prints gracing the chairs.

At the Old Faithful Snow Lodge. www.yellowstonenationalpark lodges.com. ℂ **307/344-7311.** Dinner reservations not accepted in summer but required in winter. Main courses $6–$18 breakfast, $15–$19 lunch (winter only), $20–$45 dinner. Late Apr to late Oct daily 6:30–10am and 5–10pm; mid-Dec to early Mar daily 6:30–10am, 11:30am–3pm, and 5–9:30pm.

WHERE TO STAY IN GRAND TETON

Several different concessionaires operate the lodges within the park (including Headwaters Lodge at Flagg Ranch, which is technically inside the adjacent John D. Rockefeller Jr. Memorial Pkwy.). **Aramark Destinations** runs the Signal Mountain Lodge (www.signalmountainlodge.com; ℂ **307/543-2831**). **Grand Teton Lodge Company** handles Headwaters at Flagg Ranch, Colter Bay Village, Jackson Lake Lodge, and Jenny Lake Lodge (www.gtlc.com; ℂ **307/543-3100**). In the Moose Junction area, Dornans runs the **Spur Ranch Cabins** (www.dornans.com; ℂ **307/733-2415**).

Most park lodges open between mid-May and early June and close in late September to early October (except for the Spur Ranch Cabins, open most of the year). As at Yellowstone, lodging books quickly and demand stays high, so make reservations months in advance (or a full year ahead). Lodges are kept intentionally unplugged: You won't find TVs or air-conditioning in the rooms, but Jackson Lake Lodge does have a pool.

Flagg Ranch Village Area

2 miles from the south entrance to Yellowstone; 5 miles from the northern boundary of Grand Teton

This sleepy outpost on the John D. Rockefeller Jr. Memorial Parkway had plenty of excitement in 2016, when the fast-moving Berry Fire forced an evacuation of the lodge and closed the road. Luckily, all lodge properties escaped unburned, but scorched trunks dominate some patches of surrounding forest. Still, the complex just off the Snake River remains an inviting getaway—or a convenient place to grab a snack and fill your gas tank in between the two parks—and it's much quieter than most of the other hotel areas.

Headwaters Lodge & Cabins at Flagg Ranch ★

Within striking distance of Grand Teton and Yellowstone, Headwaters is convenient if you're exploring both parks. Properties are all cabins with private bathrooms, log-cabin furnishings, and porches; ask for one that overlooks the Snake River. Budget-minded travelers can snag a camper cabin—a sparse room with bunk beds but no linens, electricity, or private bathrooms—but I'd opt for a site in the campground (you'll rough it only slightly more and save money; RV sites are available, too; see p. 153). A few short hiking trails take off from the property, as do guided horseback rides. The main lodge features a restaurant, saloon, convenience store, gift shop, and coffee shop.

At Flagg Ranch. www.gtlc.com. ⓒ **307/543-2861.** 92 cabins, 39 camper cabins, 94 RV sites, 32 tent sites. $102 camper cabin; $348–$449 cabin double; $117 RV site; $59 tent site. Early June to late Sept. **Amenities:** Restaurant; lounge; free Wi-Fi.

Colter Bay Village Area

11 miles from the park's northern boundary; 10 miles from the Moran (east) entrance

This complex of lodging, dining, shopping, and activities on Jackson Lake is one of the most happening spots in the park. You can even soak up a bit of culture at the visitor center.

Colter Bay Village ★

You won't get bored by basing yourself out of this bustling resort. Sign up for a wide range of activities on-site, including paddling, fishing excursions, horseback riding, and scenic lake cruises; a swimming beach and marina also grant access to DIY water recreationists. Lodging is cabin-style: Rustic buildings have gingham curtains and log wall interiors. The sparse tent cabins have pull-down bunks and thin mattresses in canvas (not bugproof) shelters; you're better off camping at the adjacent campground and saving money (p. 153). An RV park rounds out the offerings.

At Colter Bay. www.gtlc.com. ⓒ **307/543-2861.** 167 cabins, 65 camper cabins, 114 RV sites, 338 tent sites. $122 cabin w/shared bath; $294–$395 cabin w/private bath; $104 tent cabin; $112–$117 RV site. Late May to late Sept. **Amenities:** 2 restaurants; free Wi-Fi in public buildings.

Jackson Lake Lodge ★★ Things take a decidedly upscale turn just 5 miles down the road at Jackson Lake Lodge, one of the two fanciest options in the park (Jenny Lake Lodge is even more luxurious). The lodge's upper lobby delivers the biggest wow factor: cozy stone fireplaces in the corners, a stuffed grizzly, and most impressively, 60-foot-wide picture windows facing the Tetons and Mount Moran. You'll also find several boutiques carrying Western wear and jewelry, plus an activities desk that can hook you up with rafting trips, horseback rides, and guided park tours. A playground and the only pool in park lodging make Jackson Lake Lodge family-friendly, too. Lodge rooms are well-appointed and have double beds; even nicer are the cottages (with patios) tucked into the woods around the lodge. In both cases, you'll pay more for a mountain view.

5 miles south of Colter Bay Village on U.S. 89. www.gtlc.com. © **307/543-3100.** 385 units. $505–$639 double lodge room; $459–$679 double cottage; $1,089–$1,539 suite. Mid-May to early Oct. **Amenities:** 2 restaurants; lounge; pool; free Wi-Fi.

Signal Mountain Area

15 miles from the north entrance; 9 miles from the Moran (east) entrance

Shoring up the southeastern corner of Jackson Lake, the Signal Mountain complex offers a campground, marina, guided activities, and a general store. The scenic drive up 7,727-foot Signal Mountain takes off a bit to the south.

Signal Mountain Lodge ★ This mix of rooms and cabins on Jackson Lake has a laid-back, summer-camp vibe, from the board-game room in the lodge to the lake-facing porches with Adirondack chairs. The simple motel-style rooms feature knotty wood furniture, but your best bet is one of the frontier-style cabins or a lakefront apartment with a balcony/patio and kitchenette. The lodge can arrange for guided fishing tours, boat rentals (pontoons, fishing boats, and kayaks), and Snake River float trips. *EV drivers take note:* Signal Mountain Lodge has the park's only vehicle charger.

4½ miles southwest of Jackson Lake Lodge on U.S. 89. www.signal mountainlodge.com. © **307/543-2831.** 79 units. $311–$366 log cabin; $373–$518 lodge room; $518–$573 lakefront; $658 double cabin. Mid-May to mid-Oct. **Amenities:** Restaurant; lounge; free Wi-Fi.

Jenny Lake Area

28 miles from the northern boundary; 17 miles from the Moran (east) entrance; 16 miles from the south entrance

The south end of lovely Jenny Lake hosts a visitor center, grocery store, and the launching point for the shuttle boat to Inspiration Point. The area's only hotel is Jenny Lake Lodge, tucked away just north of the lake.

Jenny Lake Lodge ★★★ Nestled among the evergreens north of Jenny Lake are the finest accommodations in the Tetons—and one of the best lodges in any national park. Land a room at this intimate resort and you'll get a taste of the A-list life, including champagne welcome receptions, croquet, free cruiser bikes, and dining at the lodge's fantastic restaurant. All rooms are in luxurious log cabins with slate bathroom floors, quilts, and porches with rocking chairs; suites add woodstoves and sitting areas, and some have Jacuzzis. The main lodge has a mountain-view porch and a cozy lounge with a fireplace. Excellent hiking trails connect to destinations such as String Lake, Leigh Lake, and Paintbrush Canyon. *Note:* The only way to book this lodge is by purchasing the "Signature Stay," a package that includes breakfast, a five-course dinner, and horseback rides.

N. Jenny Lake Rd. www.gtlc.com. © **307/543-3100.** 37 units. $956 double; $1,139–$1,401 suite. Rates include breakfast and dinner, horseback riding, and use of bicycles. Early June to early Oct. **Amenities:** Restaurant; lounge; free Wi-Fi.

Moose Area

36 miles south of the northern boundary; 18 miles from the Moran (east) entrance; 8 miles south of Jenny Lake

The Dornans area just west of Moose Junction serves as a mini village, with a couple of restaurants; shops specializing in fly-fishing, cycling, and paddling gear; a rafting outfitter; groceries; and a wine shop. Just east, on Mormon Row, several ranch buildings from the early 20th century still squat where early Mormon settlers established a small community.

Spur Ranch Cabins ★ This family-owned clutch of cabins near the Snake River, just east of park headquarters, offers comfortable quarters for a decent price. The log cabins have one or two bedrooms, plus fully equipped kitchens, living rooms, and patios with charcoal grills. Though they're within easy walking distance of the Dornans complex, the cabins are tucked away and quiet. Picnic tables and Adirondack chairs allow for riverside lounging where moose sightings are frequent.

At Moose Junction. www.dornans.com. 📞 **307/733-2415.** 12 units. $295–$395 double; $395–$495 two-bedroom. Lower rates fall–spring. Closed Apr. **Amenities:** 2 restaurants; lounge; free Wi-Fi.

WHERE TO CAMP IN GRAND TETON

As in Yellowstone, the campgrounds in Grand Teton National Park provide a top-notch experience for a bargain price—and few developed campgrounds *anywhere* boast better views than the mountain vistas waiting outside your tent flap in many spots in this park. Concessionaires run all six developed options: The Grand Teton Lodge Company handles Headwaters Campground at Flagg Ranch, Colter Bay, Gros Ventre, and Jenny Lake, while Aramark Destinations runs Lizard Creek and Signal Mountain. Grand Teton also boasts some of the best backcountry camping in the USA; find details about permits and regulations at **www.nps.gov/grte/planyourvisit/back.htm** or call the Backcountry Office at 📞 **307/739-3309.**

GETTING A CAMPSITE All six of the Grand Teton (and John D. Rockefeller Jr. Memorial Pkwy., in the case of Headwaters) campgrounds require reservations, which you can make up to 6 months in advance (some also release a few more sites 2 weeks ahead of time). Sites get snapped up quickly, so mark your calendar and grab one as far ahead as possible. To book a site at any of the six, visit **www.recreation.gov**.

Most campgrounds can accommodate RVs, and Colter Bay RV Park and Headwaters sites offer full hookups; Signal Mountain and Gros Ventre have electric hookups only. If you have a larger RV, Colter Bay, Headwaters, and Gros Ventre are your best bets; vehicle size is limited to 25 feet at Lizard Creek and 30 feet at Signal Mountain.

THE CAMPGROUNDS All of Grand Teton's campgrounds provide a similar (and excellent) experience: With the exception of Jenny Lake and Lizard Creek, all are mid-size to large campgrounds with running water, flush toilets, picnic tables, and fire rings. Colter Bay, Headwaters, and Signal Mountain add showers and laundry. Jenny Lake, with just 61 tent-only sites, is the park's most popular. For details on prices, opening dates, and specific amenities for each campground, see the chart on p. 142.

NORTH

Headwaters Campground at Flagg Ranch ★

Mostly an RV resort (97 of the 131 sites are earmarked for RVs), Headwaters is tucked into a spruce-fir forest near the Snake River adjacent to a grocery store, restaurant, and hiking trails.

Lizard Creek ★★

On the smaller side, this 60-site campground on the north side of Jackson Lake has a remote, away-from-it-all feel. A few sites even have lake views.

Colter Bay/Colter Bay RV Park ★

Adjacent to one of the park's busiest hubs, the Colter Bay campgrounds offer easy access to a restaurant, swimming beach, boat launch, grocery store, and guided activities. The 469-site campground, one of the park's largest, sits in an evergreen forest and is within walking distance of Jackson Lake; tent sites are nicer and more private than the RV spots.

Signal Mountain ★★

Smaller, quieter, and more intimate than nearby Colter Bay, Signal Mountain's 80 sites sit in a lovely wooded area; some have views of Jackson Lake through the trees. A restaurant, bar, and grocery store are a quick stroll away.

SOUTH

Jenny Lake ★★★

The smallest, nicest campground in the Tetons sits just off Jenny Lake and has grandstand views of the peaks. Plan ahead if you want to stay here—it's the park's most coveted campground for good reason.

Gros Ventre ★★

This expansive campground lies in a sagebrush field dotted with cottonwoods, close to the Gros Ventre River. It's a great place to spot moose and pronghorn or try your luck landing a trout.

WHERE TO CAMP NEAR GRAND TETON

Several lovely campgrounds can be found along the outskirts of the park—many of them significantly cheaper than in-park sites (and a mere fraction of the cost of even the most affordable hotels in Jackson). The Bridger-Teton National Forest operates a handful of small, primitive (read: running water but pit toilets and no showers) campgrounds. **Curtis Canyon** is just 8 miles from Jackson, just outside the National Elk Refuge, and **Atherton Creek** and **Crystal Creek** are a bit farther, just east of Kelly along the Gros Ventre Road. Just east of the park you'll find **Hatchet** and **Pacific Creek,** the latter poised on the edge of the Teton Wilderness. These forest service campgrounds cost $13 to $20 per night and usually open sometime in May and close sometime in September.

For an even more remote experience, head west on Grassy Lake Road from the Flagg Ranch area. Twenty free, primitive campsites line the road, each with a picnic table, pit toilet, and bear-resistant food storage box (BYO water).

WHERE TO EAT IN GRAND TETON

The dining options in the Tetons run the scale from quick cafeteria grub to one of the finest restaurants in the entire national park system (that would be the Jenny Lake Lodge

Amenities for Each Campground: Grand Teton National Park

CAMPGROUND	TOTAL SITES	RV HOOKUPS
Colter Bay	469	Yes
Gros Ventre	322	Yes
Headwaters at Flagg Ranch*	131	Yes
Jenny Lake**	61	No
Lizard Creek	60	No
Signal Mountain	81	Yes

* On John D. Rockefeller Jr. Memorial Pkwy.
** Only tents are allowed here.

Dining Room), so there's something for every taste. Dinner reservations are a must at the higher-end spots during the high summer season.

Near the Northern Boundary

Looking for a kick-back meal? **Sheffields** at the Headwaters Lodge serves three meals a day, with a focus on loaded burgers, steaks, elk, and fish. For something a bit more casual, **Leeks Marina & Pizzeria** dishes up New York–style pizza with loads of toppings, plus pasta and sandwiches, with a fantastic lake view.

Colter Bay

This busy hub on Jackson Lake has two quick dining options—pizza, subs, and salads at **Café Court Pizzeria** and deli picks at the **General Store.**

John Colter Ranch House ★ AMERICAN/BARBECUE Colter Bay's signature dining room runs with the cowboy theme: wagon wheels on the walls, cattle-drive scenes on the salad bar, and a bar singed with the brands of local ranchers. The menu is heavy on meaty staples like steak, roasted chicken, and short ribs, but herbivores will find a nice variety of salads and a few vegetarian pastas. *Tip:* Check out the expansive bar menu to enjoy a tasty sandwich and burger while saving a few bucks.

Colter Bay Village. www.gtlc.com. (✆ **307/543-2811.** Reservations not accepted. Main courses $12–$22 breakfast, $18–$22 lunch, $18–$39 dinner. Late May to late Sept daily 6:30–10:30am, 11:30am–1:30pm, and 5:30–9pm.

DUMP STATION	FLUSH TOILETS	DRINKING WATER	SHOWERS	FIRE PITS/ GRILLS	LAUNDRY	FEES	OPEN
Yes	Yes	Yes	Yes	Yes	Yes	$59–$117	Late May to late Sept
Yes	Yes	Yes	No	Yes	No	$57–$77	Early Apr to mid-Oct
Yes	Yes	Yes	Yes	Yes	Yes	$59–$117	Early May to late Sept
No	Yes	Yes	Yes	Yes	No	$56	Early May to early Sept
No	Yes	Yes	No	Yes	No	$49	Mid-June to mid-Sept
Yes	Yes	Yes	Yes	Yes	Yes	$55–$79	Early May to mid-Oct

Jackson Lake Junction

You have several choices at both Jackson Lake and Signal Mountain lodges. Jackson Lake's **Blue Heron Lounge** is the place for small plates and creative cocktails. **Signal Mountain General Store** offers the only grab-and-go food options, but they're better than most: Think quinoa bowls and veggie sandwiches. For something a little different (and more affordable), head to the Jackson Lake Lodge's **Poolside Cantina,** where you'll have your pick of tacos and burritos served on picnic tables by the pool.

The Mural Room ★★ SEAFOOD/WILD GAME   Jackson Lake Lodge's marquee restaurant could serve you a bowl of Easy Mac and you'd still come away raving, thanks to the stunning view of the Tetons from its floor-to-ceiling windows. Luckily, the entrees aim as high as the mountain scenery: This is a place to savor impressive dishes such as elk bolognese, bison osso bucco, and Idaho ruby red trout. Breakfast and lunch are memorable too, from housemade pastries to smoked trout salad. Tear your eyes away from the peaks long enough to check out the historic Carl Rotors murals adorning the opposite wall.

At Jackson Lake Lodge. www.gtlc.com. ⓒ **307/543-3463.** Reservations recommended. Main courses $9–$28 breakfast, $18–$21 lunch, $29–$52 dinner. Mid-May to early Oct daily 7–9:30am, 11:30am–1:30pm, and 5–9pm.

Pioneer Grill ★ AMERICAN   Jackson Lake Lodge's casual eatery is a mash-up of 1950s-style diner and homesteader museum: You'll grab a stool at a counter under displays of old wagon wheels and farm tools. The food is a mix of roadside-diner classics and Wyoming specialties. Think breakfasts of huckleberry pancakes and trout and eggs. The lunch and dinner menu features burgers, sandwiches, and several types of loaded fries, plus decadent desserts.

At Jackson Lake Lodge. www.gtlc.com. ⓒ **307/543-3100.** Reservations not accepted. Main courses $9–$25 breakfast, $10–$23 lunch, $10–$39 dinner. Mid-May to early Oct daily 6–10:30am, 11am–10pm.

Trapper Grill ★ AMERICAN/MEXICAN   At nearly double its original size after taking over the now-defunct Peaks Restaurant left behind in 2020, Trapper boasts a lovely lake view and a commitment to sustainable ingredients. The wide-ranging menu should satisfy varied appetites, from trout tacos to local burgers to veggie wild rice. But the star of the show is the Mountain of Nachos, a cheesy pile of chips, beef/cage-free chicken/black beans, and all the fixings, which can certainly fill up four people. The full menu is also available in the adjacent **Deadman's Bar,** which claims one of the park's only TVs, a roaring fireplace, and a nice selection of local microbrews, wines, and cocktails.

At Signal Mountain Lodge. www.gtlc.com. ✆ **307/543-2831.** Main courses $10–$17 breakfast, $15–$35 lunch and dinner. Mid-May to mid-Oct daily 7am–10pm.

Jenny Lake

You can pick up snacks and limited groceries at the **Jenny Lake Store** near the visitor center on the lake's south side.

Jenny Lake Lodge Dining Room ★★★ CONTINEN-TAL   I haven't found a restaurant in any national park that comes close to the all-star quality of this intimate retreat. Here, a talented chef prepares a five-course dinner starring local Wyoming ingredients whipped up in creative, surprising, and delicious ways. First-course offerings might include seared scallops, latkes with caviar, or trout gravlax, followed by soup and salad. Main course options could be Wagyu rib-eye, lobster tagliatelle, or rack of lamb. The wine list is extensive, and service is warm and attentive. It all happens in a rustically elegant dining room with log walls and iron chandeliers. Reservations are essential for dinner, and lodge guests get the first crack at them. Lunch is a less pricey option.

At Jenny Lake Lodge. www.gtlc.com. ✆ **307/543-3100.** Dinner reservations required; lunch reservations highly recommended. Prix-fixe breakfast $39; lunch main courses $17–$30; prix-fixe dinner $125, not including alcoholic beverages. Early June to early Oct daily 7:30–9:30am, 11:30am–1pm, and 5:30–8:30pm.

Moose Junction

The **Dornans** complex (www.dornans.com) has two casual, relatively affordable restaurants. The **Chuckwagon Grill,** with outdoor seating, dining tepee, and Teton views is the more fun of the two; look for simple menu choices like burgers, sandwiches, and brisket. The **Pizza & Pasta Company** offers just that, plus salads and sandwiches.

GATEWAYS TO YELLOWSTONE & GRAND TETON

8

You'll find civilization waiting outside almost every park entrance, but the gateway towns vary considerably in amenities and vibe, from a remote frontier outpost to a ritzy getaway packed with art galleries and high-end restaurants. Read on to choose your ideal basecamp.

WEST YELLOWSTONE, MONTANA ★

At the west entrance of Yellowstone National Park

West Yellowstone has a tiny year-round population, but it bustles with travelers most of the year. It sprouted up around the Union Pacific Railroad's Yellowstone Special line starting in 1907. Though much of the town is hotels, souvenir shops, and overpriced restaurants, Yellowstone's western gateway also offers excellent access to outdoor pursuits both inside and outside the park. A few historic buildings from the early 20th century remain in town, and a surprisingly good wildlife park is probably the top in-town attraction.

Essentials

GETTING THERE For information on air service and car rentals, see "Getting There & Getting Around," in chapter 10. West Yellowstone is 90 miles from Bozeman via U.S. 191 and 108 miles from Idaho Falls via U.S. 20.

VISITOR INFORMATION   Stop by or contact the **West Yellowstone Chamber of Commerce,** 30 Yellowstone Ave. (P.O. Box 458), West Yellowstone, MT 59758 (www.destinationyellowstone.com; ☏ **406/646-7701**).

Getting Outside

Just a few blocks from Yellowstone's west entrance, West Yellowstone is also an easy drive from the Caribou-Targhee and Gallatin national forests and all the outdoor opportunities therein. To the north, the Madison Range and the Lee Metcalf Wilderness offer fantastic hiking trails, and nearby Hebgen Lake hosts paddlers, sailors, boaters, and swimmers. Fly-fishing is huge here, thanks to the trout-rich waters of the Madison, Gallatin, Yellowstone, and Henrys Fork of the Snake rivers. When the snow flies, West Yellowstone transforms into a mecca for snowmobiling and snowcoach tours, and the Rendezvous Trail system draws devoted Nordic skiers. For more details on these activities, see chapter 4.

Seeing the Sights

Beyond the attractions below, history buffs will get a kick out of the free, self-guided **Historic Walking Tour,** which guides you past hotels and railroad structures from the early 1900s. Pick up a map and guide at the Museum of the Yellowstone (see below).

Earthquake Lake Visitor Center ★★   One terrifying August night in 1959, a 7.5-magnitude earthquake triggered a massive landslide along the Madison River, sending 80 million tons of rock into the water—forming Earthquake Lake—and killing 28 people. This small but fascinating center perched above the lake takes a hard look at the event, from the geologic and seismic forces at play to eyewitness accounts and stories from survivors. A short trail leads to a memorial boulder, and you can easily see the scars the quake left on the landscape from the overlook, including a naked hillside and ghostly tree trunks still standing in the water.

27 miles northwest of West Yellowstone on U.S. 287. www.fs.usda.gov/detail/custergallatin/specialplaces. ☏ **406/682-7620.** Free. Late May to mid-Sept daily 10am–5pm.

Grizzly & Wolf Discovery Center ★★   The Discovery Center is no mere roadside attraction: This nonprofit center houses rescued wolves, grizzly bears, otters, and raptors, and features naturalist programs, educational displays, and a small museum. The wolves are always visible in their outdoor habitats, while employees rotate the grizzlies through their enclosure. Kid programs, bear spray demos, and ranger-led presentations round out the offerings. ***Bottom line:*** It's a good cause, and unlike inside the national park, charismatic megafauna sightings are guaranteed.

201 S. Canyon St. (in Grizzly Park). www.grizzlydiscoveryctr.org. © **800/257-2570** or 406/646-7001. $16.50 adults; $15.50 seniors; $11.50 children 5–12; free for kids 4 and under (good for 2 consecutive days). Summer daily 8:30am–7pm; shorter hours the rest of the year.

Museum of the Yellowstone ★

Take a step back into the early days of Yellowstone travel at this museum inside the 1909 Union Pacific depot. Exhibits cover the development of the town, early tourism, and transportation before the age of the automobile. Highlights include several old stagecoaches and a stuffed grizzly bear nicknamed Old Snaggletooth, a once-famous dumpster bear.

104 Yellowstone Ave. www.museumoftheyellowstone.org. © **406/646-1100.** $10 adults; $8 seniors; free for children up to age 17 (good for 2 consecutive days). Mid-May to mid-Oct daily 9am–6pm.

Where to Stay

The smartest travelers book rooms well ahead of time—especially in high summer and around the holidays. Things quiet down in the spring and fall, but the popularity of the area's snowmobile trails makes snowy winters quite lively. West Yellowstone is the closest gateway town with a wide variety of options (Cody, Wyoming has quite a few, but it's 50 miles from the park entrance), ranging from basic motels to swanky modern lodges to cabins and guest ranches.

Most hotels in town are independents, but a few chains have a presence. You can grab a double at **Days Inn,** 301 Madison Ave. (www.wyndhamhotels.com; © **406/646-7656**), notable for its pool and 100-foot waterslide, starting at $339 in summer. The newly renovated **Holiday Inn,** 315 Yellowstone Ave. (www.ihg.com; © **406/646-7365**), is a step up in quality, with doubles for $409, plus a pool, arcade, and airport shuttle. **Kelly Inn,** 104 S. Canyon (www.yellowstonekellyinn.com; © **800/259-4672**), is luxuriously modern, with rooms for $340 to $420.

For something more unique, try **Yellowstone Cabins and RV,** 504 Highway 20 (www.yellowstonecabinsandrv.com; ✆ **406/646-9350**), for small 1940s-era cabins (since refurbished) in a lodgepole-pine stand that run $215 to $265. The surprisingly affordable **Alpine Motel,** 120 Madison Ave. (www.alpinemotelwestyellowstone.com; ✆ **406/646-7544**), is a comfortable spot downtown, with rooms and suites from $140 to $240. The 1912 **Madison Hotel,** 139 Yellowstone Ave. (www.madisonhotelmotel.com; ✆ **406/646-7745**), onetime host to the likes of Clark Gable and Herbert Hoover, stands out with its historic lodge and motel rooms ($115–$255) and hostel rooms with shared bathrooms ($89). **Moose Creek Inn,** 119 Electric St. (www.moosecreekinn.com; ✆ **406/646-7952**), is a hidden gem with cabin-style motel rooms and suites for $259 to $339.

1872 Inn ★★   You'd never know this sophisticated hotel on the outskirts of downtown used to be a hardware store. Now, it's all mountain glam, with locally made wooden beds, leather armchairs, and antler chandeliers. The guest rooms at this adults-only getaway all feature king beds, small private fireplaces, and large double showers, and the hotel serves breakfast (included) in its modern-meets-rustic lobby. This is a good bet if you're looking for a quiet, upscale retreat in the busiest Yellowstone gateway.

603 Yellowstone Ave. www.1872inn.com. ✆ **406/646-1025.** 18 units. $409 double. Rates include continental breakfast. **Amenities:** Fitness center; sauna; computer/printer; free Wi-Fi.

Evergreen Motel ★   Built in 1931, this is more than your generic motel, thanks to thoughtful decor, comfortable rooms, and friendly service. Rooms are a tad small by today's standards, but they're lovingly appointed with locally made log furnishings and fake evergreen boughs, with pinecones and moose on the walls and lamps. Suites have kitchenettes.

229 Firehole Ave. www.theevergreenmotel.com. ✆ **406/646-7655.** 17 units. $235–$275 double; $275–$295 suite with kitchenette. **Amenities:** Free Wi-Fi.

Golden Stone Inn ★★   Anglers coming to ply the world-famous Madison River will feel right at home in this chic retreat (non-anglers welcome too, of course). Cabins at this intimate resort, which opened in 2019, feature sleek, modern interiors, patios with Adirondack chairs, vivid trout paintings on the walls, and dedicated spots to stash waders and rods. The inn serves a full breakfast in the lobby around a rustic wood stove and hosts evening microbrew tastings or s'mores roastings. Partner company Big Sky Anglers can hook you up with a guided fly-fishing trip.

115 S. Faithful St. www.goldenstoneinn.com. ✆ **406/646-5181.** 15 units. $409 triplex room; $459 double cabin. Lower rates fall to spring. **Amenities:** Firepits; free Wi-Fi.

Hibernation Station ★★ This complex of cabins feels a bit like a Christmas village even in the middle of summer, thanks to its cozy, log-*everything* interiors and rooflines adorned with wooden cutouts of horses and evergreens. Newly remodeled in 2021 and 2022, each room has its own decor theme (such as stagecoaches or mustangs), and styles range from simple, spacious doubles to 980-square-foot vacation homes complete with kitchens, jetted tubs, and dining rooms. Outside, you'll find a playground, grills, and a waterfall fountain. You can visit in winter for a real Santa's workshop vibe, but only a handful of cabins remain open in the off-season.

212 Gray Wolf Ave. www.hibernationstation.com. ✆ **406/646-4200.** 50 units. $339–$499 cabin. Lower rates fall to spring. **Amenities:** Lounge with 3 computers; Jacuzzi; firepit; free Wi-Fi (lounge only).

Three Bear Lodge ★ One of West Yellowstone's old-timers—it was first built in the 1930s—Three Bear Lodge has had several facelifts after various damaging fires, including the 2008 blaze. Today, the place features modern amenities, a Western-chic lobby with a stone fireplace, and an outdoor pool. The owners salvaged much of the wood from the original building, turning it into bedframes, towel racks, and other guest room furnishings. Lodge rooms are spacious, and some have balconies; at the adjoining motel, choose among simple doubles, suites, and rooms with huge Jacuzzi tubs. The lodge arranges summer van tours of Yellowstone and winter snowcoach and snowmobile outings.

217 Yellowstone Ave. www.threebearlodge.com. ✆ **800/646-7353** or 406/646-7353. 74 units. $279–$359 double. Lower rates fall to spring. **Amenities:** Restaurant; lounge; fitness center; Jacuzzi; pool (seasonal); business center; free Wi-Fi.

Where to Eat

Morning pick-me-up? You'll find two of the best in unusual places. Head to **Mocha Mammas** coffee bar in the Freeheel and Wheel bike/ski shop, 33 Yellowstone Ave. (www.freeheelandwheel.com; ⓒ **406/646-7744**), for espresso and smoothies, or to **Book Peddler** in Canyon Square (ⓒ **406/646-9358**) for tasty sandwiches and salads along with the usual caffeine. For a quick bite, try one of the town's taco buses, **La Jungla** at 21 N. Canyon St. (ⓒ **208/760-8174**), or **Taqueria Malverde,** 132 Firehole Ave. (ⓒ **208/403-1157**).

Firehole Bar-B-Que Company ★ BARBECUE This Central Texas–style joint delivers worthy barbecue. Well-executed classics like pulled pork, turkey, and brisket fill out the simple menu, supported by tangy slaw and rich mac-and-cheese sides. Opt for a reasonably sized sandwich or go whole hog with a full rack of pork ribs or a pile-it-on meat plate. Decor is sleek meets country, with picnic tables in the dining room and corrugated metal walls hung with cowhides.

120 Firehole Ave. www.fireholebbqco.com. ⓒ **406/641-0020.** Main courses $11–$32. Daily noon–sold out.

Madison Crossing Lounge ★★ STEAKS/SEAFOOD By all accounts the best place in town, Madison Crossing makes for a classy night out: Enjoy attentive service and excellent food in a warmly lit, Montana-chic setting. Its 1918 building was the first school in town. The place prides itself on its extensive wine list, but the beer and cocktail menus are also lengthy (the latter heavy on fine whiskeys). Entrees are classic and well-prepared, from steaks to elk to a tasty Idaho trout and Mediterranean pasta. You'll also find a few bison dishes, like tenderloin and meatloaf.

121 Madison Ave. www.madisoncrossinglounge.com. ⓒ **406/646-7621.** Main courses $24–$57. Daily 5–9pm.

Yellowstone Beer Company ★ MICROBREWERY West Yellowstone got a brewery of its own in 2023, a bright, welcoming space on the basketball court of the town's first school (the scoreboard is still here). Besides producing its own brews—with names like Red Dog red ale, a nickname for a bison calf, and Bear Necessities, a hefeweizen—the taproom also pours a dozen more local beers and serves a full menu of elevated pub grub. Options range from bison jambalaya to hot chicken to a catfish po'boy, all of it tasty and reasonably priced for a gateway town. A few unobtrusive TVs tuned to sports and a mezzanine sporting pool, foosball, and shuffleboard tables makes this a fine place to hang out.

121 Madison Ave. www.yellowstonebeercompany.com. © **406/646-7621.** Main courses $14–$17. Daily 1–10pm.

GARDINER, MONTANA ★

At the north entrance to Yellowstone National Park

Yellowstone's northern gateway feels worlds away from the tourist trappings of West Yellowstone and the swanky sights of Jackson: basically a few downtown blocks, limited dining and lodging, deer and elk lounging in front yards, and peace and quiet. The Yellowstone River cuts through town, and views of the scrublands and hills of north Yellowstone rise just beyond. If you're more interested in playing outside by day and stargazing by night than souvenir shopping, this laid-back town is for you. In winter, the north entrance is the only way cars can enter the park when the snow piles up.

Gardiner is back on its feet after a rough few years. First came the 2020 double whammy of the COVID-19 pandemic and a devastating fire that destroyed most of a downtown block, including several restaurants. Then catastrophic flooding in June 2022 washed out the North Entrance Road, severing Gardiner's tie to the park for months. Luckily, the park quickly rebuilt the road, restoring business as usual to this friendly little burg.

Essentials

GETTING THERE   For information on air service and car rentals, see "Getting There & Getting Around" in chapter 10. Gardiner is 78 miles south of Bozeman on U.S. 89.

VISITOR INFORMATION   Contact the **Gardiner Chamber of Commerce,** 216 Park St. (www.visitgardinermt.com; © **406/848-7971**). The nonprofit **Yellowstone Forever** (www.yellowstone.org; © **406/848-2400**), whose headquarters are downtown at 308 Park St., also has a staffed information desk, along with a gift shop.

Getting Outside

Proximity to the mighty Yellowstone River makes **whitewater rafting, floating,** and **fly-fishing** big here, and several outfitters base themselves in Gardiner. Options range from mellow 2-hour floats to multiday trips with riverside camping. For rafting and floating, try **Flying Pig Adventures,** 511 Scott St. (www.flyingpigrafting.com; ⓒ **888/792-9193**), or **Wild West Whitewater Rafting,** 129 U.S. Highway 89 (www.wildwest rafting.com; ⓒ **406/848-2252**). **Parks' Fly Shop,** 202 2nd St. S. (www.parksflyshop.com; ⓒ **406/848-7314**), is the place to sign up for guided fly-fishing outings or fishing lessons. **Horseback riding** (including multiday pack trips) and **hiking** in the Gallatin National Forest are also popular. **Hell's A-Roarin' Outfitters,** 164 Crevice Rd. (www.hellsaroarin outfitter.com; ⓒ **406/848-7578**), offers rides ranging from an hour to a day (and rents cabins and canvas wall tents). In winter, you can hop on guided **snowcoach** tours, though West Yellowstone is the true mecca for oversnow enthusiasts.

Seeing the Sights

Heritage and Research Center ★   This treasure trove of Yellowstone history houses 720,000 cultural and historic items, an archaeology lab, herbarium, research library, and the park's archives. We highly recommend reserving a spot on the free, weekly behind-the-scenes tour (late May to early Sept, Wed at 4pm) for an up-close look at wildlife specimens, rare native plants, historic photos, original Thomas Moran sketches, and more.

20 Old Yellowstone Trail. www.nps.gov/yell/learn/historyculture/ collections.htm. ⓒ **307/344-2264.** Free admission. Mon–Fri 9am–4pm.

Yellowstone Hot Springs ★   Be a part of Gardiner's long-standing love affair with hot springs, dating back to the earliest area resort in 1899, at this unpretentious resort featuring a secluded set of outdoor pools along the Yellowstone River. There's nothing so relaxing as a dip in one of the naturally heated tubs—the main pool hovers around 102°F (37°C), and there is a 104°F (40°C) hot pool as well as a cold plunge that dives into the 60s (upper teens Celsius)—with views of

surrounding peaks. ***Bonus:*** You can stay overnight in a cabin, tent, or RV campsite ($295 cabin, $25–$65 campsite).

24 E. Gate Rd. www.yellowstonehotspringsmt.com. ℭ **406/848-4141.** $18 adults; $10 children 4–12; free for kids 3 and under. Tues–Sun 9am–9pm.

Where to Stay

Gardiner has long been known for friendly, no-frills lodging—and while there are still plenty such options, swankier, boutique-style hotels have been cropping up, and several chain hotels maintain a presence. If you're planning a guided tour while in town, check with your outfitter: Some of them offer rooms on the side.

The **Antler Lodge,** 107 Hellroaring St. (www.gardiner antlerlodge.com; ℭ **406/848-7536**), makes an effort to look like it fits in, with log walls and antlered heads mounted in the lobby. Doubles go for $252 to $266. Gardiner's **Super 8,** 702 Scott St. W. (www.wyndhamhotels.com; ℭ **406/848-1081**), offers doubles for $244 to $272. The **Roosevelt Hotel,** 1014 Scott St. W. (www.yellowstonehotelbooking.com; ℭ **406/848-5130**), has doubles for $229 to $259; there are also a few cabins. At the riverfront **Absaroka Lodge,** 310 Scott St. W. (www.yellowstonemotel.com; ℭ **406/848-7414**), $235 will net you a double and $260 a kitchenette suite.

The family-run **Hillcrest Cottages,** 400 Scott St. W. (www. hillcrestcottages.com; ℭ **406/848-7353**), are a good bet for budget-minded travelers: You get a stand-alone cottage, some with a kitchenette, for a nice price, but some are *very* small. Units go for around $185 to $275, May to mid-October only. Or check out the **Park Hotel** (www.parkhotelyellowstone. com; ℭ **406/223-7007**), in a renovated 1902 building at 107 Main St. that holds a handful of cozy rooms and suites, each decorated differently. High-season prices range from $275 for a double to $285 to $475 for a suite.

406 Lodge ★ A couple blocks off the main drag, this Montana-chic boutique hotel pays attention to the little things: Wood headboards, vintage travel posters, kitschy quilts, and cowhide rugs adorn each space. Each room at the lodge, which opened in 2019, is spacious and quiet, and the upper-level ones share a small balcony. The property also offers a few larger one- and two-bedroom suites and a handful of one-bedroom riverside cabins.

204 3rd St. S. www.406lodge.com. ℂ **406/848-9956.** 16 units. $250–$270 lodge double; $320 cabin; $335–$425 suite. **Amenities:** Free Wi-Fi.

Jim Bridger Explorer Cabins ★★ *Little House on the Prairie,* this ain't: The modern one- and two-bedroom cabins at this new-in-2022 outfit would be at home on any stylish urban street. Spacious interiors feature living rooms with pullout couches, kitchenettes, and fireplaces, and each has an exterior spiral staircase leading to a rooftop patio facing Yellowstone's hills (use the included binoculars to scope for antelope and elk over your morning coffee). A communal firepit hosts complimentary s'mores roasts, and you also get access to the pool, hot tub, and sauna at sister property Ridgeline Hotel. Ridgeline's more standard (and pet-friendly; $50/stay) hotel rooms are also worth a look, and considerably cheaper (starting at $259).

905 Scott St. W. www.yellowstonevacations.com. ℂ **406/848-4160.** 9 units. $499–$609 cabin; $15/day seasonal amenity fee. **Amenities:** Restaurant; Jacuzzi; indoor pool; 2 saunas; firepit; free Wi-Fi.

Riverside Cottages ★★ These delightful homes-away-from-home range from artsy suites that comfortably sleep six to motel-style efficiency rooms. A large deck provides a common space to chill in lounge chairs or grill up a bison burger; the path down the bluff is one of the only ways in town to get close to the Yellowstone River. The extremely friendly service is icing on the cake.

521 Scott St. W. www.yellowstoneriversidecottages.com. ℂ **406/848-7719.** 16 units. $229 efficiency; $279–$379 cottage; $299–$499 suite; lower rates fall–spring. **Amenities:** Free Wi-Fi.

Wonderland Lodge ★★ Owners Stacey and Brad Orsted brought a designer's eye to the classy collection of studios and suites sitting above their organic cafe. With wood floors, granite countertops, reclaimed wood furniture, and fancy industrial showers, each unit feels more like staying at your most fashionable friend's apartment than a hotel. Every room has a full kitchen, and some add balconies, laundry, a gas fireplace, and California king beds. Arresting photos of local wildlife (Brad is a pro photographer) also grace the walls. *Note:* There's no elevator, so you have to schlep your bags up a fairly long staircase or two.

206 Main St. www.wonderlandcafeandlodge.com. ℂ **406/224-2001.** 6 units. $250 double; $325–$475 suite. **Amenities:** Free Wi-Fi.

Where to Eat

Early wildlife-watchers can grab a quick coffee and breakfast, plus to-go lunches, at the tiny **Tumbleweed Bookstore and Café,** 501 Scott St. W. (ℂ **406/848-2225**). **The Corral,** 711 Scott St. W. (ℂ **406/848-7627**), stands out among burger joints for its local and organic ingredients. The best place for ice cream is **Yellowstone Perk** at 208 Park St. (ℂ **406/600-7553**). After hours, the **Iron Horse Bar & Grill,** 212 Spring St. (ℂ **406/848-7888**), lays claim to the town's best riverfront patio.

Cowboy's Grille ★ BARBECUE/STEAKS   Sometimes in a place like Gardiner, a big ol' plate of barbecue feels just right—and this is the best place in town to satisfy that craving. The lengthy menu is chock-full of burgers, pulled pork, ribs, chicken, and steaks, with classics such as mashed potatoes and coleslaw on the side. But you can also mix it up with a number of different burritos. A new-in-2022 two-story patio adorned with horseshoes and wagon wheels grants river views to guests eating alfresco. *Bonus:* local beers and decadent desserts.

208 Stone St. www.cowboyslodgeandgrille.com. ℂ **406/848-9175.** Main courses $14–$42. Mon–Sat 7:30am–10pm; Sun 11:30am–10pm.

Two Bit City ★ STREET FOOD   In a superb example of making lemonade out of lemons, the people behind several bars that burned down in 2020 reimagined their businesses as an alfresco food court. Now, a collection of food trucks (plus a hut for the **Blue Goose Saloon**) sit on a corner of downtown, along with shaded picnic tables and lawn games. The four trucks offer a range of casual options like hearty sandwiches, hot dogs, BBQ, and espresso drinks; the Goose pours a number of cocktails with liquor from local distilleries, plus Montana craft beers. Even better: Watch for live music acts in summer.

107 2nd St. S. www.twobit.city. Main courses $5–$14. Daily 11am–8pm (bar until 2am). May–Sept (Blue Goose open year-round).

Wonderland Cafe ★★ AMERICAN   This sustainably minded, farm-to-table restaurant brings some fresh air to burger-heavy Gardiner, offering Montana-raised rib-eye,

Flathead Lake trout, baked elk chili mac, and stuffed mushrooms (and yes, a tasty burger too). In the morning, grab espresso plus scones or savory muffins. A stone fireplace, wildlife photography from co-owner Brad Orsted, and communal games complete the cozy vibe.

206 Main St. www.wonderlandcafeandlodge.com. © **406/223-1914.** Main courses $12–$18 lunch, $13–$45 dinner. Daily 7am–8:30pm.

PARADISE VALLEY, MONTANA ★★

Up to 50 miles from the north entrance to Yellowstone National Park

The gorgeous valley sandwiched between the Gallatin and Absaroka ranges just north of Yellowstone has become a destination unto itself. Here you'll find a handful of outstanding resorts, quiet hiking trails, and blue-ribbon fly-fishing on the Yellowstone River. It's *almost* enough to make you forget about the national park altogether.

Lodging options in Paradise are swanky enough to attract Hollywood types (and they do come through, many because of a Western movie set called Yellowstone Film Ranch). Since 1900, travelers have been drawn to **Chico Hot Springs Resort,** 163 Chico Rd., Pray (www.chicohotsprings.com; © **406/333-4933**), and its large geothermal pools (day soaking available for $14/day). Overnight options range from historic lodge rooms with shared bathrooms to motel rooms to upscale cabins to Conestoga glamping wagons; you'll pay anywhere from $105 to $335 per night. The fabulous **Chico Dining Room** serves well-executed classics such as pork chops and prime rib, and its Sunday brunch also draws rave reviews.

Comparative newcomer (it opened in 2018) **Sage Lodge,** 55 Sage Lodge Dr., Pray (www.sagelodge.com; © **855/400-0505**), is even more luxurious. Located on 1,200 acres in the shadow of Emigrant Peak, Sage offers hot tubs, a spa, a stocked fishing pond, and private Yellowstone tours on top of its spacious lodge rooms and four-bedroom houses. High-season rates for the lodge start at $1,184 (2-night minimum). A couple of excellent restaurants round out the top-shelf experience.

And in 2023, glamping giant **Under Canvas** launched its North Yellowstone-Paradise Valley location, 139 Pine Creek

Rd., Livingston (www.undercanvas.com; © **888/496-1148**), along the Yellowstone River, complete with lavishly furnished wall tents and an on-site smokehouse restaurant. Rates start at $494 per night.

COOKE CITY, MONTANA ★

5 miles from the northeast entrance to Yellowstone National Park

Rough-and-tumble Cooke City sprang up in the 1880s, when prospectors struck gold, but the mining heyday is long gone. Nowadays, the remote, tiny town (roughly 100 year-round residents) is all about outdoor recreation, surrounded by Yellowstone and the Custer, Gallatin, and Shoshone national forests. Hiking, fishing, and paddling opportunities abound, and snowmobiling is huge. If you're planning to cruise the ultrascenic Beartooth Highway (and you should; see p. 49), Cooke City offers the only services until Red Lodge, 68 twisty miles away. Like Gardiner, Cooke City was hit hard by the June 2022 floods. High waters didn't affect the town itself, but major damage to the roads in and out left the village temporarily isolated and cut off its full access to Yellowstone for months.

The **Colter Pass/Cooke City/Silver Gate Chamber of Commerce** (www.cookecitychamber.org; © **406/838-2495**) operates a visitor center at 206 W. Main St.; it's open daily in summer. The small, free **Cooke City Montana Museum** on-site (www.cookecitymontanamuseum.org; © **406/838-2203**) is worth a quick browse for its 19th-century settler artifacts and mining equipment. Also worth a stop: **Cooke City General Store,** 101 Main St. (www.cookecitystore.com; © **406/838-2234**), which has been offering a little of everything since it opened in 1886—these days, that means soap, wine, and T-shirts.

Cooke City and its even smaller neighbor, Silver Gate, offer the best lodging deals of any gateway town: You can still snap up a midsummer room for less than $200. **The Grizzly Lodge,** 102 U.S. 212 W. (www.yellowstonelodges. com; © **406/838-2219**), in Silver Gate, is less than a mile from the park entrance and features motel-style rooms and cabins along Soda Butte Creek for $165 to $230.

Just down the road in Cooke City, the cabins and cozy lodge rooms at **Elk Horn Lodge,** 103 Main St.

(www.elkhornlodgemt.com; © **406/838-2332**), are traveler favorites and go for $210 to $260. **Antlers Lodge,** 311 Main St. E. (www.cookecityantlerslodge.com; © **866/838-2432**), has log-style and modern cabins, plus motel rooms, grouped around a central lodge and restaurant. Small cabins and motel rooms go for $190 to $295, with two-room cabins for $325. A few private rental homes and cabins are also in the area; check with the chamber of commerce.

Cooke City's dining pickings are slim but tasty. Main Street's **Beartooth Café** (© **406/838-2475**) has the best burgers and steaks, plus made-from-scratch desserts. Also on Main Street, try **Cooke City Coffee** (© **406/539-4049**) for espresso, sandwiches, and to-go breakfasts.

JACKSON, WYOMING ★★★

Near the south entrance of Grand Teton National Park

Jackson has changed from the days when its only visitors were Native Americans hunting for summer game and, later, mountain men seeking beaver pelts. From settlements established in the 1890s a thriving tourism hub has sprung, catering to everyone from outdoor adventurers to glitterati on holiday. Packed with opportunities for outdoor fun, fine dining, and shopping, Jackson is unlike any other gateway town and well worth a stop.

You may have heard this area referred to as Jackson Hole, and that's correct: In mountain man parlance, a "hole" was a high valley surrounded by peaks. The town itself is Jackson, while Jackson Hole is the surrounding valley. Jackson centers on the old-timey Town Square, a small park marked by four famous arches fashioned from antlers.

You'll find no shortage of outfitters ready to set you up on your outdoor adventure. The Snake River provides easy access to whitewater rafting, float trips, and trout fishing, and dude ranches can get you in the saddle. In winter, Jackson Hole Mountain Resort attracts black-diamond skiers, cross-country ski trails abound, and sleigh rides at National Elk Refuge are a classic winter excursion.

Climbers and hikers can come in from a day outside and rub elbows with the high society in the town's five-star hotels, elegant restaurants, and ritzy jewelry and art galleries. If your dream national park vacation involves dropping 30 grand on a giant moose statue or indulging in elaborate spa treatments, Jackson is the place for you. More interested in microbrews beside the campfire? You'll be right at home, too.

Essentials

Chapter 10 discusses air service to Jackson and available rental-car agencies.

GETTING THERE If you're coming south from Yellowstone, Jackson is an hour and 15 minutes' drive from the south entrance on U.S. 89. You can also approach from points west (such as Idaho Falls) via U.S. 26 or over Teton Pass on WY 22 (gorgeous if the weather's nice). From the south, take U.S. 89, 189, or 191 north to reach town. For up-to-date weather information and road conditions, call © **888/996-7623** or 511, visit www.wyoroad.info, or contact the **Jackson Hole Chamber of Commerce** (info below).

VISITOR INFORMATION The **Jackson Hole Chamber of Commerce** (www.jacksonholechamber.com; © **307/733-3316**) provides info on lodging, dining, and attractions in the area. The **National Elk Refuge & Greater Yellowstone Visitor Center** at 532 N. Cache St. is another great resource and is staffed by rangers from surrounding parks. It's open 9am to 5pm in summer.

GETTING AROUND Cars are the easiest way around Jackson Hole (rental cars are available at the airport and in town), but you can get away with not having one. The **Jackson Hole Shuttle** (www.jhshuttle.com; © **307/200-1400**) provides service between the airport and Jackson, Teton Village, or Jackson Lake Lodge in Grand Teton National Park (rates $65–$150 one-way), as well as private tours. Several taxis operate in town; for a list of taxi services, visit www. jacksonholeairport.com/travelers/transportation. Note that many of the hotels and car-rental agencies in the Jackson area offer free shuttles to and from the airport.

The **Southern Teton Area Rapid Transit (START)** system (www.startbus.com; © **307/733-4521**) offers daily bus trips around town and to/from Teton Village. Rides in town are free, and it'll cost adults $3 for a one-way fare to Teton Village (free for children 8 and under). Buses come roughly every 15 minutes (in town) to 1 hour (Teton Village).

SPORTS EQUIPMENT & RENTALS If you're here to climb the Tetons, **Teton Mountaineering,** 170 N. Cache St. (www.tetonmtn.com; ✆ 307/733-3595), can equip you with top-of-the-line backpacking, mountaineering, and backcountry skiing gear. **Hoback Sports,** at 530 W. Broadway Ave. #3 (www.hobacksports.com; ✆ 307/733-5335), specializes in skis, snowboards, and bikes, and also offers rentals. **Skinny Skis,** 65 W. Deloney Ave. (www.skinnyskis.com; ✆ 307/733-6094), is a popular downtown shop carrying apparel and equipment for every mountain-related sport; it also rents gear, including mountaineering boots. **Teton Backcountry Rentals,** at 565 N. Cache St. (www.tetonbcrentals.com; ✆ 307/828-1885), rents a wide range of summer and winter gear and even delivers to your hotel. Shop for quality used gear at **Headwall Sports,** 520 U.S. 89 (www.headwallsports.com; ✆ 307/734-8022).

SUMMER SPORTS & ACTIVITIES

BIKING Like many ski hills these days, the major Teton resorts offer mountain biking when the snow melts, and riding the lift uphill lets you skip right to the speedy downhill bit. **Jackson Hole Bike Park** at Jackson Hole Mountain Resort, 3395 Cody Lane, Teton Village (www.jacksonhole.com; ✆ 307/733-2292), has beginner to advanced trails and jump tracks, plus bike and gear rentals; day passes cost $44. To get to **Grand Targhee Bike Park,** cross the ridge at Grand Targhee Resort, 3300 Ski Hill Rd., Alta, WY (www.grandtarghee.com; ✆ 307/353-2300). It offers more than 70 miles of downhill and cross-country bike trails, along with gear rentals. An adult lift ticket sets you back $60.

Those looking for a wilder experience will find numerous mountain bike trails throughout the public lands in Jackson Hole and the Teton Valley. Check out **www.mountainbiketetons.org** for trail maps and descriptions. Road biking more your thing? Paved, off-street paths connect the town of Jackson to Jenny Lake in Grand Teton National Park, Wilson, and Teton Village. And naturally, Jackson has jumped on the electric bike craze; e-bikes are allowed on the area's multiuse pathways. **Pedego Electric Bikes,** 1745 High School Rd. (www.pedegoelectricbikes.com/dealers/jackson; ✆ 866/973-3346), rents bikes, starting at $50 for 2 hours.

FISHING Both Yellowstone and Grand Teton national parks have incredible fishing in their lakes and streams; see the "Fishing" sections in chapters 4 and 6 for details.

The Snake River emerges from Jackson Lake Dam as a broad, strong river, with decent fishing from its banks in certain spots—such as right below the dam—and better fishing if you float the river. Fly-fishers should ask advice at local stores on recent insect hatches and good stretches of river, or hire a guide. Outdoor gear stores will provide all the tackle and ample information on fishing conditions. **JD High Country Outfitters,** at 50 E. Broadway (www.jdhcoutfitters. com; ℂ **307/733-3270**), runs guided trips on three local rivers and also offers casting lessons. For in-the-know local insight into the best places to cast, book a trip with **Grand Teton Fly Fishing,** 565 N. Cache St. (www.grandtetonflyfishing.com; ℂ **307/690-0910**), or **Grand Fishing Adventures,** P.O. Box 582 in Teton Village (www.grandfishing.com; ℂ **307/734-9684**). Both are licensed concessionaires with Grand Teton National Park. Expect to pay $595 to $720 for a half-day trip.

GOLF It's hard to imagine a golf course with more impressive views than the swanky **Jackson Hole Golf & Tennis Club,** 5000 Spring Gulch Rd. (www.jhgtc.com; ℂ **307/733-3111**), with its Tetons vistas. The 18-hole Robert Trent Jones II course offers fine dining at **North Grille** and a pool. Daily greens fees cost $300 in summer, cart included. The other public option in town, **Teton Pines Country Club,** 3450 N. Clubhouse Dr. in Wilson (www.tetonpines.com; ℂ **307/733-1005**), is no slouch in the scenery department, either, and features a tasty restaurant and tennis. Daily greens fees at the Arnold Palmer– and Ed Seay–designed 18-hole course are $295 in high season, cart included.

HIKING Grand Teton National Park is a hiker's paradise (see chapter 6), but the trails can get a mite crowded during the high season. Fortunately, the 3.4-million-acre **Bridger-Teton National Forest** extending north, south, and east of Jackson encompasses equally gorgeous mountain scenery—with a fraction of the people, and without permit red tape. The **Shoshone National Forest,** just east, and the **Caribou-Targhee National Forest,** northwest, add to the embarrassment of riches. Those who strike out to explore the Bridger-Teton trails will find 13,000-plus-foot peaks, turquoise lakes, glaciers, and wildlife. For details, hike suggestions, and trail conditions, head over to the **National Elk Refuge & Greater Yellowstone Visitor Center** at 532 N. Cache St. to chat with rangers, or contact the forest service directly (www.fs.usda.gov/btnf; ✆ **307/739-5500**).

HORSEBACK RIDING   Besides the stables inside Grand Teton National Park (see chapter 6), several Jackson outfitters offer rides ranging from 2-hour jaunts to multiday trips. Try the family-owned **Mill Iron Ranch** (www.milliron ranch.net; ✆ **307/733-6390**) or **Willow Creek Horseback Rides** (www.willowcreekhorsebackrides.com; ✆ **307/733-7086**). Half- to full-day rides range from $165 to about $895.

KAYAKING, CANOEING & PADDLEBOARDING   The Snake River attracts river rats from the world over, but local lakes also offer excellent paddling. For lessons and guided tours in river and lake kayaking and stand-up paddleboarding, check out **Rendezvous River Sports,** 945 W. Broadway (www.jacksonholekayak.com; ✆ **307/733-2471**).

RAFTING   Rafting trips on the Snake River come in two flavors: wild and mild. The Grand Canyon of the Snake, a deep gorge about 20 miles south of Jackson, hosts the area's classic whitewater trip—an 8-mile stretch of turbulent water, featuring up to 10 Class II and III (on a scale of I–VI) rapids. The mellower float trips take place in and near the national park and west of Jackson on the Snake's flatwater sections. Where whitewater trips are all about adrenaline and splashy action, float trips focus on scoping the banks for moose, bald eagles, bears, otters, and more aquatic wildlife. Several operators run float trips in the park (see chapter 6).

If you must pick just one, go for the whitewater: The wild ride is great for older kids but still plenty thrilling for adults. Jackson has so many top-notch rafting outfitters, chances are you'll have an excellent time no matter which one you choose. Some of the very best are **Jackson Hole Whitewater** (www.jhww.com; ✆ **800/700-7238**), **Mad River Boat Trips** (www.mad-river.com; ✆ **307/734-8898**), **Sands Whitewater** (www.sandswhitewater.com; ✆ **866/312-4957**), **Dave Hansen Whitewater** (www.davehansenwhitewater. com; ✆ **307/733-6295**), and **Lewis & Clark River Expeditions** (www.lewisandclarkrafting.com; ✆ **307/733-4022**).

Eight-mile, 3-hour whitewater trips usually cost around $110 for adults.

ROPES COURSES & ZIPLINES   Channel your inner Indiana Jones on one of Jackson's aerial adventure courses: You'll catwalk across hanging logs, scramble up rope nets, and zip through the trees. **Snow King Mountain,** 402 E. Snow King Ave. (www.snowkingmountain.com; ✆ **307/201-5464**), debuted its **Zip Line** in 2022: With a 36-degree grade, it's the steepest in North America and reaches speeds up to 60mph ($110 adults). Snow King also has a **Treetop Adventure** course that gets progressively more challenging, plus a closer-to-the-ground kids' version ($85 adults; $60 children 7–11). The $200 Big King Ultimate Pass grants access to one go at both, plus the resort's roller coaster, alpine slide, bungee trampoline, and more. **Jackson Hole Mountain Resort,** 3395 Cody Lane, Teton Village (www.jacksonhole.com; ✆ **307/733-2292**), has its **Aerial Ropes Course** ($55), part of a summer park complete with a bungee trampoline, Via Ferrata (climbing course), and disc golf course.

WINTER SPORTS & ACTIVITIES

CROSS-COUNTRY SKIING   Though it's best known for fab alpine ski resorts, Jackson offers fantastic opportunities for skinny skis, too. Classic and skate skiers can hit groomed trails at several Nordic centers, while those with more wanderlust can glide into the backcountry of the Bridger-Teton National Forest or Grand Teton (see chapter 6).

Teton County Parks and Recreation (www.tetonparks andrec.org; ✆ **307/733-5056**) grooms areas for free Nordic skiing from mid-December to mid-March, including Cache Creek Canyon and Wilson Centennial Pathway. A bit farther afield, just outside Wilson, you'll find **Trail Creek Nordic Center** (www.jhskiclub.org; ✆ **307/733-0296**), an excellent spot for skate skiing. The Jackson Hole Ski and Snowboard Club maintains its 10 miles of groomed trails; day passes cost $20. Also near Wilson, the Teton Pines golf course becomes the **Teton Pines Nordic Center** (www.tetonpines nordiccenter.com; ✆ **307/732-4130**) in winter, with 9.9 miles of groomed, Teton-view trails; day passes are $25. On the other side of the valley, **Turpin Meadow Ranch** (www.turpin meadowranch.com; ✆ **307/543-2000**) operates a Nordic Center with 9.3 miles of rolling terrain near Moran; day passes cost $25. And on the other side of the mountains, **Grand Targhee Resort** (www.grandtarghee.com; © **307/353-2300**) operates a 9.3-mile Nordic Trail System, accessible for $25. Check the Jackson Hole Nordic website at **www.jhnordic.com** for grooming details for local areas.

DOGSLEDDING   No need to fly to the Yukon to careen over the snow behind a team of huskies—**Jackson Hole Iditarod Sled Dog Tours** (www.jhsleddog.com; © **307/733-7388**) can make that happen right in Jackson. Run by eight-time Iditarod racer Frank Teasley, the outfitter offers guided half- and full-day trips through the Bridger-Teton National Forest, and yes, you get to try your hands at the reins. A half-day trip costs $360, covers 12 miles, and includes a light picnic lunch. If you can, go for the full-day option ($460), which cruises to Granite Hot Springs (a 20-mile round-trip) for a soak and a hot lunch.

DOWNHILL SKIING   Alpine skiers the world over dream about Jackson's slopes: Three resorts within striking distance (two of them top-tier destinations), abundant snow, and a reputation for exhilarating black-diamond runs make it a true skier's paradise.

The crown jewel of the Jackson ski scene is **Jackson Hole Mountain Resort ★★**, 3395 Cody Lane, Teton Village (www.jacksonhole.com; © **307/733-2292**). Half of the resort's runs are single or double black diamonds, and thrill seekers come for super-steep trails such as the infamous Corbet's Couloir, a daunting chute. But the resort has expanded and improved its blue runs in recent years, too. Thirteen lifts grant access to 2,500 acres of in-bounds snow. The Sweetwater Gondola whisks you from base to peak in 7½ minutes; also check out the iconic Aerial Tram, a 100-skier sky bus to Rendezvous Bowl. Jackson Hole is on the Ikon and Mountain Collective passes, and adult lift tickets are $269/day, though you can sometimes pre-buy them online for a slight discount.

Grand Targhee Resort ★★, 3300 Ski Hill Rd., Alta (www.grandtarghee.com; © **307/353-2300**), offers a mellower experience over on the west side of the Teton Range. This much smaller ski area is blessed with killer views and more than 500 inches of powder a year, and the new-for-2023 Colter Lift to Peaked Mountain opens up 600 more acres of intermediate to advanced slopes. With lift tickets from $140 to $170, it's quite the deal compared to its ritzier neighbor (it's also on the Mountain Collective pass).

The locals' hill is **Snow King Mountain,** at 402 E. Snow King Ave., Jackson (www.snowkingmountain.com; ✆ **307/ 201-5464**), the smallest of the area ski resorts. The hill anchors the south side of town, and indeed, you can walk there from downtown Jackson. Runs trend toward the steep end of the spectrum. Snow-tubing, a roller coaster, and a scenic gondola ride round out the activities. Lift tickets cost $85.

SNOWMOBILING   Although West Yellowstone is the most popular base for snowmobiling in the Yellowstone area, Jackson has a growing contingent of snowmobile aficionados and outfitters keen on exploring Grand Teton, Yellowstone, Bridger-Teton National Forest, the Continental Divide Snowmobile Trail, and especially Togwotee Pass.

Outfitters run guided day or multiday trips near Jackson and as far north as Yellowstone. Check **Scenic Safaris,** 1255 S. U.S. 89 (www.scenic-safaris.com; ✆ **307/734-8898**); **Teton Tour Company,** 1050 S. U.S. 89 (www.tetontourco.com; ✆ **307/733-8800**); and **Old Faithful Snowmobile Adventures,** Jackson (www.snowmobilingtours.com; ✆ **307/733-9767**). Tours range from $400 to $525 per driver (passengers cost a bit less). Renting your own sled? **Leisure Sports,** 1075 S. U.S. 89 (www.jacksonholefun.com; ✆ **307/733-3040**), has a variety for $185 to $240 per day, plus helmets, suits, and other essentials.

BIRD'S-EYE VIEWING

BALLOONING   Add an extra shot to your latte for one of **Wyoming Balloon Company**'s (www.wyomingballoon. com; ✆ **307/739-0900**) sunrise "float trips" over a private ranch with in-your-face Tetons views (winds are calmest early in the day). The hour-long hot-air-balloon rides soar up to 1,000 feet. Prices are $425 adults and $325 children ages 6 to 12 (kids 5 and under not allowed).

WILDLIFE-WATCHING

National Elk Refuge ★   As cold temps and snow arrive, Jackson Hole's elk gather on the lower-elevation plains of the National Elk Refuge in a kind of 7,000-strong elk family reunion. You can watch thousands of the antlered animals tussle, forage, and, most often, just hang out in this protected space measuring 10 miles long and 6 miles wide at its fattest point. Besides essentially guaranteed elk sightings from December to April or May, you might spy bison, coyotes, bald eagles, trumpeter swans, and the occasional wolf.

You can drive the Refuge Road yourself, but the most fun way to see the refuge's wintering elk is on one of Double H Bar's hour-long winter **horse-drawn sleigh rides** ★. Pick up tickets at the National Elk Refuge & Greater Yellowstone Visitor Center at 532 N. Cache St. ($38 adults; $23 children 5–12; free for ages 4 and under), then hop the free shuttle to the departure point. Rides depart from 10am to 4pm daily and reservations are recommended (✆ **307/733-0277**).

Located 3 miles north of Jackson on U.S. Hwy. 26/89, main access in northeast Jackson on Broadway and National Elk Refuge Rd. www. fws.gov/refuge/national_elk. ✆ **307/733-9212.** Free admission. Visitor Center daily 9am–5pm.

Area Attractions

One could almost be forgiven for neglecting the actual destination—Grand Teton and Yellowstone—and getting caught up in Jackson's activities, shops, restaurants, and attractions. That's how lively this upscale mountain town is.

Town Square is a fine place to begin your Jackson explorations; show up at 6pm in summer and you'll be treated to a free Old West shootout reenactment from the chamber of commerce and Jackson Hole Playhouse (except Sun). Dig deeper into the lives of the Native Americans, ranchers, and homesteaders of Jackson Hole's past at **History Jackson Hole,** at 175 E. Broadway Ave. (www.jacksonholehistory. org; ✆ **307/733-2414**). Admission is $12 for adults, free for children 5 and under.

Astoria Hot Springs ★★   South of town by 25 minutes and a world away from Jackson's bustle, this tranquil hot springs retreat is tucked into the Snake River Canyon. What was once a simple community pool has been saved from private development by Astoria Park Conservancy and reimagined as a collection of steamy soakers. The smallest and hottest (101°F/38°C to 104°F/40°C) of the four pools sits closest to the river; there's also a larger, 101°F (38°C) leisure pool and a cooler children's pool. The hot springs opened in 2020, and now the park is working on a trail system across its 95 acres as well as wetland restoration and a nature playground. ***Bottom line:*** This is one of the best developed hot springs I've ever visited.

25 Johnny Counts Rd (16 miles south of Jackson on U.S. 89). www.astoriahotspringspark.org. © **307/201-5925.** Reservations highly recommended. $22 adults; $16 children 2–12; free for children 1 and under. Thurs–Tues 9am to 8pm.

Jackson Hole Aerial Tram ★ The same cherry-red tram that carries skiers to the top of Jackson Hole Mountain Resort's Rendezvous Mountain in winter remains in operation for hikers and sightseers in the warmer months—and though it's pricey, the 12-minute ride to 10,449 feet is one of Jackson's iconic thrills. You'll get unbeatable views of the Teton Range, Jackson, and the Snake River Valley from the new-in-2024 **Grand Teton Skywalk** viewing platform, plus easy access to a network of trails that dips into Grand Teton National Park and the Jedediah Smith Wilderness. At the top, **Corbet's Cabin** is a must-stop for loaded waffles (peanut butter and bacon or berry compote and whipped cream are popular toppings) and beer.

3395 Cody Lane, Teton Village. www.jacksonhole.com. © **307/733-2292.** Tickets $40/$50 seniors/adults; $32 children 5–17; free for children 4 and under. Mid-May to early Oct daily 9am–5pm.

National Museum of Wildlife Art ★★ This unique museum on a hill opposite the National Elk Refuge asks a provocative question: How do we see the animals that share our world? Well-curated galleries answer it with everything from 19th-century oil paintings of bighorn sheep and grizzlies to an outdoor sculpture trail. You'll find contributions from Carl Rungius, Georgia O'Keefe, Charles M. Russell, Henri Rousseau, and John Gutzon de la Mothe Borglum (of Mt. Rushmore fame).

2820 Rungius Rd. (3 miles north of town on U.S. 191). www.wildlifeart.org. © **307/733-5771.** $18 adults; $10 first child 5–18, $5 additional children; free for kids 4 and under. Daily 10am–5pm (closed Mon Nov–Apr).

Snow King Observatory & Planetarium ★ Stars, galaxies, solar flares, and nebulae await at this mountaintop observatory, which became the first such stargazing outfit at a North American ski resort when it opened in 2024. Daytime visitors can get a close-up of the sun's surface through a solar telescope and watch one of a rotating series of space

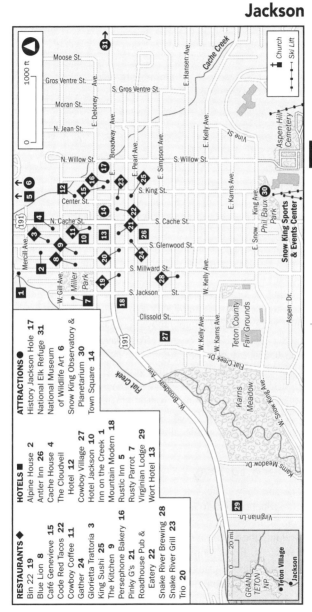

Jackson

RESTAURANTS ◆

Bin 22 **19**
Blue Lion **8**
Café Genevieve **15**
Code Red Tacos **22**
Cowboy Coffee **11**
Gather **24**
Glorietta Trattoria **3**
King Sushi **25**
The Kitchen **9**
Persephone Bakery **16**
Pinky G's **21**
Roadhouse Pub &
  Eatery **22**
Snake River Brewing **28**
Snake River Grill **23**
Trio **20**

HOTELS ■

Alpine House **2**
Antler Inn **26**
Cache House **4**
The Cloudveil
  Hotel **12**
Cowboy Village **27**
Hotel Jackson **10**
Inn on the Creek **1**
Mountain Modern **18**
Rustic Inn **5**
Rusty Parrot **7**
Virginian Lodge **29**
Wort Hotel **13**

ATTRACTIONS ●

History Jackson Hole **17**
National Elk Refuge **31**
National Museum
  of Wildlife Art **6**
Snow King Observatory &
  Planetarium **30**
Town Square **14**

movies in an immersive, dome-shaped theater. But after dark is when the place really comes alive, when you can peer at the heavens through the enormous, 1.0-meter PlaneWave telescope (and a number of smaller ones, too). It's a cool experience, but the attraction is small and very expensive, making it best for real astronomy buffs. *Tip:* Tickets are half-price if you skip the gondola ride and hike to the observatory, a very steep 1- to 3-hour endeavor (daytime only).

100 E. Snow King Ave. www.snowkingmountain.com. ℰ **307/201-5464.** Daytime $60 adults, $50 students; nighttime $125 adults, $100 students; both free for kids 5 and under. Daily 10am–5pm and 9–midnight.

ART GALLERIES

Jackson is home to more than 30 galleries, most of them clustered around Town Square. And while the town's reputation as a hotbed for Western art is well-deserved—you'll find soulful mustangs, romanticized cowboys and Native Americans, and bronze moose in droves—more surprising works pop up in some of the edgier galleries.

Rare Gallery, 55 N. Glenwood St. (www.raregallery jacksonhole.com; ℰ **307/733-8726**), features modern paintings, sculpture, and photography. **Maya Frodeman Gallery,** 66 S. Glenwood St. (www.mayafrodemangallery.com; ℰ **307/733-0555**), exhibits contemporary work from noted artists in a sleek space. **Two Grey Hills Indian Arts & Jewelry,** 110 E. Broadway (www.fineindianart.com; ℰ **307/733-2677**), showcases jewelry, pottery, rugs, and weavings from Southwest Indigenous artists. The **Jackson Hole Gallery Association** (www.jacksonholegalleryassociation.com) is a great resource.

Where to Stay

The good news: Jackson and Teton Village have no shortage of excellent places to lay your head. The bad news: It'll cost you. In high season, rates at even the mediocre hotels soar well into the $300s, and the finest properties can set you back thousands. Book rooms as early as possible and ask about reduced rates in spring and fall.

Downton Jackson's answer to a hostel is **Cache House,** 215 B. N. Cache St. (www.thecachehouse.com; ℰ **800/234-4507**), a tastefully decorated spot where $96 per night gets you a private cubby in a shared room. A couple of blocks off Town

Teton Village

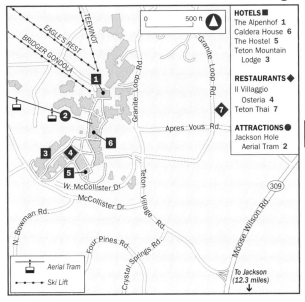

HOTELS ■
The Alpenhof **1**
Caldera House **6**
The Hostel **5**
Teton Mountain
  Lodge **3**

RESTAURANTS ◆
Il Villaggio
  Osteria **4**
Teton Thai **7**

ATTRACTIONS ●
Jackson Hole
  Aerial Tram **2**

8

GATEWAYS TO THE PARK

Jackson, Wyoming

Aerial Tram
●–●–● **Ski Lift**

Square, **Antler Inn,** 43 W. Pearl Ave. (www.townsquareinns. com; ⓒ **307/733-2535**), is a good bet, with a big hot tub and knotty wood bedframes. In summer, doubles range from $339 to $379 (it has suites, too). On the more luxurious side of the spectrum, **The Cloudveil Hotel,** 112 Center St. (www.the cloudveil.com; ⓒ **307/699-6100**), is one of downtown's most sophisticated options. High-season doubles start at $1,016.

On the north side, **Inn on the Creek,** 295 N. Millward St. (www.innonthecreek.com; ⓒ **307/739-1565**), is a cozy, country-style B&B on Flat Creek; room amenities might include fireplaces, patios, Jacuzzis, or kitchens. Summer doubles cost $429 and suites $469. **Rustic Inn,** 475 N. Cache St. (www.rusticinnatjh.com; ⓒ **800/323-9279**), sits on an aspen- and evergreen-shaded property against Saddle Butte and Flat Creek; the 12-acre space includes firepits and a tepee, plus a pool, sauna, and hot tub. Guest rooms ($469–$619 doubles), stand-alone cabins ($489–$629), and spa suites ($1,129–$2,179) are luxe. And **Bentwood Inn** in Wilson, 4250 Raven Haven Rd. (www.bentwoodinn.com;

© **307/739-1411**), feels more like bunking in a chic friend's home than a hotel. There's a kick-back lounge, front porch, and home-cooked breakfasts plus three-course dinners. Doubles go for $609 to $649.

IN JACKSON

Alpine House ★★   This intimate, Scandinavian-style inn just might be the friendliest lodging in town. With 22 unique rooms, a library with a crackling fireplace, and a sunny atrium where the chef serves eggs Benedict and homemade granola for breakfast, Alpine House is more B&B than hotel. Every room is different, but all share a bright white color scheme, blond wood, and touches such as antique furniture or lofted beds. Perks include free use of cruiser bikes.

285 N. Glenwood St. www.alpinehouse.com. © **307/201-5535.** 22 units. $474–$678 double; $914–$974 suite. Rates include full breakfast. Lower rates Oct–May. **Amenities:** Sauna; gym; free Wi-Fi.

Cowboy Village Resort ★   Set slightly apart from the bustle of downtown, this unassuming complex has the feel of a summer camp—except *these* cabins come with comfy beds and cable TV. The mostly small but nicely decorated log cabins all have kitchenettes, private bathrooms, and pullout couches; some options have two rooms. Of the two lodge rooms, one is a family suite with bunk beds and a full kitchen.

120 S. Flat Creek Dr. www.townsquareinns.com. © **307/733-3121.** 84 units. $400–$530 lodge; $404–$504 cabin. Rates include continental breakfast (winter only). Lower rates in winter. **Amenities:** Pool; Jacuzzi; gym; business center; free ski shuttle to Teton Village (winter); free Wi-Fi.

Hotel Jackson ★★★   If you're looking for the coolest lodging in town, this is it: From the walls paneled with salvaged Wyoming barnwood to the custom-photo-printed curtains and pillows, every meticulously considered design detail here comes together perfectly. Rooms in this LEED-certified boutique hotel are done up in a chic brown-and-white palette and include gas fireplaces; some have mountain views, and suites include private patios and soaking tubs. The restaurant, **Figs,** serves creative Mediterranean fare.

120 N. Glenwood St. www.hoteljackson.com. © **307/733-2200.** 55 units. $1,449–$1,549 double; $1,789–$2,389 suite. Lower rates fall–spring. **Amenities:** Restaurant; hot tub; gym; free ski shuttle to Teton Village (winter); free Wi-Fi.

Mountain Modern ★   It may bill itself as a motel, but a bare-bones road stop this ain't. Rooms in this sprawling complex a few blocks from Town Square are done up with subway tile, lumberjack plaids, and oversize photos of mountains or bison, and all have storage space for extra gear. Suites are particularly cushy, with fireplaces, balconies, and full kitchens, and some rooms have bunk beds. There are two pools and two hot tubs (one indoor, one outdoor) to choose from, plus three on-site restaurants serving Korean, BBQ, and American dishes.

380 W. Broadway. www.mountainmodernmotel.com. ✆ **307/733-4340.** 194 units. $569–$629 double; $769–$1,369 suite. Lower rates fall–spring. **Amenities:** 3 restaurants; 2 pools; 2 hot tubs; firepit; free Wi-Fi.

Rusty Parrot ★★   The 2019 fire that gutted this charming, family-owned lodge couldn't keep the Parrot down—in 2024, the hotel reopened with an updated look but its original warm spirit intact. Some of the tasteful guest rooms (think wildlife sketches on the walls and leather furniture) have fireplaces and balconies, and suites add sitting rooms. The Body Sage Spa is also back, offering massage, facials, and yoga sessions, and the 48-seat **Wild Sage Restaurant** focuses on local fare. For anyone seeking a friendly, pampering stay in Jackson, it's a welcome resurrection indeed.

175 N. Jackson St. www.rustyparrot.com. ✆ **888/739-1749.** 40 units. $995–$1,095 double; $1,585–$1,695 suite. Lower rates fall–spring. **Amenities:** Restaurant; lounge; spa; hot tub; firepit; free ski shuttle to Teton Village (winter); free Wi-Fi.

Virginian Lodge ★   A Jackson institution since 1965, the Virginian got a major makeover in 2022. Don't worry, the midcentury-modern charm is still intact—but now you'll find rain showers and comfy pillowtop mattresses along with the retro furniture. The motor lodge–style hotel features perhaps the best courtyard in Jackson, with a heated pool, two hot tubs, and shared firepits with a mountain view. Other on-site perks include a saloon, burger joint, bottle shop, and an outdoor adventure center. Doubles are simple yet upscale, while the suites add sitting rooms, kitchenettes, or family-friendly bunk beds. The Virginian also has an RV park.

750 W. Broadway. www.outboundhotels.com/the-virginian. ✆ **307/733-2792.** 160 units. $597–$667 double; $657–$867 suite. Lower rates fall–spring. **Amenities:** Restaurant; lounge; burger joint; liquor store; outdoor adventure center; pool; Jacuzzi; free Wi-Fi.

Wort Hotel ★★★ Part elegant historic hotel, part art gallery, and part lively bar/music space, the Wort Hotel is one of a kind. The stately stone building in the center of downtown has been hosting guests since the family of late-19th-century homesteader Charles Wort opened it in 1941, and it remains one of Jackson's iconic buildings. The lobby is filled with some 200 paintings, sculptures, furniture, and photos, and a grand staircase leads to one of two cozy fireplaces. Rooms are in "New West" style, with leather chairs and cowboy-themed art, and some have wet bars; the Grand Rooms and suites are enormous (the Silver Dollar Suite is 1,100 sq. ft.), with sitting areas and posh bathrooms. The hotel's **Silver Dollar Bar** is a Jackson institution, named for the 2,032 silver dollars inlaid in the bar.

50 N. Glenwood St. (at Broadway). www.worthotel.com. © **307/733-2190.** 55 units. $869–$1,014 double; $1,013–$2,691 suite. Lower rates fall–spring. **Amenities:** Restaurant; lounge; gym; Jacuzzi; business center; free ski shuttle to Teton Village (winter); free Wi-Fi.

NEAR JACKSON

Fireside Resort ★ If you're into ultramodern architecture, you'll love this collection of sleek, wooden, modular cabins on wheels on the highway between Jackson and Teton Village. Each LEED-certified cabin features a fireplace, full kitchen, small deck, pullout couch, and cool furniture (pony-print ottomans, iron-accented coffee tables). A few have lofts with platform beds. Firepits provide still more hangout space, and the creek winding through the property makes for frequent moose sightings. There's also an RV park on-site ($105–$135 per night), and you can arrange for rental jeeps and RVs through the resort.

2780 N. Moose Wilson Rd., Wilson. www.firesidejacksonhole.com. © **307/733-1177.** 25 units. $579–$769 cabin (2-night min. in summer). Lower rates fall and spring. **Amenities:** Firepits; free Wi-Fi.

Jackson Hole Hideout ★★ Though it's just 15 minutes from downtown Jackson, this delightful B&B on the top of a steep, winding forest road feels a world away. With its many edges, corners, nooks, and crannies, the sprawling inn resembles the Burrow, the Weasley House of Harry Potter fame. Each plush room has a private bathroom, and all but one have a private deck with valley views (the Wrangler Room even has a swing). An outdoor firepit and indoor fireplace offer cozy corners for lounging. The tasty breakfast menu might include skillets, waffles, or bread pudding French toast, and the house provides essentials like bear spray, sunscreen, and trekking poles.

6175 Heck of a Hill Rd., Wilson. www.jacksonholehideout.com. 𝄐 **307/733-3233.** 5 units. $359–$799 double, includes breakfast (3-night min.). Lower rates fall–spring. **Amenities:** Free Wi-Fi.

Spring Creek Ranch ★★★

For a positively opulent experience, look up—about 1,000 feet above the valley floor, where Spring Creek Ranch sits atop East Gros Ventre Butte, on a 1,000-acre wildlife sanctuary. The Teton views are incredible, and you might even spot deer or moose wandering past your windows. Accommodations range from deluxe (rooms with fireplaces and balconies) to lavish (one- to four-bedroom townhomes with sunken living rooms and fancy full kitchens) to sumptuous (mountain villas that start at 4,000-plus sq. ft.). The resort can help plan guided hiking, climbing, and rafting excursions, and there are on-site horseback riding stables and naturalist programs.

1600 N. East Butte Rd., Jackson (on top of the East Gros Ventre Butte). www.springcreekranch.com. 𝄐 **307/733-8833.** 75 units. $495 double; $445–$3,400 condo or home. Lower rates fall–spring. **Amenities:** Jacuzzi; pool; spa; gym; tennis; firepit; free area shuttle; free Wi-Fi.

IN TETON VILLAGE

You can take advantage of the attractions of Jackson, to the south, and Grand Teton, to the north, without suffering the crowds by journeying to Teton Village, which is approximately equidistant from both. Located at the foot of Jackson Hole Mountain Resort, the village and surrounding area offer several fine dining establishments, and activities nearby include skiing, ballooning, and hiking in Grand Teton National Park. During winter months, this is the center of activity in the valley. While lodging in the town of Jackson tends to be significantly cheaper in the winter than the summer, Teton Village is reversed—rooms by the ski hill often get more expensive after the snow falls. For a wide range of basic condos and deluxe vacation homes, contact **Jackson Hole Resort Lodging** (www.jhrl.com; 𝄐 **307/732-3655**) or check out Airbnb's numerous options.

The Alpenhof ★★

Teton Village's oldest and most unique lodge has been bringing a touch of Bavarian flavor to the mountain since 1965. The lodge's original owners were Swiss and German, and they designed the Alpenhof to echo the country inns of the Alps: gingerbread-house balusters, fireplaces, and ornately carved wooden beams. The in-house **Alpenrose** (winter only) serves up all manner of strudels, schnitzels, and fondues. Rooms are all a little different, featuring Bavarian-style furnishings and stenciled art on the walls; some have their own fireplaces and/or balconies. Suites have roomy decks.

3255 W. Village Dr. www.alpenhoflodge.com. ✆ **307/733-3242.** 42 units. $647–$923 double; $1,140–$1,810 suite. Lower rates spring and fall. Closed Nov and Apr. **Amenities:** 2 restaurants (1 in summer); lounge; Jacuzzi; pool; sauna; spa; ski shop; free Wi-Fi.

Caldera House ★★★

Hitting the slopes with friends or extended family? This ultra-posh boutique retreat next door to the ski resort's aerial tram is hands-down the best home away from home for groups. Suites sleep up to 12 in a combination of king bedrooms and kid-perfect bunk rooms and plentiful bathrooms; the living rooms are spacious and include media retreats, making for ample hangout space. The eight opulently decorated suites feature warm, modern, Western-meets-Scandi furniture and linens, and feature patios and fireplaces. Depending on the suite, you might also enjoy mountain views, firepits, and private hot tubs. The in-house concierge can set you up with adventures; upon your return, unwind in the heated infinity pool or order an in-room hot-stone massage. Enjoy a meal at the on-site **Corsa** Italian trattoria, or invite a chef to your rooms to prepare a private meal. You'll sleep like a movie star—but when you split the rates among multiple families, the splurge becomes almost manageable.

3275 W. Village Dr. www.calderahouse.com. ✆ **307/200-4220.** 8 units. $7,000–$10,000 2-bedroom suite; $12,000–$20,000 4-bedroom suite (7-night min. peak winter season). Rates include breakfast. Lower rates spring–fall. **Amenities:** 2 restaurants; spa; sauna; pool; gym; concierge; ski shop; free Wi-Fi.

The Hostel ★

Ski-bum paradise meets European-style travelers' hub in this low-key lodge. Considering its prime location just steps from the ski mountain, it's shockingly affordable, and by far the best value in Teton Village. All rooms are private, some with a king bed and some with four twins (plus bathrooms). When not out playing, guests gather in a lively common area reminiscent of a 1970s rec room, with board games, table tennis, foosball, and comfy couches, as well as flatscreen TVs and DVD players. The lodge has a ski waxing station and ski storage, and in summer, barbecue grills next to a small brook.

3315 Village Dr. www.thehostel.us. ✆ **307/733-3415.** 58 units. $99–$269 double/private quad. Lower rates spring and fall. **Amenities:** Free Wi-Fi.

Teton Mountain Lodge ★★ Checking in to this classy hotel, which was renovated in 2024, is like stepping into your favorite mountain living magazine: With wooden beams and a stone fireplace meeting mod-style furniture, the decor walks the line between rustic lodge and city condo. Room options are cozy, all with jetted tubs and granite countertops and some with fireplaces and kitchenettes; two- and three-bedroom suites offer plenty of space to spread out. On-site perks include a large indoor pool (and an outdoor one), five hot tubs (the adults-only rooftop one fits 15), a spa, and a ski valet. Extremely personable service is the cherry on top.

3385 Cody Lane. www.tetonlodge.com. ✆ **307/201-6066.** 145 units. $821–$931 double; $940–$2,081 suite. Lower rates spring and fall. **Amenities:** Restaurant; lounge; concierge; gym; 5 Jacuzzis; 2 pools; spa; free Wi-Fi.

Where to Eat

Jackson has more quality restaurants than you'd ever fit into a single vacation. Yes, options tend to be upscale and pricey, but you can also find a few gems in the casual category. This is a meat town, so expect all kinds of steak, elk, and bison to hold down the local menus, plus other locally sourced ingredients and even seafood. For a quick breakfast, try **Cowboy Coffee Co.,** 125 N. Cache St. (www.cowboycoffee.com; ✆ **307/733-7392**), for egg sandwiches and huckleberry espresso drinks, or the James Beard semifinalist **Persephone Bakery,** 145 E. Broadway (www.persephonebakery.com; ✆ **307/200-6708**), a purveyor of delicate pastries, rustic breads, and hot sandwiches.

EXPENSIVE

The Blue Lion ★★ NEW AMERICAN   Homey and cozy, this Jackson institution has occupied the same 1930s home since it opened in 1978. Tables are grouped under stained-glass windows, and in summer, the shady front patio hosts live acoustic music. The place is known for its rack of lamb, elk and beef tenderloins, and sautéed fish. The French onion soup appetizer and Russian cream with raspberries dessert are standouts.

160 N. Millward St. www.bluelionrestaurant.com. © **307/733-3912.** Reservations recommended. Main courses $28–$66. Summer daily 5:30–10pm; hours may be reduced in winter.

Gather ★★ NEW AMERICAN   This community favorite combines a casual, welcoming spirit with seriously great food. Inside the midcentury modern–meets–industrial chic restaurant, you'll find a little bit of everything on the menu, from classics like fried chicken to Korean-style rib-eye, elk bolognese, and sweet corn curry (and the staff are quick to recommend the pork buns and crispy Brussels sprouts). The wine and cocktail lists are both impressive.

72 S. Glenwood St. www.gatherjh.com. © **307/264-1820.** Reservations recommended. Main courses $24–$54. Daily 5pm–close.

Glorietta Trattoria ★★ ITALIAN   Downtown Jackson's upscale Italian spot is made for lingering—and if the unfussy country kitchen atmosphere doesn't keep you here, the food will. Fresh antipasti and *primi* like eggplant caponata, bone marrow, and calamari provide the first act, while handmade pastas with accompaniments like local mushrooms, pork ragu, and kale pesto headline the menu. Other stars on the menu include wood-fired bison teres major (a tender shoulder cut) or Idaho trout. *Bonus:* The team behind New York City's legendary bar Death & Co designed the inventive cocktail menu.

242 Glenwood St. www.gloriettajackson.com. © **307/733-3888.** Reservations recommended. Main courses $27–$72. Daily 5–10pm.

Il Villaggio Osteria ★★ ITALIAN   This high-end pizza and pasta spot brings a true taste of Italy to Teton Village. Inspired by the community-focused restaurants of the Italian countryside, this one features indulgent freshly made pastas; mains like bison short ribs, salmon with romanesco, and roasted Cornish chicken; wood-fired pizzas topped with the likes of dried figs, bechamel, and salumi; and inventive antipasti. The wine list is long and varied, with plenty of Italian bottles, and the cocktail menu is creative.

In the Hotel Terra, 3335 W. Village Dr., Teton Village. www.jhosteria. com. © **307/739-4100.** Main courses $15–$32 brunch; $18–$68 dinner. Daily 7am–close.

King Sushi ★★ JAPANESE   Exquisite fish in landlocked Jackson? This intimate spot will make you a believer. Settle into one of the handful of tables or bar stools in this tiny log cabin (reservations are a must) and flex your chopsticks skills on King's elaborate sashimi and house rolls. Basic sushi rolls starring tuna and salmon are available, but the specialty options are where it's at: Try concoctions featuring lobster claw and Wagyu beef, salmon with mango and hamachi, or scallops and yuzo chili aioli. Creative versions of Japanese classics like pork belly ramen and tempura shrimp round out the menu, and sake and bright cocktails make fine accompaniments.

75 S. King St. www.kingsushijh.com. ⓒ **307/264-1630.** Reservations recommended. Main courses and rolls $18–$42. Tues–Sun 4:30–9pm.

Snake River Grill ★★★ NEW AMERICAN   This rustic-yet-fancy restaurant on Town Square is all about consistency: A mainstay of the dining scene since 1993, it's perennially touted as the town's best restaurant by adoring locals and travelers alike. The inventive eats are wide-ranging: You might start with Hamachi crudo or the famous steak tartare pizza, then move on to Wagyu flank steak or roasted duck breast. The ice cream bars with caramel dipping sauce are longtime favorites. The wine list has more than 200 choices, and a great cocktail menu includes zero-proof sips.

84 E. Broadway (on Town Square). www.snakerivergrill.com. ⓒ **307/733-0557.** Reservations recommended. Main courses $29–$205. Mon–Wed 5–9pm; Thurs–Sat 5–9:30pm. Closed Nov and Apr.

Trio ★★ NEW AMERICAN   Jackson's dining scene can be a web of interconnections, with top chefs hopping between restaurants or opening their own hot spots. So it is with Trio, started by three chefs from the excellent Snake River Grill (one is still at Trio's helm). This spinoff is now one of the best upscale restaurants in town. Dishes tend toward well-executed classics such as steak with fingerling potatoes or pork chops, with a few surprises (snap pea risotto, game sausage pasta), plus a selection of pizzas. Locals rave about the waffle fries, topped with bleu cheese fondue and scallions.

45 S. Glenwood St. www.bistrotrio.com. ⓒ **307/734-8038.** Reservations recommended. Main courses $21–$48. Mon–Sat 5pm–close.

MODERATE

Bin 22 ★★ TAPAS   Co-owner Gavin Fine (a sommelier and co-owner of the Kitchen, Roadhouse Pub, and Il Villaggio Osteria, to name a few) envisioned Bin 22 as a one-stop shop: a laid-back place to pick up a bottle of wine and a few groceries as well as sit down to Spanish- and Italian-style small plates. Choose a bottle from the well-stocked wine shop (or order from the beer and cocktail menu) and take it to your table to pair with tasty tapas: salumi, cheeses, and excellent shareables such as grilled octopus, pork belly bravas, and the fresh mozzarella with several toppings.

200 W. Broadway. www.bin22jacksonhole.com. ⓒ **307/739-9463.** Shared plates $8–$35. Daily 10am–10pm.

Café Genevieve ★★ NEW AMERICAN/SOUTHERN The log cabin housing this welcoming cafe doesn't just look old, it *is* old: Early settlers built it in the early 1900s. The cafe serves Southern-inspired food with local, seasonal flair. Every day starts with a hearty brunch (until 3pm) of fried chicken and waffles and Cajun eggs Benedict. Lunch, from 10:30am, consists of soups, salads, and burgers. Do sample the cafe's specialty, pig candy: candied bacon crumbled over a salad or served as an appetizer. The patio offers fine alfresco dining in summer.

135 E. Broadway. www.genevievejh.com. ⓒ **307/732-1910.** Main courses $16–$22 brunch; $14–$24 lunch. Daily 8am–3pm.

The Kitchen ★★ NEW AMERICAN   Visiting the Kitchen is a bit like dining inside a warm, inviting spaceship, thanks to the streamlined architecture and curved wall aglow with soft lighting. One of Jackson's favorite restaurants, the Kitchen serves artfully presented dishes that draw from various culinary influences, from Asian to Mountain West. Seafood plays a major role, from the raw bar to entrees of salmon with fennel compote and scallops. It's a nice mix of classics (burgers, pork chops) and more fanciful dishes (wild mushroom ramen, miso duck breast). Take your pick from a long list of cocktails, sake, and wines by the glass.

155 N. Glenwood St. www.thekitchenjacksonhole.com. ⓒ **307/734-1633.** Reservations recommended. Main courses $23–$47. Tues–Sat 5:30pm–close (usually 9:30pm).

Roadhouse Pub & Eatery ★★ MICROBREWERY   This unusually delicious pub was born when Gavin Fine (of Jackson restaurant juggernaut Fine Dining Group fame) and local home brewer Colby Cox teamed up to create a beer joint with culinary flair. The result serves an eclectic mix of sandwiches, flatbreads, and intriguing entrees such as moo shu pork lettuce wraps and Korean fried chicken. Then there's the beer—a fun mix of a half-dozen IPAs, plus pilsners, golden ales, Belgians, and a few guest taps. Tuck into it all in the industrial-chic, upper-level space, or grab a spot on the patio overlooking Town Square. Bonus points for Roadhouse: It's a certified B Corp with sustainability built into its manufacturing.

20 E. Broadway. www.roadhousebrewery.com. © **307/739-0700.** Main courses $18–$33. Daily 11:30am–9pm.

INEXPENSIVE

Code Red Tacos ★ MEXICAN   When the newest member of the Fine Dining Group family opened in 2023, it brought a welcome change of pace to fancy bistro-heavy Town Square. The casual, East LA–style taqueria specializes in a la carte tacos in flavors like beef birria, citrus-braised pork, and elk carne asada, all swaddled in house-made tortillas. But you'll also find burritos, loaded bowls of pozole, and rice bowls, with a long beer list and tequila/mezcal cocktails to sweeten the deal.

20 E. Broadway. www.coderedtacos.com. © **307/249-3015.** Tacos $5–$6; main courses $12–$18. Daily 10am–10pm.

Nora's Fish Creek Inn ★ AMERICAN   Jackson Hole breathed a collective sigh of relief when two local restauranteurs rescued this beloved brunch spot from closing, launching a reimagined Nora's in 2022. Don't worry, the huevos rancheros and banana bread French toast are still here (as is the giant trout on the roof), and the homey log cabin vibes didn't change. The rest of the breakfast menu is equally hearty: trout and eggs, chicken-fried steak, biscuits and gravy. New lunch and dinner menus take an upscale turn; think prime rib, chicken pot pie, and trout amandine, plus pizza.

5600 W. Wyo. 22, Wilson. www.norasfishcreekinn.com. © **307/733-7662.** Main courses $7–$26 breakfast; $13–$24 lunch; $22–$54 dinner. Daily 6:30am–2pm, 5–9pm.

Pinky G's ★ PIZZA   Sometimes all you need is a New York–style slice served on a piece of waxed paper—or a whole pie, for that matter. Build your own or go for one of the specialty pizzas, such as the Abe Froman (Italian sausage and fresh mozzarella) or the Flyin' Hawaiian (pineapple, ham, and jalapeños). You'll also find salads and calzones. Exposed brick walls and neon signs give the place a hip, casual vibe; the full bar helps, too.

50 W. Broadway. www.pinkygs.com. ✆ **307/734-7465.** Pizzas $22–$35. Sun–Wed 11am–9pm; Thurs–Sat 11am–10pm.

Snake River Brewing ★★ MICROBREWERY   First-rate beers, and food that's a significant cut above your average pub fare—is it any wonder this casual brewery is hopping most nights? Jacksonites pack the place to scarf down rich pastas, loaded pizzas, burgers, fish-and-chips, and an impressive array of hearty salads and starters. Wash it down with one of their popular beers: The Jenny Lake Lager, Snake River Pale Ale, and Pako's IPA have all taken home awards. A dog-friendly lawn and live music make this a family-friendly place to spend an evening.

265 S. Millward St. www.snakeriverbrewing.com. ✆ **307/739-2337.** Main courses $16–$30. Daily 7am–11pm.

Teton Thai ★ THAI   Five-alarm flavor devotees love this family-owned joint in Teton Village for its very spicy options (milder palates won't want to go past 2 on the spice scale), while everyone appreciates its summer patio. The extensive menu features Thai classics, from stir-fries to noodles to soups to curries; meat options include crispy duck on top of the usual proteins and veggies. Also look for starters such as fried tofu, chicken satay, and egg rolls. The bar menu offers sake and tropical cocktails along with beer and wine.

7342 Granite Loop Rd., Teton Village. www.tetonthaivillage.com. ✆ **307/733-0022.** Main courses $13–$28 lunch; $24–$36 dinner. Mon–Sat noon–9pm.

Jackson After Dark

Jackson packs a whole lot of culture into a small mountain town. It's always worth checking out what's going on at the **Center for the Arts,** 240 S. Glenwood St. (www.jhcenterforthearts.org; ✆ **307/734-8956**), a nonprofit, shared community arts campus. The complex includes a 500-seat theater and puts on dance performances, art shows, writing workshops, live music, and lectures.

In summer, the **Grand Teton Music Festival** (www.gtmf. org; ✆ **307/733-1128;** box office during the festival) showcases talent from all over the country, plus Canada. The classical music celebration extends for 8 weeks, with performances taking place in an amphitheater in Teton Village. Tickets range from about $30 to $85 (ages 17 and under get $5 tickets). Find still more live music at the summer weekly free ($5 suggested donation) **Music on Main** shows in Victor, Idaho (www.tetonvalleyfoundation.org; ✆ **208/399-2884**).

As for the local bar scene, the **Million Dollar Cowboy Bar,** 25 N. Cache St. (www.milliondollarcowboybar.com; ✆ **307/733-2207**), is Jackson's quintessential watering hole. The bar stools are saddles, the pillars knotty pine, and the scene raucous, thanks to frequent live country-music shows and dancing—what's not to love? Fuel up for the night at the excellent **Million Dollar Cowboy Steakhouse,** located under the bar. For a more chill vibe, **Sidewinders American Grill,** 945 W. Broadway (www.sidewinderstavern.com; ✆ **307/734-5766**), is the town's favorite sports bar, with 30 flatscreen TVs and 24 beers on tap. And you can't go wrong at the **Stagecoach Bar,** 5755 W. Hwy. 22 (www.stagecoachbar.net; ✆ **307/733-4407**), Wilson's favored place to party since 1942. Thursday nights bring a disco dance-a-thon, and every Sunday, the Stagecoach Band gets the crowd dancing to country-western tunes.

CODY, WYOMING ★★

53 miles from the east entrance to Yellowstone

Welcome to the Wild West: More than any other Yellowstone gateway town, Cody has staked its identity on keeping the bygone era of frontier cowboys alive and kicking. No wonder, considering the town's history: The famed Old West entertainer William F. "Buffalo Bill" Cody helped found the place in the 1890s, and his work securing a railroad stop and dam spurred the town's growth. Today, that Wild West flavor permeates Cody, from the main drag shootout reenactments to the rebuilt historic Old Trail Town to the thousands of cowboy hats and belt buckles you'll spy downtown.

Set in the gorgeous Bighorn Basin and ringed by three mountain sub-ranges (the Bighorns, Absarokas, and Owl Creeks), this area would be an outdoor haven even without its proximity to Yellowstone. The Shoshone River flows right through town, and the 50-mile scenic drive from Cody through the Wapiti Valley to Yellowstone is the second-most visually stunning way to approach the park. Number one? That'd be the Chief Joseph Scenic Byway, a 17-mile stretch beginning just north of Cody and climbing high into the gorgeous Absaroka Mountains to link up with the Beartooth Highway and Yellowstone's Northeast Entrance. After you're through playing outside, Cody makes a primo basecamp for browsing Western art galleries, catching a rodeo, and checking out a collection of stellar museums.

Essentials

For info on air service to Cody and rental-car agencies, see "Getting There & Getting Around" in chapter 10.

GETTING THERE   Cody is a 4-hour, 177-mile drive from Jackson if you take U.S. 89 north and U.S. 14/16/20 east through Yellowstone; it's another hour if you go via U.S. 26 east and WY 120 west outside the park borders (which you'll have to do fall through early summer). From Sheridan, it's 147 miles and 3 hours away on U.S. 14 west. If you're traveling from Cheyenne, take I-25 north and U.S. 20 west 392 miles and nearly 6 hours to get to Cody. Winter storms can quickly make the roads treacherous: Call ✆ **888/996-7623,** or 511 (in state) for road and travel information. Online, visit **www.wyoroad.info**.

VISITOR INFORMATION   The visitor center at the **Cody Chamber of Commerce,** 836 Sheridan Ave. (www.codychamber.org; ✆ **307/587-2777**), is open daily 8am to 7pm in summer (to 5pm fall–spring). The **Park County Travel Council** (www.codyyellowstone.org; ✆ **800/393-2639**) is another great source of info.

Getting Outside

The very best outdoor recreation opportunities around Cody are in Yellowstone itself. Beyond that, the **Shoshone National Forest** lies between the park and town and offers trails that grant access to the North Absaroka and Washakie wildernesses, plus some peaceful campgrounds along the

North Fork of the Shoshone River. Closer to town, there's **Buffalo Bill State Park,** a small preserve on the shores of **Buffalo Bill Reservoir.** If water sports such as boating, fishing, waterskiing, and windsurfing are your thing, it's well worth a stop; two campgrounds accommodate RVs, and waterfront picnic areas abound. In winter, **Sleeping Giant Ski Area** attracts local alpine skiers, Nordic fans glide several groomed trails, and ice climbers flock to the South Fork Valley. **Sunlight Sports,** 1131 Sheridan Ave. (www.sunlight sports.com; ✆ **307/587-9517**), carries camping, climbing, and skiing equipment plus rentals. **Sierra Trading Post,** 1402 8th St. (www.sierra.com; ✆ **307/578-5802**), sells top-brand gear and apparel for steep discounts.

Several Cody outfitters also run tours into Yellowstone, which are great for people who don't want to deal with mountain driving over Sylvan Pass or high-season traffic hassles in the park. Among them are **Cody Wyoming Adventures** (www.codywyomingadventures.com; ✆ **307/587-6988**), **Experience Yellowstone Tours** (www.experience yellowstonetours.com; ✆ **844/262-9160**), and **Grub Steak Expeditions** (www.tourtoyellowstone.com; ✆ **307/527-6316**). Expect to pay anywhere from $229 to $800, depending on tour length and type.

CLIMBING   The canyon of the Shoshone River on the way to Yellowstone is a magnet for rock and ice climbers, offering routes from rookie-friendly to challenging. **Montana Alpine Guides** (www.mtalpine.com; ✆ **406/586-8430**) runs ice climbs in winter starting at $250/day.

FISHING   Trout-laden waters and dependable solitude make Cody an angling heaven. Fly-fishing is tops on the easy-access **Shoshone River,** including its **North Fork** and **South Fork.** The **Clark's Fork of the Yellowstone,** Wyoming's only designated Wild and Scenic River, is another favorite. About 80 miles south of town, the slow-moving **Big Horn River** appeals to beginners. Boat anglers cast into the waters of **Buffalo Bill Reservoir,** home to lake trout, browns, cutthroats, and rainbows. **North Fork Anglers,** 1107 Sheridan Ave., Unit A (www.northforkanglers.com; ✆ **307/527-7274**), carries all the equipment you'll need and can lead you right to the fish on a variety of guided trips, from floats to riverside strolls. Rates start at $500–$575 for a half-day trip.

FLOAT TRIPS/RAFTING The supremely scenic and relatively mild (most sections are Class II or III on a six-point scale) **Shoshone River** makes Cody a fine place to get out on the water. The long-standing outfitter **Wyoming River Trips,** 233 Yellowstone Ave. (www.wyomingrivertrips.com; ✆ **307/ 587-6661**), guides scenic rafting trips in the lovely Red Rock Canyon, the Lower Canyon, and the North Fork. **River Runners of Wyoming,** 730 Yellowstone Ave. (www.riverrunners ofwyoming.com; ✆ **307/527-7238**), also offers floats in Red Rock Canyon and the North Fork. Trips range from $47 to $142.

HIKING Cody has no shortage of excellent trails nearby. Closer to town, hoof up the steep **Sheep Mountain** or **Heart Mountain** trails for big views of the Bighorn Mountains. The **Shoshone National Forest** also offers several hikes along mountain creeks, into wildlife-packed basins, and up to the high-elevation Beartooth Plateau.

SKIING **Sleeping Giant Ski Area,** 348 North Fork Hwy. (www.skisg.com; ✆ **307/587-3125**), is a fraction of the size of the resorts around Jackson, but lift tickets also cost a fraction ($70) of what you'd pay there. This two-lift operation is a great spot for families. Cross-country skiers find almost 12 miles of track at **North Fork Nordic Trails,** 183 North Fork Hwy. (www.pcnsawy.org), near Pahaska Tepee Resort, just outside Yellowstone's east entrance.

SNOWMOBILING Private permits for snowmobiling inside Yellowstone are tough to get, so sledding on a guided tour is often your best bet. **Gary Fales Outfitting,** 2750 North Fork Hwy. (www.garyfalesoutfitting.com; ✆ **307/587-3970**), is the only Cody-area park concessionaire and leads day trips among the geysers and in the Canyon area; trips cost $400 per double snowmobile. DIY sledders can explore an extensive trail network in the Beartooth Mountains, the Bighorns, the Wyoming Range, and along the Continental Divide; check the **Wyoming State Trails Program** website (https://wyospcr.wyo.gov) for trail maps.

WINDSURFING Wyoming's strong winds make the 8-mile-long, 4-mile-wide **Buffalo Bill Reservoir** a popular windsurfing destination. It's best experienced from June to September. A boat ramp is near the campground on the north side of the reservoir, just off U.S. Hwy. 14/16/20. *Note:* BYO windsurfing board; no one in the area rents them at this time.

Special Events

The five museums of the **Buffalo Bill Center of the West** (www.centerofthewest.org; ✆ **307/587-4771**) hold several fun, fascinating events during the year. Tops among them is the September **Rendezvous Royale,** a Western art show and auction with lectures and workshops. Contact the center for details. If you've never been to a rodeo (and even if you have), don't miss the annual **Cody Stampede Rodeo** (www. codystampederodeo.com; ✆ **307/587-5155**) leading up to the Fourth of July: It's a classic Western good time, with a parade, craft fair, and plenty of ropin' and ridin'.

Seeing the Sights

Buffalo Bill Center of the West ★★★   Undeniably the top attraction in Cody (and one of the state's best cultural centers), this complex of five museums can absorb you for an entire day. The center is affiliated with the Smithsonian and interprets the story of the American West through the lens of science, art, history, and culture.

The **Buffalo Bill Museum ★★** is the complex's flagship, and it has come a long way since its humble beginnings as a log cabin in 1927. Trace the life, work, and family of William F. "Buffalo Bill" Cody, the famous Army scout, frontiersman, entertainer, and entrepreneur; exhibits include footage of his Wild West Show and personal artifacts. Get up close to the flora and fauna of the Greater Yellowstone Ecosystem at the **Draper Natural History Museum ★★★**, which features everything from the tiny pika to the enormous grizzly bear. Staff naturalists and interactive exhibits bring the region to life—stop by here before your Yellowstone trip, if possible. At the **Whitney Western Art Museum ★★**, giant bronze elk share space with paintings and prints from both contemporary and historically significant artists, including Albert Bierstadt, Thomas Moran, and Charles M. Russell, for a look at the landscapes, animals, people, and legends that make up the Western art genre. The highly interactive **Plains Indian Museum ★★** displays beautiful examples of beadwork, headdresses, and moccasins. Listening booths and videos delve into what life is like for modern tribal members, too. The renovated-in-2019 **Cody Firearms Museum ★** has 7,000-plus guns, the world's most comprehensive collection of American firearms. Exhibits trace the evolution of weapons, from a 650 B.C.–era crossbow to Colts to modern examples; explain the science of firing a gun; and pay homage to famous gun designers.

Special exhibits, a research library, educational programs, and demos (like the popular live raptor show) complete the experience. The small cafe and coffee bar can be revitalizing should museum overload set in.

720 Sheridan Ave. www.centerofthewest.org. ✆ **307/587-4771.** $23 adults; $16 children 6–17; free for kids 5 and under. Admission is good for 2 consecutive days. May to mid-Sept daily 8am–6pm; mid-Sept to Oct daily 8am–5pm; Nov daily 10am–5pm; Dec–Feb Thurs–Sun 10am–5pm; Mar–Apr daily 10am–5pm.

Buffalo Bill Dam & Visitor Center ★

Stand on the top of the 325-foot Buffalo Bill Dam to watch the North Fork of the Shoshone River unfurl at your feet, winding its way through a canyon toward Cody. Completed in 1910, the Buffalo Bill Dam supports irrigation projects in the Bighorn Basin—and forms **Buffalo Bill Reservoir,** an oasis for boating, windsurfing, and fishing. The visitor center plays a short movie about the dam project and displays exhibits on the dam's history, Wyoming wildlife, and prehistoric life in the Bighorn Basin (did you know an *Allosaurus* was discovered in nearby Greybull?).

4808 North Fork Hwy., 6 miles west of Cody. www.bbdvc.com. ✆ **307/527-6076.** Free admission. Visitor center: May–Sept Mon–Fri 9am–6pm, Sat–Sun 9am–5pm.

Cody Heritage Museum ★

True history buffs will appreciate this tiny but well-curated museum. Housed in a 1907 building, it traces Cody's development, from when the Crow tribe lived in the area to late-19th-century settlement and on through early tourism and the oil industry's heyday.

1092 Sheridan Ave. www.codyheritagemuseum.org. ✆ **307/586-4272.** $2 adults; free for children 6 and under. Summer Tues–Sat 10am–4pm, Sun noon–4pm; winter hours by appointment.

Cody Nite Rodeo ★★

If barrel racing, saddle broncs, and bull riding sound like something you'd like to see, don't miss the nightly rodeo action at Stampede Park. Taking place every summer night since 1938, Cody Nite Rodeo bills itself as the world's longest-running rodeo. Get there early for a chance to take a picture with a rodeo bull, learn real roping skills, or get your face painted courtesy of a rodeo clown.

Stampede Park (519 W. Yellowstone Ave.). www.codystampederodeo. com. ⓒ **307/587-5155.** $24 adults; $12.50 children 7–12; free for children 6 and under. June–Aug nightly at 8pm; gates open at 7pm.

Cody Trolley Tours ★   There's no more entertaining way to learn about Cody than by hopping on one of these restored trolleys for an hour's ride. Guides take you through Cody highlights, with an emphasis on town founder Buffalo Bill. You'll hear about unsolved mysteries, bygone bank robberies, and modern life in Cody while passing historic homes, public art, and the Buffalo Bill Dam and Reservoir.

1192 Sheridan Ave. (at the Irma Hotel). www.codytrolleytours.com. ⓒ **307/527-7043.** $28 adults; $16 children 6–17; free for children 5 and under. Tours late May to early Oct daily 9am, 11am, 1pm, and 3pm (less often in spring and fall).

Heart Mountain Interpretive Center ★★   Between 1942 and 1945, almost 11,000 Japanese Americans were forced to live in barracks here—part of a dark chapter in the U.S.'s involvement in World War II. Heart Mountain is just one of several Japanese internment camps dotted throughout the most desolate regions of the U.S. This engaging and sobering center walks you through that era with historic photos, original writings, newspaper and film clips, and artifacts from the camp. Home movies of forced removals in the aftermath of Pearl Harbor and video interviews with survivors breathe life into the past, and you can walk inside a reconstructed barracks building. This is one of a few internment camps now open to the public and a potent reminder of the dangers of racism and xenophobia.

1539 Rd. 19, Powell (13 miles north of Cody on U.S. 14). www.heart mountain.org. ⓒ **307/754-8000.** $14 adults; $10 kids 11–17; free for children 9 and under. Mid-May to early Oct daily 10am–5pm; Oct to mid-May Wed–Sat only.

McCullough Peaks Wild Horse Herd Management Area ★   Here's something most of us don't see every day: wild mustangs running free! The hundred-plus wild horses who call this high desert preserve home are descended from the ones the Spanish brought to America in the 1500s, and they come in a multitude of colors—black, white, strawberry roan, and everything in between. Chances of spotting them grazing, galloping, or even sparring are quite good. **Cody Wyoming Adventures** (www.codywyomingadventures. com) offers guided tours of the area for $89.

12 to 27 miles east of Cody on U.S. 14/16/20. www.blm.gov. ✆ **307/578-5900.** Free admission.

Old Trail Town ★ Part ghost town and part museum, this assemblage of weathered old storefronts and clapboard cabins from Wyoming and Montana in the late 1880s is a worthy spot to spend an hour. A wooden boardwalk takes you past several notable old structures, including an 1883 cabin where Butch Cassidy and the Sundance Kid once conspired; the cabin of a Crow scout who worked with General Custer's expedition; and the 1897 home of Cody's first mayor. There's also a museum filled with relics, a suite of old wagons, and the relocated graves of many Western notables.

1831 DeMaris Dr. www.oldtrailtown.org. ✆ **307/587-5302.** $12 adults; $6 children 6–12; free for children 5 and under. Mid-May to Sept daily 8am–6pm.

Where to Stay

Cody's lodging options include high-class inns, historic hotels, and budget-friendly basics. **Hampton Inn & Suites,** 8 Southfork Rd. (www.hilton.com; ✆ **307/587-4505**), has a small pool and great views from the upper floors. Doubles go for $239 in summer.

If you seek a larger cabin or rental home, check out the cabins, guesthouses, and ranches managed by **Cody Lodging Company,** 1371 Sheridan Ave. (www.codylodgingcompany. com; ✆ **307/587-6000**). **Airbnb** (www.airbnb.com) listings in Cody are strong, with affordable choices; **VRBO** (www. vrbo.com) offers several upscale homes in the Shoshone River canyon.

Buffalo Bill Village: Holiday Inn, Comfort Inn, and Buffalo Bill Cabin Village ★ It's not so much a "village" as it is a convenient cluster of accommodations within walking distance of downtown, but this three-hotel complex has a lot going for it. The stand-alone log cabins at Buffalo Bill Cabin Village look rustic, but each one features modern hotel amenities and bathrooms. The Holiday Inn and Comfort Inn are standard examples of their chains and a half-step up from the cabins in caliber. The three share an outdoor heated pool, restaurant, and bar; the Holiday Inn adds a fitness center.

1701 Sheridan Ave. www.blairhotels.com. © **307/587-5555.** Comfort Inn: 74 units. $250–$260 double. Holiday Inn: 186 units. $225 double. Historic cabins: 83 units. $160–$200. Cabins closed Oct–Apr. **Amenities:** Restaurant; lounge; gym (Holiday Inn); pool; free Wi-Fi.

The Chamberlin Inn ★★★ Utterly charming and packed with historic bona fides, the Chamberlin is Cody's finest hotel. First opened as a boardinghouse in 1903 and lovingly restored since then, the boutique hotel is full of elegant nooks and crannies: a leafy conservatory, a sun porch, and a lobby with a fireplace and tin ceiling. There's also a large courtyard with stately trees and summer croquet games. Ernest Hemingway famously stayed here as he finished *Death in the Afternoon* in 1932; you can even sleep in his room, the Hemingway King Studio Suite. Rooms range from doubles to suites to apartments to the expansive Courthouse, all different and featuring historic furniture, exposed brick walls, and wrought-iron accents.

1032 12th St. www.chamberlininn.com. © **307/587-0202.** 23 units. $346–$384 double; $376–$493 suite or apt. Lower rates fall–spring. **Amenities:** Lounge; gym; business center; free Wi-Fi.

The Cody ★★ This deluxe hotel on the west side of town (near the rodeo grounds) is one of Cody's finest options. From the moment you step into the expansive lobby, the place sets a warm, inviting tone: dark, heavy woods; comfy couches set in small groups; and Western-style paintings and accents. Or hang out on the outdoor patio, where a firepit makes alfresco relaxation an option year-round. Rooms are simple and chic: Some doubles have patios or balconies (the ones on the west side have the best views of Shoshone River Canyon), and the suites boast fireplaces and Jacuzzis.

232 W. Yellowstone Ave. www.thecody.com. © **855/746-3431.** 75 units. $269–$408 double; $439 suite. Rates include buffet breakfast. Lower rates fall–spring. **Amenities:** Gym; Jacuzzi; pool; business center; firepit; free Wi-Fi.

The Irma Hotel ★ Naturally, the town that Buffalo Bill built contains one of his hotels—first opened in 1902 to cater to early Yellowstone tourists, hunters, and ranching barons, and named after his youngest daughter. The man himself kept a couple of private suites here (one of which you can still bunk in today). The Irma has taken steps to preserve its historic nature, from the old-fashioned guest room options to the elaborate cherrywood bar anchoring the on-site Silver Saddle Saloon—a gift from Queen Victoria, and a longtime draw. You have two choices for rooms: standards, which are modern and unremarkable, or the much more character-filled historic rooms, which feature period touches such as rose wallpaper, ornate tasseled curtains, and pull-chain toilets. Among its other charms: the free shootout reenactment that takes place daily in summer right outside, and the popular prime-rib buffet at the **Irma Restaurant.**

1192 Sheridan Ave. www.irmahotel.com. 𝄢 **307/587-4221.** 30 units. $225 double; $235–$255 historic double; $320 suite. Lower rates fall–spring. **Amenities:** Restaurant; lounge; free Wi-Fi.

Ivy Inn & Suites ★★   Those looking for thoroughly modern accommodations will do well at this Best Western Premier property, one of Cody's nicest options. Contemporary design is the name of the game, with rooms boasting arty black-and-white cowboy photography and funky patterned rugs; the soaring lobby centers around a sleek stone fireplace. Standard rooms are comfortable, with upscale bathrooms and dreamy beds; upgrade to a suite for a separate living area. The **8th Street Restaurant** serves three meals daily, and there's also a large pool plus hot tub.

1800 8th St. www.bestwestern.com. 𝄢 **307/587-2572.** 70 units. $359–$434 double; $409–$474 suite. Lower rates fall–spring. **Amenities:** Restaurant; lounge; pool; Jacuzzi; gym; free Wi-Fi.

Where to Eat

Cody has a reputation as a steak-and-potatoes town—and you'll have no trouble finding a burger or a T-bone—but more variety has crept into the dining scene lately. The **Station by Cody Coffee,** 919 16th St. (www.codycoffee.com/the-station; 𝄢 **307/578-6661**), serves espresso, plus delicious crepes and pastries, on a large patio with a firepit (indoor seating available, too). **Proprietress,** 1128 12th St. (𝄢 **307/587-4472**), offers tastings of Wyoming whiskey, mead, and wine Tuesday through Saturday. And one of the liveliest rodeo hangouts you're likely to visit, the **Proud Cut Saloon,** 1227

Sheridan Ave. (www.proudcutsaloon.com; ✆ **307/527-6905**), offers monster steaks and burgers. That name? It's an homage to a stallion that stays feisty even after gelding.

Annie's Soda Saloon ★ SANDWICHES/DESSERT   This establishment manages to feel both old-fashioned and cutting-edge. Barnwood-style paneling and a tin ceiling put you in the mood for Annie's signature treats: ice cream sodas like the ones you used to get at the five-and-dime. You can also cool off with a shake, sundae, or plain old cone. But don't skip right to dessert: Pancakes, biscuits, and omelets start off the day, and the creative panini and salads are tasty, too.

1202 Sheridan Ave. www.anniessodasaloon.net. ✆ **307/578-8400.** Main courses $7–$15 breakfast, $9–$18 lunch; ice cream sodas $7. Mon–Sat 7am–2pm.

Blanca Tatanka ★★ AMERICAN   The cocktails may be creative, and the wine/beer lists long, but this urban-cowboy outpost is a lot more than a bar. Blanca Tatanka serves well-executed small plates (wonton nachos, pork belly tacos, lemon pepper wings) along with hearty fare like sliders made with local Wagyu beef and buffalo chicken wraps in a chic space studded with nice touches: sagebrush chandeliers, a patio lounge. Live music and a small dance floor liven things up some nights.

1455 Sheridan Ave. www.theblancatatanka.com. ✆ **307/527-6293.** Main courses $12–$20 lunch and dinner. Mon–Tues 11am–9pm; Wed–Sat 11am–10pm.

Pat's Brew House ★ MICROBREWERY   When Norfleet Montgomery bought the local-favorite Pat O'Hara's Brewing Company in 2021, it became Wyoming's first female-owned and -operated brewery. Beer remains front and center—the bar wraps around a collection of shiny fermentation tanks—but Pat's also serves bar food that's a cut above. Brats, burgers, and hearty salads join unique appetizers like chicken "lollipops" (brined and fried winglets) and Irish eggrolls stuffed with corned beef and cabbage. In summer, a garage door–style entrance rolls up to expand the patio. And that beer? A nutty brown ale, smooth blonde, and juniper-tinted IPA, among others, draw plenty of fans.

1019 15th St. www.patsbrewhousewy.com. ✆ **307/586-5410.** Main courses $13–$27 lunch and dinner. Wed–Sun 11am–9pm.

Sitti's Table ★★ MEDITERRANEAN   Inspired by the "explosion of freshness" the owner's grandma served at her own table (*sitti* is Lebanese for grandmother), two local caterers launched this fantastic little spot in 2022. Diners enjoy a fusion of Middle Eastern, Mediterranean, and French flavors and techniques over a handful of tables. Sample lamb kefta in a tangy yogurt sauce, halloumi grilled cheese, or Israeli salad topped with falafel. Breakfast is equally delicious, starring mains like *shakshuka* (eggs in stewed tomatoes) and mushroom tartine, with fancy lattes to boot. Afterward, browse the attached market for olives, fancy chocolate, and kombucha. Grandma would be proud.

1034 13th St. www.sittistable.com. ℂ **307/213-0378.** Main courses $12–$18 breakfast, $14–$17 lunch. Tues–Sat 8am–10:30am, 11am–2pm (market open until 4pm).

Trailhead ★★ PIZZA/PASTA/STEAK   Pair a casual, bustling atmosphere with thoughtfully sourced, upscale dishes, and you have the convivial downtown Trailhead. Wood-fired pizzas with toppings like fig and honey or chorizo and pineapple are the top draw, but you'll also find inspired pastas and meaty mains like elk medallions and several huge steaks. The chef-owner makes a point of using local ingredients and switches up the menu seasonally. Live music and plenty of cocktail and wine choices sweeten the deal.

1326 Beck Ave. www.trailheadcody.com. ℂ **307/578-8510.** Main courses $9–$20 brunch, $13–$18 lunch, $17–$46 dinner. Tues–Fri 11am–2pm and 3–9pm (until 10pm Fri); Sat 11am–2pm and 3–10pm.

Cody After Dark

Of the two cowboy music shows in town, **Cody Cattle Company,** 1910 Demaris Dr. (www.thecodycattlecompany.com; ℂ **307/272-5770**), is more family friendly and features a buffet dinner and a live "cowboy band." It's open late May to mid-September. **Dan Miller's Cowboy Music Revue,** at 1601 Stampede Ave. (www.cowboymusicrevue.com; ℂ **307/899-2799**), takes the show's music side a bit more seriously; performances run early June to late September.

The long-standing **Cassie's,** 214 Yellowstone Ave. (www.cassiessteakhousecody.com; ℂ **307/527-5500** hosts live music and dancing most summer nights. The **Silver Dollar Bar,** 1313 Sheridan Ave. (ℂ **307/527-7666**), is a local favorite watering hole with pool tables, a large patio, and live music.

A PARKS NATURE GUIDE

Yellowstone and Grand Teton National Parks have distinct differences. One is an immense wilderness plateau that sits atop a caldera seething with molten lava; the other is a striking set of peaks rising from a broad river plain. One encloses some of the most remote backcountry in the lower 48 and provides crucial habitat for rare species; the other is a short drive from a chic resort town and includes an airport and grazing cattle in its mixed-use approach. What they *do* share is the affection of millions of visitors who come here annually to renew their ties to nature through the parks' mountains, alpine lakes, majestic elk, and astonishing geysers.

The **Greater Yellowstone Ecosystem** is an interdependent network of watersheds, mountain ranges, wildlife habitats, and other components extending beyond the two parks into seven national forests, the Wind River Reservation, three national wildlife refuges, and nearly a million acres of private land. It is one of the largest intact temperate ecosystems on the planet and covers an area as vast as Connecticut, Rhode Island, and Delaware combined.

It's also a massive source of water. West of the Continental Divide, snowmelt trickles into creeks, streams, and rivers that run through Yellowstone before draining into the Snake River, traveling through Grand Teton National Park and Idaho, and running into the Columbia River, which winds its way west through Oregon and into the Pacific

Ocean. Water on the eastern slopes of the divide passes through Yellowstone in the form of the Madison and Gallatin rivers, which meet the Jefferson River west of Bozeman, Montana, and merge into the Missouri River, which flows into the Mississippi and, ultimately, the Gulf of Mexico.

THE PARKS TODAY

It has long been a challenge for park managers to make the parks accessible to their more than 4 million annual visitors. It necessitates the construction of new facilities and ongoing road maintenance and repair. At the same time, the parks are wild preserves, and the National Park Service must cope with the impact of almost 9 million pairs of feet on the forests, meadows, and thermal areas, as well as on the lives of the millions of animals that inhabit the area.

Some pivotal issues in the parks today center on the impact of climate change; the reintroduced gray wolves and the resulting livestock losses in and around the parks; the inadequacy of the park's infrastructure to cope with the crush of visitors each year; invasive species; and the reduction of habitat surrounding the parks, coupled with elk and bison seeking forage beyond park boundaries.

Possible solutions are often "too little, too late," layering complex management strategies on an ecosystem that might do better if it were allowed to work things out naturally. The problem is that Grand Teton and Yellowstone have already been altered significantly by humans, so "natural" becomes a relative concept.

As the world awakens to the accelerating loss of vital species in shrinking wild habitats, it becomes ever more imperative to find ways to preserve the planet's relatively unspoiled ecosystems, like that of Greater Yellowstone.

LANDSCAPE & GEOLOGY

The Yellowstone and Grand Teton region is one of the most dynamic seismic areas in the world—wracked by earthquakes, cracked by water boiling to the surface, and littered with the detritus of previous volcanic eruptions. Today, the bowels of the Yellowstone caldera are again filling with magma. Geologic studies show that, for the past 2 million years, the plateau has blown its top every 600,000 years or so—and the last explosion was about 640,000 years ago. That means that a titanic blow—bigger than anything seen in recorded history—could happen, well, any century now, give or take thousands of years. The good news is that the big one is not imminent; geologists say things need to heat up considerably first.

As you'll learn when you visit the exhibits on the park's geology at Moose, Mammoth, and the various geothermal areas, what you see on the surface—great layers of ash and the core of volcanic vents, such as Mount Washburn and Bunsen Peak—is only a fraction of the story of Yellowstone and Grand Teton.

On 2.2 million acres, Yellowstone is significantly larger than its sister to the south. Encompassing 3,472 square miles, Yellowstone has 310 miles of paved roads and 1,000 miles of backcountry trails. It is home to more geysers and hot springs than the combined total in the rest of the world.

Although it can't match Yellowstone's size, Grand Teton National Park is nothing to sneeze at. It has towering mountain spires that have been compared to cathedral towers, reaching almost 14,000 feet skyward; picturesque glacial lakes; and a great deal of interesting topography. The roughly 320,000 acres of Grand Teton contain about 160 miles of paved roads and more than 250 miles of hiking trails.

The Faces of Yellowstone

By the end of the 1872 Hayden expedition, explorers had identified several distinct areas in the park, each with its own physical characteristics. Less spectacular than the craggy mountain scenery of Grand Teton, and less imposing than the vast expanses of the Grand Canyon in Arizona, Yellowstone's beauty is subtle, reflecting the changes it has undergone during its explosive past.

Although Yellowstone has its share of mountains, much of the park is a high mountain plateau. The environment changes dramatically as you ascend the mountain slopes from the foothill zones in the valleys—the elevation at the entrance at West Yellowstone is 6,666 feet, for example, compared to 5,314 feet at the Gardiner entrance. Because the park lies about halfway between the equator and the North Pole, its summers consist of long, warm days that stimulate plant growth at the lower elevations.

At the lowest elevations, down around 5,300 feet above sea level, you'll find **grassy flats** and sagebrush growing on dry, porous soils, with creeks and rivers cutting through to form wildlife-rich **riparian zones.** Deposits of glacial moraines dot the **foothills,** which slope upward toward peaks. Douglas fir, pine, and other conifers, as well as aspen, clad these slopes. Marshes and ponds are fed by the spring snowmelt. Shrubs and flowers, such as huckleberry and columbine, favor these wet, shady spots.

Then comes the **mountain zone** (6,000–7,600 ft.) with its thickening forests dominated by lodgepole pine and broken by meadows where deer, elk, and moose often graze. The transition between the highest forest and the bare surface above timberline is known as the **subalpine zone** (7,600–11,300 ft.). Finally, we come to the bare rock at the very top of the continental shelf, where small, hardy plants bloom briefly after the annual thaw.

Although the park is most famous for its geysers, visitors can choose among very different environments; this diversity reflects the long-term effects of geologic activity and weather.

The limestone terraces at **Mammoth Hot Springs** give testimony to the region's subsurface volcanic activity. The park sits atop a rare geologic hot spot where molten rock rises to within 2 miles of the Earth's surface, heating the water in a plumbing system that still mystifies scientists.

The **northern section of the park,** between Mammoth Hot Springs and the Tower-Roosevelt region, is a high-plains area defined by mountains, forests, and broad expanses of river valleys created by ice floes.

The road between the Tower-Roosevelt junction and the northeast entrance winds through the **Lamar Valley,** an area that has been covered by glaciers three times, most recently during an ice age that began 25,000 years ago and continued for 10,000 years—in geologic terms, just yesterday. Because this area was a favorite of Theodore Roosevelt, it is often referred to as "Roosevelt Country." Glacial ponds strewn with boulders deposited by moving ice dot the beautiful valley where elk, bison, and wolves live together.

Farther south are **Pelican** and **Hayden valleys,** the two largest ancient lake beds in the park. They feature large, open meadows where abundant plant life provides food for a population of bison and elk.

In the warm months, you'll enjoy the contrast between the lush green valleys and **Canyon Country,** in the center of the park. The Grand Canyon of the Yellowstone, a colorful, 1,000-foot-deep, 24-mile-long gorge, is to many people just as dramatic as its cousin in Arizona. The Yellowstone River cuts through the valley, in some places moving 64,000 cubic feet of water per second, and creating two waterfalls, one of which is more than twice the height of Niagara Falls.

When you arrive at the **southern geyser basins,** you might feel that you've been transported through a geologic time warp. Here you will find the largest collections of thermal areas in the world—the park itself has perhaps 600 geysers and 10,000 geothermal features—and the largest geysers in Yellowstone. The result: boiling water catapulted skyward and barren patches of sterile dirt; hot, bubbling, and unimaginably colorful pools; and, of course, the star of this show, the geyser **Old Faithful.**

You'll see the park's volcanic activity on a 17-mile journey east to the **lake area,** the scene of three volcanic eruptions that took place more than 600,000 years ago. When the final eruption blasted more than 1,000 square miles of the Rocky Mountains into the stratosphere, it created the Yellowstone caldera, a massive depression measuring 28 by 47 miles, and Yellowstone Lake basin, some 20 miles long and 14 miles wide, reaching depths of 390 feet. The landscape here consists of flat plateaus of lava that are hundreds of feet thick.

The Spires of Grand Teton

Your first sight of the towering spires of the **Cathedral Group**—the *trois tetons* (three breasts), as lonesome French trappers called them—will create an indelible impression. A bit of history makes them even more interesting.

The formation of the spires began more than 2.5 billion years ago when sand and volcanic debris settled in an ancient ocean that covered this entire area. Scientists estimate that roughly 40 to 80 million years ago, a compression of the Earth's surface caused an uplift of the entire Rocky Mountains from Mexico to Canada. This was just the first step in an ongoing series of events that included several periods during which a miles-thick crust of ice covered the area. Then, 6 to 9 million years ago, the shifting of the Earth's tectonic plates caused movement along the north-south Teton fault that produced a tremendous uplift. The valley floor also dropped precipitously. These simultaneous forces pushed the rock that is now the **Teton Range** to its present site, from a position 20,000 to 30,000 feet *below* what is today the floor of Jackson Hole. The west block of rock tipped upward to create the Teton Range, and the eastern block swung downward to form the valley that is now called **Jackson Hole**—kind of like a pair of horizontal swinging doors that moved the ground 5 miles.

After this upheaval, and after eons of erosion and glacial activity, **Grand Teton,** the centerpiece of this 40-mile-long fault area, towered 13,770 feet above sea level—more than a mile above the visitor center at Moose Junction. Eleven other peaks in the park are more than 12,000 feet high today, with conditions that support mountain glaciers. As you gaze upward at this magnificent range, you will notice that many cliffs are more than a half mile in height.

Geologic explorations of **Mount Moran** (elevation 12,605 ft.) discovered that erosion had removed some 3,000 feet of material from its summit, meaning that it once must have been more than 15,000 feet high. Equally remarkable is the fact that the thin layer of Flathead sandstone on top of this peak is also found buried at least 24,000 feet below the valley's surface—further evidence of the skyward thrust of the mountains.

Although this is the youngest range in the Rockies, the rocks here are some of the oldest in North America, consisting of granitic gneisses and schists, which are the hardest and least-porous rocks known to geologists.

The Teton area experienced a cooling trend about 150,000 years ago, during which glaciers more than 2,000 feet thick flowed from higher elevations, and an ice sheet covered Jackson Hole. When the sheet melted for the final time, some 60,000 to 80,000 years ago, it left behind the 386-feet-deep, 16-mile-long depression now known as **Jackson Lake.**

The receding layers of ice also left other calling cards. The ice created several beautiful **glacial lakes,** including Phelps, Taggart, Bradley, Jenny, String, and Leigh; it polished the sides of **Cascade Canyon;** carved glacial lakes, called **cirque lakes,** at the heads of canyons; and sharpened the peaks of the mountains to their present jagged edges. Five glaciers have survived on Mount Moran. The best trail for glacial views is the Cascade Trail, which leads to the Schoolroom Glacier. But you shouldn't walk on the Mount Moran glaciers unless you are experienced and have the proper gear; the terrain is icy and can be unstable. Like glaciers in many parts of the world, Grand Teton's glaciers are retreating due to climate change.

PLANT LIFE IN THE PARKS

When it comes to the variety of plants in the two parks, the only limiting factor is the high altitude—otherwise, the diversity of terrain, weather, and soils permits a fairly wide range of vegetation. Estimates vary, but there are more than 1,500 native plant varieties in the Greater Yellowstone Ecosystem. Some species are found living on the dry valley beds in hostile soil, close to other species that predominate in lush meadows and riverbeds. Some thrive in thermal areas, while others do well in alpine areas, near mountain lakes, and in cirques near glaciers.

Examination of plant fossils indicates that life began during the Eocene epoch, approximately 55 million years ago, and continued for 17 million years. The inspection of petrified tree stumps in Yellowstone's Lamar Valley led to the identification of 27 distinct layers of forests, one atop the other. Climatic conditions during the Eocene epoch were similar to those in the southeastern and south-central United States. Difficult as it might be to imagine, the area was once a warm, temperate zone in which rainfall might have averaged 50 to 60 inches per year at what was then an elevation of 3,000 feet above sea level.

These days, the elevation ranges from 5,000 to 13,000 feet, the average low temperature is approximately 30°F (−1°C), and hundreds of inches of snow fall each year. Plants have adapted to a growing season that is a mere 60 days in duration. Consequently, forests once populated with hardwoods, such as maple, magnolia, and sycamore, are now filled with conifers, the most common of which are pine, spruce, and fir. A smattering of cottonwoods and aspens also thrive in the cool park temperatures.

The parks have several growing zones. Above 10,000 feet in the alpine zone, plants adapt to wind, snow, and lack of soil by growing close to the ground, flowering soon after the snows melt. You'll find such flora on trails near Dunraven Pass in Yellowstone and in Cascade Canyon in Grand Teton.

In Yellowstone, the canyon and subalpine regions, at 7,000 to 10,000 feet, are known for **conifer forests** and open meadows of **wildflowers.** As elevation increases, wildflowers are abundant and healthy, while trees are stunted and shrublike.

In the valley in Grand Teton, at 6,400 to 7,000 feet, the porous soil supports plants that tolerate hot and dry summertime conditions. **Sagebrush, wildflowers,** and **grasses** thrive and predominate. Plants bloom in a pageant of colors from early June to early July.

Identifying the plants described below does not require a degree in botany, but Kurt F. Johnson's *A Field Guide to Yellowstone and Grand Teton National Parks* (Farcountry Press, 2013) is a handy addition to your trip kit.

Trees

Coniferous trees are most common in the parks because of the high altitude and short growing season, but there are some hardy deciduous trees as well, such as cottonwood and aspen. The most common cone-bearing trees in the parks are lodgepole pines, which cover as much as 80% of Yellowstone, and Douglas firs, subalpine firs, Engelmann spruces, blue spruces, and whitebark pines. The key to identification is the trees' basic shape, the shape of their needles, and various characteristics of their cones.

Lodgepole Pine This familiar tree grows tall and slender, with bare trunk at the bottom and needles near the top resulting in dense stands that look like the spears of a closely ranked army. The needles of the lodgepole are clustered in pairs, typically around 3 inches long. You'll see logs from this tree supporting tepees and forming the walls of cabins.

Lodgepole Pine

Douglas Fir "Doug fir" is actually a member of the pine family, with prickly cones and dark, deeply etched bark. This tree has flat, flexible, single needles that grow around the branch, giving an appearance of fullness. Another giveaway is that its cones hang downward and do not disintegrate aloft; instead, they litter the forest floor. These trees like the north-facing side of the mountain.

Douglas Fir

Subalpine Fir You can distinguish firs by their needles, which sprout individually from branches instead of in clusters, like a pine; and by their cones, which grow upright on the branch until they dry up and blow away. Look for the slender, conical crown of this tree. When heavy snows weigh down the lower branches, they often become rooted, forming a circle of smaller trees called a snow mat. You'll find subalpine firs at high elevations near the timberline.

Subalpine Fir

Engelmann Spruce This tree also likes the higher elevations, growing in shaded ravines and in the canyons of the Teton Range above 6,800 feet and sometimes much higher. Look for it near Kepler Cascades, Spring Creek, and the south entrance of Yellowstone National Park. It is distinguished by

Engelmann Spruce

single needles that are square and sharp to the touch, and by cones with papery scales that are approximately 1½ inches long.

Blue Spruce The Engelmann spruce's cousin, this tree is most common along the Snake River near Jackson. True to its name, it is characterized by its bluish appearance and by cones that are twice the size of the Engelmann's.

Blue Spruce

Other Plants

Here's a brief listing of some of the most common and interesting plants in the ecosystem.

Glacier Lily A member of the lily family with a nodding bloom on a 6- to 12-inch stem, this bright yellow spring flower is found in abundance in both parks at elevations of more than 7,500 feet. Also known as the fawn lily, trout lily, and adder's-tongue, it is especially common near Sylvan Pass and on Dunraven Pass, both in Yellowstone.

Glacier Lily

Indian Paintbrush This is the Wyoming state flower. It has a distinctive narrow, bright scarlet bloom that is most commonly found from mid-June to early September in the Snake River bottomland. Other species are white, yellow, orange, and pink.

Indian Paintbrush

Plains Prickly Pear This member of the cactus family is one of two such species found in the parks, usually in the Mammoth area and near the Snake River. It is distinguished by thick, flat green stems armed with spines and, in midsummer, a conspicuous yellow flower with numerous petals. Native Americans recognized prickly pear's medicinal qualities and treated warts by lacerating them and then applying juice from the plant.

Plains Prickly Pear

To successfully record your discovery of the parks' flora, consider using a microlens that will allow you to focus within 6 inches of blossoms. Speeds of 200 ISO or faster will add to the chances of proper exposure, even on cloudy days.

Fringed Gentian This member of the gentian family is the official flower of Yellowstone Park, where it is common and blooms throughout the summer. Its purple petals are fused into a 2-inch-long corolla and sit atop 1- to 3-foot-tall stems. It is also found below Jackson Lake Dam in Grand Teton.

Fringed Gentian

Silky Phacelia This is one of the most photogenic and easily recognized species in the parks. Growing in purple clumps alongside the road at Dunraven Pass, the flower derives its name from the silvery pubescence that covers its stems and leaves. It's best photographed in July and August.

Silky Phacelia

Shooting Star The shooting star is characterized by pinkish ½- to 1-inch-long flowers that dangle earthward like meteorites from a 12-inch stem; they bloom in June. It is commonly found near thermal areas, streambeds, and Yellowstone Lake.

Shooting Star

Yellow Monkey Flower This flower exhibits a bright yellow petal that, together with orange spots, attracts insect pollinators near streambeds at elevations of 7,000 to 9,000 feet all summer. It is also found near thermal areas and Yellowstone Lake.

Yellow Monkey Flower

Fairy Slipper (also known as the Calypso Orchid) Finding this beautiful orchid might require some serious detective work. It is one of 15 orchid species in the parks and is considered by many to be the most beautiful and striking. Seen during May and June, it usually has one small, green leaf and a red-pink flower that resembles a small

Fairy Slipper (aka Calypso Orchid)

lady's slipper. It is found in cool, deep-shaded areas and is becoming rare because its habitat is disappearing.

Bitterroot The state flower of Montana, the bitterroot makes its first appearance in early June in dry, open, sometimes-stony soil and in grassy meadows. Its fleshy rose-and-white petals extend up to 1 inch in length. It was a source of food for Native Americans, who introduced it to Captain Meriwether Lewis of Lewis and Clark fame, hence its botanical name, *Lewisia rediviva.*

Bitterroot

Columbia Monkshood This purple flower has a hood-shape structure with two sepals at its side and two below (all of which make up the *calyx,* the leafy parts surrounding the flower). It varies in height from 2 to 5 feet. You'll see these flowers in wet meadows and stream banks from June to August, often near thermal areas and Yellowstone Lake.

Columbia Monkshood

WILDLIFE IN THE PARKS

For many, the primary reason for a visit to these parks is the wildlife: bears, bighorn sheep, bison, elk, bald eagles, river otters, and moose all wandering free, often near roadsides. Yellowstone and Grand Teton are home to the largest concentration of free-roaming wildlife in the lower 48. This includes one of the largest herds of elk in North America, the

> **Ready for Their Close-Ups**
>
> Photographers need a telephoto lens, preferably a zoom, to get good shots of wildlife. Even the biggest animals in the park present minimal risks to humans, unless you move in for a close-up. Invest in a 300mm lens, or a 100- to 300mm zoom, and you should get good shots without disturbing the wildlife or putting yourself at risk.

largest free-roaming herd of bison in the U.S., and one of the lower 48's only populations of grizzly bears.

Also in the parks are pronghorns, mountain goats, and two species of deer (totaling eight species of *ungulates,* or hoofed mammals); black bears; three species of wildcats; coyotes; wolverines; pine martens; about 60 species of smaller mammals; and 322 species of birds. Add to that the gray wolves reintroduced in 1995—they now number more than 500 in the entire Greater Yellowstone Ecosystem—and you have a rich array of wildlife. Most creatures steer clear of humans. But humans want to get ever closer to the animals, and that can cause problems. Unlike the critters that inhabit petting zoos, the animals in the Greater Yellowstone Ecosystem are wild and pose an unpredictable threat to the safety of visitors.

Death is a day-to-day affair in the parks. In the spring, you'll see carcasses of elk and bison that died during the long winter, attracting bears and other carnivores looking for a free lunch. That's part of the picture when you vow to interfere as little as possible with nature's way.

Park naturalists generally agree that every major vertebrate wildlife species that was present during the most recent ice age (more than 10,000 years ago) is a resident of the parks today, as are several rare or endangered species, the most notable being the grizzly bear and the bald eagle.

Mammals

Bear (Black & Grizzly)   In recent years, grizzly bears have enjoyed a comeback, in part because of the reintroduction of gray wolves, which create plenty of carcasses for bears to scavenge. However, unless you have the patience to spend weeks outdoors in bear country, such as the Lamar and Hayden valleys, your chances of seeing a grizzly in

Yellowstone or Grand Teton aren't all that good—you might have to go to the zoo in West Yellowstone.

Estimates vary, but probably about 965 grizzly bears live in the Greater Yellowstone Ecosystem today, as well as an equal or greater number of black bears. Rangers say you're more likely to spot the black bears, especially during the spring months after they emerge with new cubs from their winter dens. However, black bears are probably more visible because they are more likely to venture near human development than grizzlies, meaning that an encounter with a grizzly is most likely to occur in the backcountry. Bears that get a taste for human food, or get too comfortable around human camp-sites, are relocated to the depths of the wilderness. Black bears are most commonly sighted in the Northern Range and the Bechler area in the park's southwest corner, where they feed on green grass, herbs, berries, ants, and carrion.

Grizzly bears are most commonly seen in the northeast area of Yellowstone, in the meadows on the hillsides of the Lamar Valley, or wandering the Hayden Valley north of Yellowstone Lake. They also feed on trout spawning in Yellowstone Lake tributaries in the late spring (campgrounds by these streams are closed during spawning). They are most active in the spring, when they emerge from hibernation hungry, and in the fall, when they're busy fattening themselves up for winter.

Grizzly bears can do you the most damage, particularly when their cubs are around or when they think you're after their food.

Black Bear

Grizzly Bear

Bighorn Sheep If a mountainside has even a hint of a foothold, a bighorn sheep will find it. Its hooves are hard and durable on the outside but soft and clamp-like underneath—perfect for maneuvering steep, rocky terrain. You'll often hear them clattering before you spot their stocky, gray-brown bodies and white rumps. Six feet long, the males weigh up to 300 pounds. Their horns are coiled; the females' are straight.

BLACK bear **OR GRIZZLY** bear?

Because a black bear can be black, brown, or cinnamon, here are some identifiers. The grizzly is the larger of the two: typically 3½ feet at the shoulder with a dish-face profile and a pronounced hump between the shoulders. The black bear's ears are rounder. The grizzly's color is typically yellowish brown, but the coat is sometimes recognized by its cinnamon color, often highlighted by silver tips. In terms of tracks, the black bear's toes follow an arc around the foot pad while the grizzly's toes are arranged in a nearly straight line. The grizzly's claws are also considerably longer.

Caution: Park rangers attempt to keep track of grizzlies to prevent human/bear encounters. But it's best to assume that they are always around; make noise when traveling in isolated spots.

Look for them on Mount Washburn, along Specimen Ridge, and in the Gallatin Range in Yellowstone; they are also occasionally seen in the Heart Mountain area in southern Yellowstone. In Grand Teton, smaller herds are found in the Gros Ventre Valley, as well as the western slopes of the Teton Range. In winter, a large herd of bighorn sheep congregates south of the town of Dubois in Whiskey Basin, in the Wind River Range east of the Teton Range.

Bighorn Sheep

Bison

Bison Bison (commonly, but incorrectly, called buffalo) appear indifferent to humans as they wander the roads and go about their grazing, but don't think for a minute that they're docile. Their prodigious size, cute calves, and fearless nature ensure that bison are very visible symbols of Yellowstone. On ballerina-thin ankles, these burly brown animals carry as much as 2,000 pounds, much of it concentrated in thick shoulders and massive chests. Those big heads help them clear snow for winter grazing, but during harsh winters they instinctively migrate to lower elevations. (Some biologists insist that both grizzlies and bison were driven up on the plateau from their natural home on the prairie.) Bison are easy to spot in the summer; you'll see them munching grass and wallowing in dust pits in Hayden Valley, Pelican Valley, the Madison River area, and the geyser areas near the Firehole River. In the winter, snowmobilers often have to make way for the shaggy beasts as bison take advantage of the snow-packed roads to travel around.

Coyote   The wily coyote is the predator most often spotted by park visitors. Looking like lanky shepherd dogs with grizzled, gray-brown coats, coyotes make their homes in burrows and caves. Numbers have dropped a bit since the gray wolf reintroduction, but coyotes are very adaptable. Active hunters year-round, they feast on small animals such as squirrels and rabbits, as well as the carcasses of animals that died naturally or were killed by larger carnivores. They are seen near park roads, in the meadows, and in the sagebrush. Coyote pups are considered a delicacy by great horned owls, eagles, mountain lions, and bears.

Coyote   *Gray Wolf*

Gray Wolf   In a controversial move, gray wolves were reintroduced to Yellowstone in 1995 for the first time since the 1920s, when they were eliminated by hunters operating under a federal predator control program designed to protect cattle herds. The population of Canadian gray wolves is thriving in its new environment (the 2024 population was estimated to be about 124). Gray wolves are high-profile occupants of the Lamar Valley, under constant observation by visitors with binoculars or spotting scopes.

WOLF OR coyote?

Wolves and coyotes both bear a striking resemblance to large dogs. Here are some ways to distinguish them:

- Coyotes grow to a height of 20 inches; wolves often grow to 34 inches and are far more massive.
- Coyotes have long, pointed ears; wolf ears are rounded and relatively short.
- Coyotes have thin, delicate legs, similar to those of a fox; wolves' legs are thick and long.

Elk It is estimated that the Yellowstone herd has 10,000 to 20,000 elk (also called wapiti) in summer and less than 4,000 in winter, and other herds spend time in the park as well. The most common large animal in both parks, elk are rather sociable and travel in small groups. Males are easily identifiable by a massive set of antlers. Although they shed the antlers every spring, by early summer, bulls are beginning to display prodigious racks that, by year's end, are the envy of their cousins in the deer family. The elk's grayish-brown body, which typically weighs as much as 900 pounds, is accented by a chestnut brown head and neck, a shaggy mane, a short tail, and a distinctive tan patch on the rump.

One herd can often be seen in the vicinity of Mammoth Hot Springs, on the lawn of the main square. Others are found throughout each park. During winter months, the northern Yellowstone herd heads to a winter grazing area near Gardiner, while their cousins in Grand Teton head for the National Elk Refuge, just north of Jackson, where the Forest Service supplements their diet with bales of alfalfa.

Elk

Moose

Moose Perhaps because of their size, their homely appearance, and their broad antler racks (which can grow to 6 ft. across), moose elicit unequaled excitement from park visitors. A typical adult male moose weighs 1,000 pounds and is most easily recognizable by a pendulous muzzle and a fleshy dewlap that hangs beneath its neck like a bell.

Sightings are most frequent on the edges of ponds and in damp, lush valley bottoms, where moose feed on willows and water plants, especially along the Moose-Wilson Road and near the Jackson Lake Lodge in Grand Teton.

The plodding, nibbling moose in a meadow is not to be approached. Cows will charge any perceived threat to a calf, and bulls become particularly ornery in the fall, so give both a wide berth.

Mountain Lion After their near-eradication in the early 1900s, there has been a relatively stable population of about 34 to 42 mountain lions (also known as cougars, panthers, or pumas) in Yellowstone for years, primarily on the Northern Range, and a smaller number in Grand Teton. Adults weigh 100 to 150 pounds, making them the largest feline in the parks and the Rocky Mountains. Largely opportunistic predators, the parks' mountain lions hunt deer, elk, and porcupines. They are seldom seen in Yellowstone but more often heard: Listeners often mistake their high-pitched wails for a human.

Mountain Lion

Mule Deer An estimated 1,900 mule deer live within park borders in summer. They are most often spotted near forest boundaries or in areas covered with grass and sagebrush. The mule deer's most distinguishing characteristics are its huge ears and a black tip on the tail that contrasts with

Most of the larger, four-legged animals roaming the parks have lavish headpieces that are either horns or antlers. What's the difference? Antlers are shed every year; horns last a lifetime. Male deer, elk, and moose shed their antlers every spring, so they're as bald as cue balls when the season begins. By early June, though, new velvet-covered protuberances are making their appearance. In comparison, both sexes of bison and pronghorn grow only one set of horns during their lifetimes.

its white rump. When mule deer run, they bounce, with all four legs in the air. Fawns are typically born in late spring, often in pairs.

Pronghorn The oft-sighted pronghorns graze near the north entrance to Yellowstone and on the valley floors of Grand Teton, but they are shy and difficult to approach or photograph because of their excellent vision and speed. Often mistakenly referred to as antelope, the pronghorn is identified by its short, black horns, tan-and-white body, and black accent stripes. They can run 45 mph, but they can't clear fences. Yellowstone's pronghorn population was 500 to 600 in 2022, including a small sub-population in the Paradise Valley.

Mule Deer

Pronghorn

BIRDS IN THE PARKS

The skies above the parks are filled with predators on the wing, including eagles and 27 species of hawks, not to mention ospreys, falcons, and owls.

Bald Eagle   Once almost wiped out by the pesticide DDT, the bald eagle holds a position in the pecking order that parallels that of the grizzly. Of all the birds in the park, this photogenic species is the one most visitors are interested in spotting. Yellowstone and Grand Teton are now home to one of the largest populations of eagles in the continental United States; in Yellowstone, there were at least eight active nests in 2022. Bald eagles are most recognizable by a striking white head, tail feathers, and wingspans up to 7 feet. The Yellowstone Plateau, Snake River, Yellowstone Lake, and headwaters of the Madison River are prime spotting areas for this spectacular bird.

Bald Eagle

Golden Eagle

Golden Eagle   The bald eagle's cousin, the golden eagle, is similar in appearance, although it is smaller and does not have a white cowl. The golden eagle goes after small mammals, such as jackrabbits and prairie dogs. They hunt in open country; sometimes you'll find one feeding on roadkill.

Osprey   The osprey, nicknamed the "fish eagle" because of its diet, is the eagle's smaller relative, growing to 21 to 24

Birding Spot

Take a picnic lunch or a relaxing break at the **Oxbow Bend** overlook in Grand Teton. Weather permitting, you can soak up some sunshine and observe great blue herons, ospreys, pelicans, cormorants, and maybe a bald eagle. Although it's a popular spot, there's always room for one more vehicle.

inches; it has a white underbody and a brown topside. Ospreys tend to create large nests made of twigs and branches on the tops of trees and power poles. Look for this handsome, interesting bird in the Snake River area and the Grand Canyon of the Yellowstone River, a popular nesting area.

Osprey   *Raven*

Raven Sporting a 50- to 60-inch wingspan, the raven is jet black and markedly larger than the crow. The most intelligent bird in the parks, the raven plays an interesting role in the Greater Yellowstone Ecosystem: Biologists have observed ravens communicating with wolves, leading them to carcasses, and even playing with pups. The relationship is symbiotic: Ravens are scavengers that benefit from wolf kills. They can be seen just about everywhere in both parks.

Trumpeter Swan The trumpeter swan, one of the largest birds on the continent, has made the Greater Yellowstone Ecosystem a sanctuary. Easily recognizable by its long, curved neck, snowy white body, and black bill, it is found in marshes and on lakes and rivers, namely the Madison River in Yellowstone and Christian Pond, Swan Lake, and Cygnet Pond in Grand Teton.

Trumpeter Swan

Other Raptors **American kestrels, prairie falcons,** and **red-tailed hawks** are seen on Antelope Flats–Kelly Road in Grand Teton, where they search for small rodents.

American Kestrel   *Prairie Falcon*   *Red-Tailed Hawk*

Other Aquatic Birds The **great blue heron,** a skinny, long-legged wading bird, is seen in wetlands and rocky outcrops, especially near the end of Jackson Lake. Yellowstone Lake is a prime viewing area for the best fisher in the park, the **American white pelican,** which captures fish in its long, yellow-pouched bill. The **American dipper,** the only aquatic songbird in North America, revels in cold, fast-flowing mountain streams. The slate-gray dipper is tiny, only 7 to 8 inches tall, and recognized by its long bill and stubby tail.

Great Blue Heron

PLANNING YOUR TRIP

F ew things can do more to ruin a much-anticipated vacation than poor planning. Taking a look over some of the crucial information in this chapter before you hit the road might make the difference between a trip you'll always remember and one you'd rather forget.

GETTING THERE & GETTING AROUND

The automobile is the main method of transport within the parks. You won't find trains or buses with regular schedules here, although many tour operators use buses. Bikes are common, but riders and drivers should exercise extreme caution: Roads are twisty and rife with wildlife, pulled-over vehicles, and jaw-dropping scenery.

10

By Plane

The closest airport to Yellowstone is **Yellowstone Airport** (**WYS;** https://yellowstoneairport.mdt.mt.gov; ℮ **406/646-7631**), just 1 mile north of the town of **West Yellowstone,** Montana (and 2 miles north of the west entrance to the park), on U.S. 191. The airport has commercial flights seasonally. **Delta Airlines** connects through Salt Lake City, May through October, and **United Airlines** flies from Denver, June through September.

Alaska, American, Delta, and **United** all have flights to and from **Jackson Hole Airport (JAC;** www.jacksonholeairport.com; ℮ **307/733-7682**), which is right in Grand Teton National Park in **Jackson,** Wyoming, and only 56 miles of scenic driving from the southern entrance of Yellowstone.

To the north, **Bozeman Yellowstone International Airport (BZN;** www.bozemanairport.com; ✆ **406/388-8321**) in **Bozeman,** Montana, provides service via **Alaska, Allegiant, American, Avelo, Delta, JetBlue, Southwest, Sun Country Airlines,** and **United.** From Bozeman, you can drive 87 miles on U.S. 191 to the West Yellowstone entrance or drive 20 miles east on I-90 to Livingston and then 53 miles south on U.S. 89 to the Gardiner entrance.

Also to the north, **Billings Logan International Airport (BIL;** www.flybillings.com; ✆ **406/247-8609**), Montana's busiest airport, is 2 miles north of downtown **Billings,** Montana. Service is provided by **Alaska, Allegiant, American, Delta, Cape Air,** and **United.** From Billings, drive 65 miles south on U.S. 212 to Red Lodge, and then 30 miles on the Beartooth Highway to the northeast Yellowstone entrance in Cooke City.

Yellowstone Regional Airport (COD; www.flyyra.com; ✆ **307/587-5096**) in **Cody,** Wyoming, serves the Bighorn Basin as well as the east and northeast entrances of Yellowstone with year-round commercial flights via Denver and **United Express.** From Cody, it's a gorgeous 53-mile drive west along U.S. 14/16/20 to the east entrance of Yellowstone.

Airfares to the small airports surrounding the parks can be pricey, so if you like to drive, consider flying into **Salt Lake City,** Utah, and driving about 300 miles to Grand Teton National Park. Even **Denver,** a drive of roughly 500 miles, is an alternative.

By Car

If interstate highways and international airports are the measure of accessibility, then Yellowstone is as remote as Alaska's Denali National Park. But more than 4 million people manage to make it here every year, on tour buses, in family vans, on bicycles, and astride snowmobiles. The car is the most common method of travel in and around the parks. Public transportation is sparse, and the lack of trains makes it hard to even get near the parks without a vehicle.

Grand Teton's gateways are from the north, south, and east. Drivers naturally enter from whichever side they approach the parks. From the west, U.S. 20 or U.S. 191 takes you to West Yellowstone, Montana. From the south, U.S. 191 runs through Jackson and the length of Jackson Hole before

Getting There & Getting Around

PLANNING YOUR TRIP

Driving Distances to Yellowstone National Park*	
Salt Lake City	390 miles
Denver	563 miles
Las Vegas	809 miles
Seattle	827 miles
Portland	869 miles
Omaha	946 miles
Washington, D.C.	2,081 miles

*The difference in distance to Grand Teton is about 70 miles, depending on your route.

entering Yellowstone. From the east, U.S. 20 bisects Cody, Wyoming, and continues west 53 miles to the east entrance of Yellowstone. The northeast entrance of Yellowstone is accessible from U.S. 212 via Cooke City, Montana. The north entrance is just outside Gardiner, Montana, on U.S. 89.

Most of the major car rental agencies have operations in the gateway city airports. Visit each airport's rental car page for details, national reservation phone numbers, and local rental desk numbers. Also consider using a third-party booker such as **Hotwire** (www.hotwire.com) or **Kayak** (www.kayak.com) for substantial savings on your rates. Bozeman Yellowstone International (www.bozemanairport.com) hosts nine car rental companies, and Billings Logan International (www.flybillings.com/815/car-rentals) has eight. Jackson Hole Airport and Jackson have eight options, with four at the airport itself (www.jacksonholeairport.com/travelers/rental-cars) and four more accessible via a free shuttle ride. Five operate out of Cody's Yellowstone Regional Airport (www.flyyra.com/transportation), and two are in West Yellowstone's Yellowstone Airport (https://yellowstoneairport.mdt.mt.gov).

One U.S. gallon equals 3.8 liters or .85 imperial gallons. Gasoline is available in the gateway cities, but at only a select few locations in the park; fill up well before empty. **Electric vehicle charging** infrastructure can be found in West Yellowstone and Gardiner as well as four locations inside Yellowstone and one in Grand Teton, with more stations added by the year. International visitors should note that insurance and taxes are almost never included in quoted rental car rates in the U.S. Be sure to ask your rental agency about additional fees for these.

By Bus or Shuttle

Public transportation options are fairly limited around the parks; a few companies will haul you from selected airports to gateway towns. For long-distance bus travel, check **Greyhound** (www.greyhound.com; ✆ **800/231-2222**) schedules for West Yellowstone, Bozeman, Jackson, and Cody. **Yellowstone Roadrunner** (www.yellowstoneroadrunner.com; ✆ **406/640-0631**) runs shuttles and vans serving the airports in West Yellowstone, Bozeman, Jackson, and Idaho Falls; call for rates. In the winter, you can catch a ride from the Bozeman airport to West Yellowstone with **Karst Stage** (www.karststage.com; ✆ **406/556-3500;** $295 round-trip). Also in winter, the **Xanterra Travel Collection** (www.xanterra.com; ✆ **307/344-7311**) runs a daily shuttle from Bozeman airport to Mammoth for $103 one-way (advance booking required).

Tips for RVers

You can drive most major roads in both parks with an RV or a trailer; large vehicles are prohibited in some areas, and most of the camping areas don't provide hookups—Colter Bay, Flagg Ranch, and Fishing Bridge are the exceptions. Keep in mind that finding a spot for a large RV rig in the parks' crowded parking lots can be a real challenge; leave campers behind in your campground, if possible, or visit busy spots early or late in the day.

TIPS ON ACCOMMODATIONS

Inside the parks, your options for lodging are fairly limited, and the seemingly limitless number of peak-season visitors makes for high occupancy and rates. And the fact that many of the parks' hostelries have historic designations might mean they don't fit some visitors' modern tastes. The gateway cities have more variety, from dorm-style hostels to luxury ski resorts. House swapping is a possibility in Jackson and Cody, but less likely in smaller gateways. In Yellowstone, lodging information is available from **Xanterra Travel Collection** (www.yellowstonenationalparklodges.com; ✆ **307/344-7311**). In Grand Teton, contact the park concessionaires: **Grand Teton Lodge Company** (www.gtlc.com; ✆ **307/543-3100**),

and **Signal Mountain Lodge Co.** (www.signalmountain
lodge.com; ☎ **307/543-2831**). For more info about where to
stay, see chapters 7 and 8.

SPECIAL PERMITS

Backcountry Permits

If you want to sleep in Yellowstone or Grand Teton backcountry, you must get a permit, follow limits for length of stay
and campfires, and stay in a designated area. The permit costs
$5 per person per night in Yellowstone (plus a $10 reservation
fee). See chapter 4 for details on how to get one. In Grand
Teton, backcountry permits cost $20 plus $7 per person per
night. At both parks, reservations must be made through www.
recreation.gov. Even when you get reservations, you still need
to pick up your permit in person upon your arrival in the park.
Yellowstone begins processing early-access lottery requests
for the current year starting in March and accepts general
permit requests starting in late April. In Grand Teton, you can
reserve a permit starting in January. If you're going during the
parks' busy season, you'd be wise to make a reservation.

  In Yellowstone, permits can be obtained at the Bechler,
Bridge Bay, Old Faithful, and South Entrance ranger stations;
Grant Village, Mammoth, and West Yellowstone visitor centers; or Tower Backcountry Office, no more than 2 days before
embarking on a trip. Reservations for high-season permits must
be made online. Phone reservations are not accepted, but if you
want information about the system, call ☎ **307/344-2160.**

  In Grand Teton, permits are issued at the Craig Thomas
(Moose) and Colter Bay visitor centers and the Jenny Lake
Ranger Station. Phone reservations are not accepted, but
information is available by calling ☎ **307/739-3309.**

Boating Permits

For motorized craft in Yellowstone, the cost is $60 for the sea-
son and $40 for 7-day permits. Fees for nonmotorized boats are
$30 for annual permits, $20 for 7-day permits. Boating permits
are required for all vessels. Motorized boating is restricted to
designated areas. Boating is prohibited on Yellowstone's rivers
and streams except for the Lewis River Channel, where hand-
propelled vessels are permitted. Boating permits are available
at the Lewis Lake Ranger Station, Grant Ranger Station, and

Bridge Bay Ranger Station; a number of other locations issue permits for angler float tubes only. In Grand Teton, the fees are $75 for motorized boats, $25 for nonmotorized; permits are available online at www.recreation.gov starting in early April each year, or pick one up at the Craig Thomas or Colter Bay visitor centers. Powerboats are permitted on Jenny and Jackson lakes; nonmotorized boats are allowed on most park lakes and the Snake River. Sailboats, windsurfers, and jet skis are allowed only on Jackson Lake. U.S. Coast Guard–approved personal flotation devices are required for each person.

Fishing Permits

In **Yellowstone,** park permits are required for anglers ages 16 and over; the permit costs $40 for 3 days, $55 for 7 days, and $75 for the season. Children 15 and under don't need a permit if they are fishing with an adult, but they need a free permit if they're fishing without supervision. Rangers prefer that you buy the permit ahead of time at www.recreation.gov, but they're also available at any ranger station, any visitor center, the Yellowstone Park General Store, and most fishing shops in the gateways. The season usually begins on the Saturday of Memorial Day weekend and continues through October. Yellowstone Lake, its tributaries, and sections of the Yellowstone River have shorter seasons; parts of the Madison and Gardner rivers have longer ones.

In **Grand Teton,** Wyoming fishing licenses are required for everyone ages 14 years and over. An adult nonresident license costs $14 per day and $102 for the season. Nonresidents under age 14 can fish for free with a licensed adult. A $21.50 Conservation Stamp is required for licenses except the 1- and 5-day varieties. Jackson Lake is closed all of October.

PLANNING A BACKCOUNTRY TRIP

While we've given the particulars for both Yellowstone (p. 80) and Grand Teton national parks (p. 122) in their respective chapters and in chapter 7, the following tips are useful.

Regulations

The theme in the backcountry is "leave no trace," and that means packing out any garbage you take in, not bringing pets, and staying on designated trails and reusing existing campsites. Fires are allowed only in established fire rings (and prohibited in some areas), and only dead and downed material may be used for firewood; backpacking stoves are allowed throughout the parks. You must have a park permit for overnight stays in the backcountry. For more information on "leave no trace" ethics, see **www.lnt.org**.

Backpacking for Beginners

Wear comfortable, sturdy, waterproof hiking shoes for an early-season hike; cotton socks are not a good idea because the material holds moisture, whereas wool and synthetics, such as fleece, wick it away from your body. Your sleeping bag should be rated for the low temperatures found at high elevations; if you bring a down bag, keep it dry or suffer the consequences. A lightweight sleeping pad is a must. An internal frame backpack with good padding, a lumbar support pad, and a wide hip belt helps ensure a comfortable trip. Be sure to try out the pack and boots before you take them on a long trip with heavy loads, so that you'll have time to break them in.

Personal Safety Issues

Do not backpack alone, but if you must, let park rangers and friends know where you'll be and how long you'll be gone. Don't leave the parking lot without the following gear: a compass, topographical maps, a first-aid kit, bug repellent, toilet paper, a headlamp, matches, a knife, food supplies, a bear-resistant food container (required in Grand Teton) if your campsite doesn't have a bear pole, and bear spray, as well as a tent, a stove, and a sleeping bag. At this altitude, sunscreen and sunglasses with UV protection are also wise. You'll also need water treatment pills, a good water filter, or a UV light purification device, because that stream could have parasites that are likely to cause intestinal disorders. Or bring water to a boil before you drink it. For more details, see "The 10 Essentials + 1," p. 83.

RECOMMENDED READING

The following books are interesting, informative, and easy to find: *A Ranger's Guide to Yellowstone Day Hikes,* by Roger

Anderson and Carol Shiveley Anderson (Farcountry Press, 2013); *Empire of Shadows: The Epic Story of Yellowstone,* by George Black (St. Martin's Griffin, 2013); *The Art of Yellowstone Science: Mammoth Hot Springs as a Window on the Universe,* by Brad W. Fouke and Tom Murphy (Crystal Creek Press, 2016); *Death in Yellowstone,* by Lee H. Whittlesey (Roberts Rinehart Publishers, 2014); *Yellowstone: The Official Guide to Touring the World's First National Park,* by the Yellowstone Association (Yellowstone Association, 2014); *Creation of the Teton Landscape: A Geologic Chronicle of Jackson Hole & the Teton Range,* by J. David Love, John C. Reed, Jr., and Kenneth L. Pierce (Grand Teton Association, 2016); *Peaks, Politics & Passion: Grand Teton National Park Comes of Age,* by Robert W. Righter (Grand Teton Association, 2014); and *Grand Teton National Park Fishing Guide,* by Dave Shorett (LakeStream Publications, 2004). **Falcon Press** also publishes a long list of hiking, fishing, climbing, and other guides to the Yellowstone/Grand Teton region.

If you can't find these publications in your local bookstore, many can be ordered from either **Yellowstone Forever** (www.yellowstone.org; ✆ **406/848-2400**) or the **Grand Teton Association** (www.grandtetonassociation.org; ✆ **307/739-3606**).

[FastFACTS] YELLOW-STONE & GRAND TETON NATIONAL PARKS

Accessibility Both parks are becoming increasingly user-friendly. Those who are blind or have permanent disabilities can obtain a free **America the Beautiful Access Pass,** which allows lifetime access to all national parks and federal fee areas. These are available at https://store.usgs.gov/access-pass, or at entrances to Yellowstone or Grand Teton.

YELLOWSTONE Wheelchair-accessible accommodations are available in all park lodges. For detailed information about accessible features throughout the park, visit www.nps.gov/yell/planyourvisit/accessibility.htm. All campgrounds have at least one **wheelchair-accessible campsite.**

Wheelchair-accessible restrooms with sinks and flush toilets are located at all developed areas except West Thumb. Accessible vault toilets are located in campgrounds and in most scenic areas and picnic areas.

Many of Yellowstone's **roadside attractions,** including the south rim of the Grand Canyon of the Yellowstone, West Thumb Geyser Basin, much of the Norris and Upper Geyser basins, Mammoth Hot Springs, and parts of the Mud Volcano and Fountain Paint Pot areas, are negotiable by wheelchair. **Visitor centers** at Old Faithful, Grant Village, Mammoth, West Thumb, West Yellowstone, and Canyon are wheelchair accessible, as are the Norris Museum and the Fishing Bridge Visitor Center.

Wheelchair-accessible parking is available at all major developed areas and some overlooks and picnic areas.

GRAND TETON Campsites at Colter Bay, Jenny Lake, and Gros Ventre campgrounds are on relatively level terrain; Headwaters Lodge & Cabins at Flagg Ranch also offers accessible campsites

and RV sites. Lizard Creek and Signal Mountain are hilly and less accessible.

Wheelchair-accessible dining facilities are located at Flagg Ranch, Leeks Marina, Colter Bay, Signal Mountain Lodge, Jackson Lake Lodge, and Jenny Lake Lodge.

Visitor centers at Moose, Colter Bay, Jenny Lake, and Flagg Ranch provide interpretive programs, displays, and visitor information in several forms, including visual, audible, and tactile.

Wheelchair-accessible parking spaces are located close to all visitor center entrances; curb cuts are provided, as are **accessible restroom facilities.**

More information is available from **Grand Teton National Park** at www.nps.gov/grte/planyourvisit/accessibility.htm.

Area Codes Yellowstone is almost entirely in Wyoming, with the area code **307.** The park also extends slightly into Montana (area code **406**) and Idaho (area code **208**). **Grand Teton** is entirely in

Wyoming, and its area code is also **307.**

Car Rental See "Getting There & Getting Around," earlier in this chapter.

Cellphones The parks have several cell towers in developed areas. Cell service is widely available on the floor of Jackson Hole throughout Grand Teton National Park; in Yellowstone, it is available in Canyon, Grant, Lake, Mammoth Hot Springs, and Old Faithful villages but largely unavailable on the roads and in wilderness areas. Cell service is available in all cities. International travelers may want to buy a pay-as-you-go phone for the trip.

Crime See "Safety," later in this section.

Customs International visitors may carry in or out up to $10,000 in U.S. or foreign currency with no formalities; larger sums must be declared to U.S. Customs and Border Protection on entering or leaving, which includes filing form FinCen105. For details regarding U.S. Customs and Border Protection, consult your nearest U.S. embassy or consulate, or **U.S. Customs and Border Protection** (www.cbp.gov).

Doctors In Yellowstone, the **clinic at Mammoth Hot Springs** (📞 **307/344-7965**) is open in summer daily and from October to June on weekdays, except some holidays. **Lake Clinic** (📞 **307/242-7241**) and **Old Faithful Clinic** (📞 **307/545-7325**) are open in summer and fall. In Grand Teton, the **Grand Teton Medical Clinic** at Jackson Lake Lodge (📞 **307/543-2514**) is open daily in summer. The next-closest clinic is in Jackson, Wyoming: **St. John's Medical Center,** 625 E. Broadway(📞**307/733-3636**), has a 24-hour emergency room.

Drinking Laws The legal age for the purchase and consumption of alcoholic beverages is 21; proof of age is required and often requested at bars, nightclubs, and restaurants. Do not carry open containers of alcohol in your car or any public area that isn't zoned for alcohol consumption. The police can fine you on the spot.

Don't even think about driving while intoxicated. Alcohol is widely available at stores in both parks and in the gateway cities.

Driving Rules Both Wyoming and Montana require that all vehicle occupants wear seatbelts and that children under 9 (under 6 in Montana) be properly secured in a child safety or booster seat. See "Getting There & Getting Around," earlier in this chapter.

Electricity Like Canada, the U.S. uses 110 to 120 volts AC (60 cycles), compared to 220 to 240 volts AC (50 cycles) in most of Europe, Australia, and New Zealand. Downward converters that change 220–240 volts to 110–120 volts are difficult to find in the U.S., so bring one with you.

Electric Vehicle Charging See "Getting There & Getting Around," earlier in this chapter.

Embassies & Consulates All embassies are in the nation's capital, Washington, D.C. Some consulates are in major U.S. cities,

and most nations have a mission to the United Nations in New York City. If your country isn't listed below, check **www.embassy.org/embassies**.

The embassy of **Australia** is at 1601 Massachusetts Ave. NW, Washington, DC 20036 (www.usa.embassy.gov.au; 📞 **202/797-3000**). Consulates are in Chicago, Honolulu, Houston, New York, Los Angeles, and San Francisco.

The embassy of **Canada** is at 501 Pennsylvania Ave. NW, Washington, DC 20001 (www.international.gc.ca; 📞 **844/880-6519**). Canadian consulates are in 12 other cities throughout the U.S., including Atlanta, Boston, Chicago, New York, Los Angeles, Miami, and Seattle.

The embassy of **Ireland** is at 2234 Massachusetts Ave. NW, Washington, DC 20008 (www.dfa.ie; 📞 **202/462-3939**). Consulates are in Austin, Atlanta, Boston, Chicago, Los Angeles, New York, Miami, and San Francisco.

The embassy of **New Zealand** is at 37

Observatory Circle NW, Washington, DC 20008 (www.mfat.govt.nz; ☏ **202/328-4800**). New Zealand consulates are in Los Angeles, Honolulu, and New York.

The embassy of the **United Kingdom** is at 3100 Massachusetts Ave. NW, Washington, DC 20008 (www.gov.uk/government/world/organisations/british-embassy-washington; ☏ **202/588-6500**). British consulates are in Atlanta, Boston, Chicago, Houston, Miami, New York, San Francisco, and Los Angeles.

Emergencies Call ☏ **911.**

Family Travel One useful guide to traveling with the kids is *An Outdoor Family Guide to Yellowstone and Grand Teton National Parks* (Mountaineers Books, 2006). Older children can learn about nature by enrolling in the **Junior Ranger Program** at both Yellowstone (p. 68) and Grand Teton (p. 113).

Gasoline See "Getting There & Getting Around," earlier in this chapter.

Health Health hazards range from mild

headaches to run-ins with wild animals, but the latter happen less frequently than car accidents in the parks. To be safe, keep a first-aid kit in your car or luggage, and have it handy when hiking. It should include at least butterfly bandages, sterile gauze pads, adhesive tape, an antibiotic ointment, pain relievers for children and adults, alcohol pads, a pocketknife with scissors, and tweezers. Healthcare is available at clinics in both parks; hospitals with 24-hour emergency rooms are located in Jackson and Cody, Wyoming, as well as in Bozeman, Montana.

o **Altitude Sickness** Adjusting to the parks' high elevations is a process that can take a day or more. Symptoms of altitude sickness include headache, fatigue, nausea, loss of appetite, muscle pain, and lightheadedness. Doctors recommend that, until acclimated, travelers should avoid heavy exertion, consume light meals, and drink lots of liquids but little caffeine or alcohol.

o **Bugs, Bites & Other Wildlife Concerns** Wildlife are to be treated with utmost respect in both parks. Keep your distance—at least 300 feet if possible—from any wild animal in either park. Mosquitoes, spiders, and ticks are the most bothersome biters, aside from the occasional rattlesnake you might see around Gardiner, Montana.

o **Waterborne Illnesses** See "Water," below.

Internet & Wi-Fi When it comes to modern telecommunications, Yellowstone and Grand Teton have extremely limited infrastructure: Lack of connectivity is the rule, not the exception. Some Yellowstone lodges have Wi-Fi, sometimes only in the lobby or other public spaces: They are Mammoth Hot Springs Hotel, Canyon Lodge, Lake Yellowstone Hotel (wired only), Old Faithful Lodge, and Old Faithful Snow Lodge. In Grand Teton National Park, Wi-Fi is available in public areas at the visitor center in

Moose, Colter Bay Village, Jackson Lake Lodge, Signal Mountain Lodge, and Jenny Lake Lodge. Internet access is widely available in all the gateways but can be notably slow in Gardiner and West Yellowstone.

Legal Aid While driving, if you are pulled over for a minor infraction (such as speeding), never attempt to pay the fine directly to a police officer; this could be construed as attempted bribery, a much more serious crime. Pay fines by mail, or directly into the hands of the clerk of the court. If accused of a more serious offense, say and do nothing before consulting a lawyer. In the U.S., the burden is on the state to prove a person's guilt beyond a reasonable doubt, and everyone has the right to remain silent. Once arrested, a person can make one telephone call to a party of their choice. The international visitor should call their embassy or consulate.

LGBTQ Travelers While Wyoming and Montana have earned reputations as intolerant destinations in the past, Yellowstone and Grand Teton National Parks are generally LGBTQ-friendly. However, LGBTQ culture and nightlife are very limited in Jackson and nearly nonexistent in other gateways.

Mail At press time, domestic postage rates were 56¢ for a postcard and 73¢ for a letter. For international mail, letters and postcards start at $1.65. For more information visit www. usps.com.

If you aren't sure what your address will be in the U.S., mail can be sent to you, in your name, c/o General Delivery at the main post office of the city or region where you expect to be. (Call ✆ **800/275-8777** for information on the nearest post office.) The addressee must pick up mail in person and must produce proof of identity (a driver's license or passport, for example). Most post offices will hold mail for up to 1 month and are open Monday to Friday from at least 9am to 5pm and Saturday from 9am to 1pm.

Always include a zip code when mailing items in the U.S. If you don't know the zip code, go to www. usps.com/zip4.

Medical Requirements Unless you're arriving from an area known to be suffering from an epidemic (particularly cholera or yellow fever), inoculations or vaccinations are not required for entry into the U.S. See also "Health," above.

Mobile Phones See "Cellphones" earlier in this section.

Money & Costs Frommer's lists exact prices in the local currency, the dollar. The currency conversions provided were correct at press time. However, rates fluctuate, so before departing consult a currency exchange website such as **www.xe.com** to check up-to-the-minute rates.

ATMs are widely available in the gateway cities and developed areas in both parks. Beware of hidden credit card fees while traveling. If you're visiting from outside the U.S., check with your credit or debit card issuer

WHAT THINGS COST IN YELLOWSTONE & GRAND TETON

	US$
Admission to both parks for a week	70.00
Double motel room in the parks, peak season	246.00–690.00
Cabin (private)	135.00–956.00
Dinner main course in a full-service hotel restaurant	8.00–48.00
Horseback riding	68.00–142.00
Basic lake cruise	23–88.00
Bus sightseeing tour (Yellowstone)	40.00–177.00
Round-trip snowcoach to Old Faithful	340.00
1 gallon/1 liter of regular gasoline (petrol)	3.89/1.03

about any fees for overseas transactions.

Newspapers & Magazines The primary papers in the region are the *Billings Gazette, Bozeman Daily Chronicle*, and the *Cody Enterprise.* In **Yellowstone,** the best source of park information is the free *Yellowstone Visitor Guide*, the free park newspaper available at all entrances and visitor centers. In **Grand Teton,** the free *Grand Teton Guide* is full of park information. In **Jackson,** the newspaper is the *Jackson Hole News & Guide.*

Packing Nothing ruins a trip to the parks faster than sore or wet feet. Bring comfortable walking shoes, even if you

plan to keep walking to a minimum. **Bring shoes that are broken in,** and if you plan to do serious hiking, get sturdy boots that support your ankles and protect against water. Early in the season, trails might be wet or muddy; late in the fall, you can get snowed on. The more popular trails are sometimes also used by horses, making stream crossings a mucky mess.

Wear your clothing in layers, and bring a small, empty backpack or fanny pack so that you have somewhere to put the clothes as you take those layers off and on as temperature, altitude, and your level of exertion change. Cotton is a

no-no in the backcountry; synthetic fabrics dry much faster. Gloves or mittens are useful before the park heats up, or in the evening when it cools down, *even in summer.*

The atmosphere is thin at higher altitudes, so protect your skin. Bring a strong sunblock, a hat with a brim, and sunglasses. we also recommend bringing insect repellent, water bottles, and a first-aid kit.

Take into account that elevations at the parks are between 5,000 and 11,000 feet; in campgrounds and on hiking trails, you'll want clothing appropriate to the temperatures—in summer, 40°F (4°C) in the evening, 75°F (24°C) during the day.

Passports Virtually every air traveler entering the U.S. is required to show a passport. All persons, including U.S. citizens, traveling by air between the U.S. and Canada, Mexico, and Bermuda are required to present a valid passport. *Note:* U.S. and Canadian citizens entering the U.S. at land and seaports of entry from within the Western Hemisphere must also present a passport or other documents compliant with the Western Hemisphere Travel Initiative. Children 15 and under may continue entering with only a U.S. birth certificate, or other proof of U.S. citizenship.

Petrol See "Getting There & Getting Around," earlier in this chapter.

Police Call ☎ **911.**

Safety The roads are the most dangerous places in Yellowstone, so be cautious while driving. Lightning and falls are also killers, but wildlife is the most unique peril in the parks. The most dangerous animal in either park might well be the grizzly bear, but all wildlife has the potential to injure a human. Keep a safe distance from bison, deer, moose, and other animals—at least 300 feet. But because a close bear encounter can happen unexpectedly, you need to know what to do. First, be aware that what matters most to a bear are food and cubs. Get between a sow and her cubs, and you could be in trouble. If a bear thinks that the food in your backpack is his, you also have a problem.

Unless bears have already developed a taste for human food, though, they won't come looking for you. Make a lot of noise on the trail through bear habitat, and *Ursus arctos horribilis* will give you a wide berth. Don't camp anywhere near the carcass of a dead animal; grizzlies sometimes partially bury carrion and return to it. Hang your food bag from your campsite's pole or use a bear-resistant food container, keep your cooking area distant from your campsite, and don't keep any food or utensils in your tent—or even clothes worn while cooking. Soaps and other perfumed items can also be attractants.

Avoid hiking at night or in the meadows of mountain areas if visibility is poor. Bears have an extremely good sense of smell but poor eyesight. Always carry bear spray. If you encounter a bear, here are some things you should and should not do:

○ **Do not run.** Anything that flees looks like prey to a bear, and it might attack. Bears can run at more than 30 mph. The bear might bluff charge, but you're best off holding your ground.

○ **Avoid direct eye contact.**

○ If the bear is unaware of you, **stay downwind** (so that it doesn't catch your scent) and **detour away from it slowly.**

○ If the bear is aware of you but has not acted aggressively, **slowly back away.**

○ **Do not climb a tree.** Although black bears have more suitable claws for climbing, grizzly bears can climb trees, too.

o **Make noise** and **act intimidating** if the bear does not retreat.

o Carry **bear spray** and be sure that it's handy when you're in possible bear habitat. If a bear charges, spray when it's 30 to 60 feet away and aim for the bear's face and eyes to create a cloud. Keep spraying until the bear changes direction. After you use it, leave the area: Bears have been seen returning to sniff an area where spray has been used.

o If you're attacked, drop to the ground face down, clasp your hands over the back of your neck, tuck your knees to your chest, and **play dead.** Keep your backpack on—it can help protect your body. Only as a last resort should you attempt to resist an attack and fight off a bear.

Smoking Montana has a statewide smoking ban in indoor public places; Wyoming does not, but smoking is banned in most public places in the park and Jackson Hole.

Taxes Lodging tax in Yellowstone and its gateways varies from 4% to 5%. There's no sales tax in Montana, but sales tax is 4% in Grand Teton Park and Jackson Hole. Every state, county, and city may levy its own local tax on all purchases, including hotel and restaurant bills and airline tickets. These taxes are not on price tags. The U.S. has no value-added tax (VAT) at the national level.

Telephones Some convenience stores and packaging services sell **prepaid calling cards** in denominations up to $50. Most long-distance and international calls can be dialed directly from any phone. **To make calls within the U.S. and to Canada,** dial 1 followed by the area code and the seven-digit number. **For other international calls,** dial 011 followed by the country code, city code, and the number you are calling.

Calls to area codes **800, 888, 877,** and **866** are toll-free. Calls to area codes **700** and **900** (chat lines, bulletin boards, "dating" services, and so on) can be expensive, with charges of 95¢ to $3 or more per minute. Some numbers have minimum charges of $15 or more.

For **reversed-charge or collect calls,** and for person-to-person calls, dial the number 0, then the area code and number; follow the automated instructions to place the call.

For **directory assistance** ("Information"), dial ✆ **411** for local numbers and national numbers in the U.S. and Canada. For dedicated long-distance information, dial 1, then the appropriate area code plus 555-1212.

Time Both parks are in the **Mountain Standard Time** zone. **Daylight saving time (summertime)** is in effect from 2am on the second Sunday in March to 2am on the first Sunday in November. Daylight saving time moves the clock 1 hour ahead of standard time.

Tipping In hotels, tip **bellhops** at least $1 per bag ($2–$3 if you have a lot of luggage) and tip the **housekeeping staff**

$2 to $5 per day (more if you've left a big mess). Tip the **door attendant** or **concierge** only if they've provided you with some specific service (for example, arranging a trip with an outfitter).

In restaurants, bars, and nightclubs, tip **service staff** and **bartenders** 20% of the check, tip **checkroom attendants** $1 per garment, and tip **valet-parking attendants** $1 per vehicle.

Tip **cab drivers** 15% of the fare; tip **skycaps** at airports at least $1 per bag ($2–$3 if you have a lot of luggage); and tip **hairdressers** and **barbers** 20%.

Toilets You won't find public toilets or "restrooms" on the streets in most U.S. cities, but they can be found in hotel lobbies, bars, restaurants, museums, department stores, railway and bus stations, and service stations. Large hotels and fast-food restaurants are often the best bet for clean facilities. Both Yellowstone and Grand Teton have vault (flushless) toilets at numerous pullouts

along the roads, and there are toilets at some trailheads, though not all.

VAT See "Taxes," above.

Visas The U.S. Department of State has a **Visa Waiver Program (VWP)** allowing citizens of the following countries to enter the U.S. without a visa for stays of up to 90 days: Andorra, Australia, Austria, Belgium, Brunei, Chile, Croatia, Czech Republic, Denmark, Estonia, Finland, France, Germany, Greece, Hungary, Iceland, Ireland, Israel, Italy, Japan, Latvia, Liechtenstein, Lithuania, Luxembourg, Malta, Monaco, Netherlands, New Zealand, Norway, Poland, Portugal, San Marino, Singapore, Slovakia, Slovenia, South Korea, Spain, Sweden, Switzerland, Taiwan, and the United Kingdom. (**Note:** This list was accurate at press time; consult https:// travel.state.gov.) Even though a visa isn't necessary, in an effort to help U.S. officials check travelers against terror watch lists before they arrive at U.S. borders,

visitors from VWP countries must register online through the Electronic System for Travel Authorization (ESTA) before boarding a plane or a boat to the U.S. Travelers must complete an electronic application, providing basic personal and travel eligibility information. The Department of Homeland Security recommends filling out the form at least 3 days before traveling. Authorizations will be valid for up to 2 years or until the traveler's passport expires, whichever comes first. Currently, there is a $21 fee for the online application. Existing ESTA registrations remain valid through their expiration dates. **Note:** As of April 1, 2016, you must have an enhanced e-passport to qualify for the VWP. Citizens of these nations also need to present a round-trip air or cruise ticket upon arrival. E-passports contain computer chips capable of storing biometric information, such as the required digital photograph of the holder. Canadian citizens may enter the U.S. without visas but will need to show passports and proof of residence.

Citizens of all other countries must have (1) a valid passport that expires at least 6 months later than the scheduled end of their visit to the U.S.; and (2) a tourist visa.

For details about U.S. visas, go to https://travel.state.gov.

Visitor Information The primary entries to Yellowstone and Grand Teton are through Montana and Wyoming, so if you want information about the surrounding areas, contact these states' travel services: **Montana Office of Tourism** (www.visitmt.com; ☏ **800/847-4868**) and **Wyoming Office of Tourism** (www.travelwyoming.com; ☏ **800/225-5996** or 307/777-7777).

To receive maps and information before your arrival, contact the parks directly: **Yellowstone National Park** (www.nps.gov/yell; ☏ **307/344-7381**) and **Grand Teton National Park** (www.nps.gov/grte; ☏ **307/739-3399**).

For information about educational programs at the **Yellowstone Forever Institute** and other resources, contact **Yellowstone Forever** (www.yellowstone.org; ☏ **406/848-2400**). The **Grand Teton Association** (www.grandtetonassociation.org; ☏ **307/739-3606**) is a not-for-profit organization that provides information about the park through retail book sales at park visitor centers; it also sells books about the park by mail.

National forests and other public lands surround the parks. For information about national forests and wilderness areas in Montana, contact the **U.S. Forest Service Northern Region** (www.fs.usda.gov/r1; ☏ **406/329-3511**). For information on Wyoming's national forests, turn to the **U.S. Forest Service Intermountain Region** (www.fs.usda.gov/r4; ☏ **801/625-5605**), and the **U.S. Forest Service Rocky Mountain Region** (www.fs.usda.gov/r2; ☏ **303/275-5350**).

The federal **Bureau of Land Management** also manages millions of acres of recreational lands and can be reached at its Wyoming state office, 5353 Yellowstone Rd., Cheyenne, WY 82009 (www.blm.gov/wy; ☏ **307/775-6256**); or its Montana state office, 5001 Southgate Dr., Billings, MT 59101 (www.blm.gov/montana-dakotas; ☏ **406/896-5004**).

Water Two waterborne hazards are *Giardia* and *Campylobacter,* with symptoms that wreak havoc on the human digestive system. Untreated water from the parks' lakes and streams should be boiled before consumption, pumped through a fine-mesh water filter specifically designed to remove bacteria, or treated with chemical water purifiers or a UV light purification device. All these water treatment methods are available in outdoor gear shops in gateway towns.

Wi-Fi See "Internet & Wi-Fi," earlier in this section.

Index

General Index

247

Map List

Photo Credits

p. i: Alyssa Mattei; p. ii: Alyssa Mattei; p. iii: Danita Delimont/Shutterstock; p. iv: Eniko Balogh/Shutterstock; p. v, top: NPS/Neal Herbert; p. v, bottom: Alyssa Mattei; p. vi, top: NPS/Ashton Hooker; p. vi, middle: NPS/Jacob W. Frank; p. vi, bottom: Fotos593/Shutterstock; p. vii, top: Ronnie Chua/Shutterstock.com; p. vii, bottom: AndreAnita; p. viii, top: Yellowstone National Park/Jim Peaco; p. viii, bottom: Kelly vanDellen/Shutterstock; p. ix, top: NPS/Neal Herbert; p. ix, middle: NPS/Neal Herbert; p. ix, bottom: Rob Crandall/Shutterstock.com; p. x, top: Ryan Kelehar; p. x, bottom: YegoroV/Shutterstock; p. xi, top: Kelly vanDellen/Shutterstock; p. xi, middle: NPS/Lehle; p. xi, bottom: NPS; p. xii, top: hutch photography/shutterstock; p. xii, bottom: Gary Saxe; p. xiii, top: Jeffrey T. Kreulen; p. xiii, middle: f11photo; p. xiii, bottom: Courtesy of Grand Teton Lodge Company; p. xiv, top: Reimar; p. xiv, bottom: Kit Leong/Shutterstock; p. xv, top: Jane; p. xv, middle: Lori Iverson/USFWS; p. xv, bottom: Michael J Magee/Shutterstock; p. xvi, top: Courtesy of Buffalo Bill Center of the West; p. xvi, middle: Don Graham; p. xvi, bottom: Lensation photos/Shutterstock.

Frommer's Yellowstone & Grand Teton National Parks, 12th Edition

Published by
FROMMER MEDIA LLC

ISBN 978-1-62887-629-1 (paper), 978-1-62887-630-7 (ebk)

Editorial Director: Pauline Frommer
Editor: Alexis Lipsitz Flippin
Production Editor: Erin Geile
Cartographer: Andy Dolan
Photo Editor: Alyssa Mattei
Cover Design: Dave Riedy
Compositor: Lissa Auciello-Brogan
Indexer: Kelly Henthorne

Front cover photo: Male bison standing in a field with flowers, Yellowstone National Park © Don Mammoser / Shutterstock

Back cover photo: Grand Prismatic Spring at Yellowstone National Park © Framalicious / Shutterstock

For information on our other products or services, see www.frommers.com.

FrommerMedia LLC also publishes its books in a variety of electronic formats. Some content that appears in print may not be available in electronic formats.

Manufactured in Turkey

5 4 3 2 1

ABOUT THE AUTHOR

Elisabeth Kwak-Hefferan is a freelance writer and editor who specializes in the environment, public lands, outdoors, travel, and science. Her work has appeared in *The New York Times*, *Sierra*, *National Geographic*, *5280*, *National Parks*, and many more. Elisabeth lives with her husband and two kiddos in Missoula, Montana, where the cross-country skiing is off the charts and the craft breweries aren't too shabby, either (classic spot for a pint: KettleHouse Southside Brewery).

ABOUT THE FROMMER TRAVEL GUIDES

For most of the past 65 years, Frommer's has been the leading series of travel guides in North America, accounting for as many as 24% of all guidebooks sold. I think I know why.

Though we hope our books are entertaining, we nevertheless deal with travel in a serious fashion. Our guidebooks have never looked on such journeys as a mere recreation, but as a far more important human function, a time of learning and introspection, an essential part of a civilized life. We stress the culture, lifestyle, history, and beliefs of the destinations we cover, and urge our readers to seek out people and new ideas as the chief rewards of travel.

We have never shied from controversy. We have, from the beginning, encouraged our authors to be intensely judgmental, critical—both pro and con—in their comments, and wholly independent. Our only clients are our readers, and we have triggered the ire of countless prominent sorts, from a tourist newspaper we called "practically worthless" (it unsuccessfully sued us) to the many rip-offs we've condemned.

And because we believe that travel should be available to everyone regardless of their incomes, we have always been cost-conscious at every level of expenditure. Though we have broadened our recommendations beyond the budget category, we insist that every lodging we include be sensibly priced. We use every form of media to assist our readers and are particularly proud of our feisty daily website, the award-winning Frommers.com.

I have high hopes for the future of Frommer's. May these guidebooks, in all the years ahead, continue to reflect the joy of travel and the freedom that travel represents. May they always pursue a cost-conscious path, so that people of all incomes can enjoy the rewards of travel. And may they create, for both the traveler and the persons among whom we travel, a community of friends, where all human beings live in harmony and peace.

Arthur Frommer